Equality of Opportunity for Sexual and Gender Minorities

T0344941

Equality of Opportunity for Sexual and Gender Minorities

Clifton Cortez, John Arzinos, and Christian De la Medina Soto

 **WORLD BANK GROUP**

Contents

Boxes

Figures

Contents

Maps

Tables

Foreword

COVID-19 (Coronavirus) has dealt a major blow to development progress, pushing 100 million more people into extreme poverty. All around us, the uneven impact of the crisis is in plain sight. From their inability to access vaccines to the lack of adequate social protection systems, the poor and vulnerable have been hit hardest, exacerbating inequality.

Sexual and gender minorities are among social groups that face greater risks as the pandemic exposes existing disparities. They struggle to achieve the three main objectives of the World Bank Group's gender strategy: improved human endowments, increased economic opportunities, and enhanced voice as well as agency. From a social inclusion standpoint, the stigma driven by homophobia and transphobia, regressive norms, and discriminatory laws fuel their exclusion.

In charting a course for the post-COVID world, we can do better and move toward more sustainable and inclusive societies. This is part of the World Bank Group's approach to achieve green, resilient, and inclusive development. Ensuring that the recovery does not leave anyone behind can reduce disparities in opportunities and outcomes.

The World Bank has been working to improve the inclusion of sexual and gender minorities in its work through policies that aim to prevent discrimination in investment lending, through training, and through research that supports positive development outcomes for LGBTI people. In many countries, however, it is particularly difficult to tackle the challenges of LGBTI exclusion due to the absence of adequate data. Only five percent of global funding for sexual and gender minorities' issues goes towards research.

The *Equality of Opportunity for Sexual and Gender Minorities (EQOSOGI)* report is part of an overall effort to address this gap. By assessing the unique legal challenges faced by LGBTI people in six important areas—education, employment, access to public services and social protection, civil and political inclusion, protection from hate crimes and from being criminalized—the report aims to influence legislative change and support research on institutions and regulations that can ultimately lead to poverty reduction and shared prosperity. It covers laws and regulations in 16 countries across diverse geographies, income, and levels of inclusion.

Laws matter for the inclusion of sexual and gender minorities. Achieving equality of opportunity for LGBTI people is a long and difficult process, but regulatory reforms can play a foundational role. The first step toward an inclusive society is understanding the legal and institutional challenges faced by sexual and gender minorities that prevent them from fully participating in, benefiting from, and contributing to the economy on an equal footing with others. Of course, the existence of inclusive laws and regulations does not always ensure that sexual and gender minorities are free from discrimination. Enforcement of these laws is crucial.

The report shows that although most countries address discrimination against sexual and gender minorities in some way, no country has achieved true equality in treatment. It offers policy recommendations that can help to prevent and eliminate discriminatory practices in all the areas covered. As the first in a proposed series, the report is expected to include a wider set of countries going forward to allow more in-depth quantitative analysis and to identify possible correlations with socioeconomic outcomes.

Rising inequality and the exclusion of different social groups from services, markets, and opportunities are impediments to development that we cannot afford to ignore. We need to do more to include diverse perspectives and involve communities in the design of policies and investment projects. We hope that this report will be a useful tool in the global effort to achieve an inclusive and sustainable future for all.

Juergen Voegele
Vice President
Sustainable Development
The World Bank

Acknowledgments

The data and analysis presented in this report were produced by a team under the direction of the World Bank's Sexual Orientation and Gender Identity (SOGI) Global Advisor, Clifton Cortez. The study was co-led by Christian De la Medina Soto and John (Ioannis) Arzinos, the primary authors of the report. The core team members were Evangelia Siska, Kwame Gyamfi Boateng, Joaquin Espinosa Alarcon, and Eduardo Calderon Pontaza. Toni Joe Lebbos also contributed to the statistical analysis. The publication was edited by Djurdja Lazic and Bronwen Brown and Hope Steele, and it was designed by Will Kemp and Veronica Elena Gadea.

The team is grateful for colleagues' valuable comments, both within and outside the World Bank Group, who supported the initiative and provided invaluable technical assistance on the connection between equality legislation and economic development. The study was peer-reviewed by Jorge Luis Rodriguez Meza (Program Manager, DECEA), Tea Trumbic (Program Manager, DECWL), and Nicholas Menzies (Senior Governance Specialist, ELCG2).

Special thanks go to Professors M.V. Lee Badgett (University of Massachusetts Amherst and UCLA Williams Institute) and Yana van der Meulen Rodgers (Rutgers University) for their review of the research. The team would also like to thank the World Bank Country Management Units (CMUs) for their valuable contributions and reviews of the countries covered in the report, as well as other topic specialists: Sabah Moyeen (Senior Social Development Specialist, SSAS1), Rita Almeida (Program Leader, HLCDR), Eric R. Lancelot (Program Leader, ILCDR), Maria Beatriz Orlando (Lead Social Development Specialist, SAR), Sudip Mozumder (Lead External Affairs Advisor, India, Sri Lanka, and Maldives, Bangladesh special projects), Nandita Roy (External Affairs Officer, India), Philarisa Sarma Nongpiur (Consultant, Social Development, India), Vickram Cuttaree (Program Leader, ILCDR), Caryn Bredenkamp (Lead Economist, HECDR), Christabel E. Dadzie (Social Protection Specialist, HAFS3), Jeffrey Waite (Advisor, HAFE2), Jason Allen Weaver (Senior Economist, HECED), Elisabeth Sedmik (Analyst, HMNED), Elizabeth N. Ruppert Bulmer (Lead Economist, HSPJB), Jimena Garrote (Senior Counsel, LEGOP), and Victor Bundi Mosoti (Chief Counsel, LEGEN).

The team is grateful for the support of Louise J. Cord (Global Director, Social Sustainability and Inclusion Global Practice), Maninder S. Gill (Global Director, Environmental and Social Framework), and Ingo Wiederhofer (Practice Manager, Social Development Global Practice) in advancing knowledge on the inclusion of sexual and gender minorities around the world.

Finally, the team acknowledges the Canadian government/Global Affairs Canada for their support of this research and the World Bank's SOGI inclusion work.

About the Authors

John (Ioannis) Arzinos is one of the co-leads of the initiative. He joined the World Bank's Development Economics (DEC) Vice Presidency of the World Bank in 2017 and has since worked on many projects, including Women, Business and the Law (WBL), Business Enterprise Surveys, and Global Indicators of Regulatory Governance (GIRG). He has been part of the SOGI Core Team since 2018, where he has been working on the global Environmental and Social Framework (ESF) engagement and SOGI-specific research.

He is also working on Social Protection in Africa and on Regulatory Advisory Services in Europe. Before joining the World Bank, he worked with organizations such as the US Chamber of Commerce and Uber Technologies in the United States. He holds a master's degree in international relations and international economics from the Johns Hopkins School of Advanced International Studies (SAIS) and a bachelor's degree in international relations from the University of Piraeus in Greece.

Clifton Cortez joined the World Bank Group in 2016 as its first Global Advisor on Sexual Orientation and Gender Identity (SOGI). Previously, he served as the United Nations Development Programme's (UNDP) global LGBTI Team Leader (2014–16), based at the UN headquarters in New York City. He led UN efforts to ensure the inclusion of LGBTI people in global development, particularly as it relates to the Sustainable Development Goals. He focused these efforts on LGBTI inclusion in economic development, political and civic participation, health, and education, and in addressing personal security and violence—including leading work in defining how countries can measure LGBTI inclusion in these important aspects of the human condition.

Before his global role, he led related efforts for UNDP in Asia, based in Bangkok, Thailand (2010–14). Prior to joining the UNDP, he was part of the United States Agency for International Development's (USAID) HIV response, including in relation to sexual orientation and gender identity (1997–2010). Over 24 years, his work has taken him to countries throughout Africa, Asia, Latin America and the Caribbean, and the Pacific. He holds a law degree from Georgetown University in Washington, DC.

Christian De la Medina Soto co-leads the EQOSOGI initiative. He joined the World Bank Group in 2013 and has been part of the Sexual Orientation and Gender Identity (SOGI) Core Team since 2018. He is also working on the Investment Climate Unit of the World Bank. Prior to joining the Investment Climate Unit and the SOGI Core Team, he worked on several projects at the World Bank, including Investing across Borders; Women, Business and the Law; and Benchmarking Public Procurement. He has worked as a foreign legal specialist in the Financial Inclusion department at the Public International Law & Policy Group, as a foreign legal consultant at the Legal Department of the Inter-American Development Bank, and at Tobin & Munoz Firm and Moarbes, LLP, in Washington, DC. He also clerked for the Mexican Federal Court for more than six years.

He holds a master's in international legal studies from American University, Washington College of Law (LL.M.); a master's in political science from El Colegio de Abogados de Madrid, Spain; and a law degree from Anahuac University in Mexico. He is bilingual in Spanish and English and has a working knowledge of French, Italian, and Portuguese.

Executive Summary

Main Findings

Sexual and gender minorities face discrimination in all sectors and all countries examined.

Although more countries have taken steps toward equality for sexual minorities, legal recognition of and protection for transgender people is not yet a reality in most.

The findings provide insight into how the COVID-19 pandemic is adversely affecting sexual and gender minorities.

Countries score best in the criminalization and access to the labor market indicator sets.

Access to inclusive education, access to public services and social protection, civil and political inclusion, and protection from hate crimes are often overlooked.

The existence of inclusive laws and regulations does not always ensure that sexual and gender minorities are free from discrimination. Enforcement of these laws is crucial.

The *Equality of Opportunity for Sexual and Gender Minorities* (EQOSOGI) report benchmarks laws and regulations that affect the lives of sexual and gender minorities. Despite important legal advances over the past two decades, sexual and gender minorities continue to face discrimination and violence in both developing and developed countries. Such marginalization has harmed sexual and gender minorities as well as the communities and economies in which they live.[1] Laws and regulations that discriminate against sexual and gender minorities not only impede social and economic prosperity for the individuals concerned, but probably limit a country's wider economic prosperity and development. Yet, the absence of data on many aspects of protective and discriminatory legislation related to sexual orientation and gender identity (SOGI), prevents meaningful cross-country comparisons and analysis.

In 2019, the World Bank launched the EQOSOGI study to collect comparable cross-country data on legal frameworks that impact sexual and gender minorities. This is a first report that pilots the application of an established methodology in a new field (SOGI inclusion in development) in a limited number of countries intended for further expansion to a larger set of countries. Currently, the small sample size of countries in this report does not allow for economic analysis, simple or sophisticated. In future reports, when more countries are included, a simple correlation analysis would allow a comparison of this initiative's findings with measures of economic growth and prosperity and would facilitate an examination of connections.

As with similar initiatives—Women, Business and the Law, for example—the more data points there are, the more robust the benchmarking features.

This report highlights the current legal situation of sexual and gender minorities in 16 countries—Bangladesh, Canada, Costa Rica, India, Indonesia, Jamaica, Japan, Kosovo, Lebanon, Mexico, Mozambique, Nigeria, South Africa, Tunisia, Ukraine, and Uruguay. This selection of countries was deliberate. It was designed to represent (a) a diversity of geographies (across all World Bank regions); (b) a range of income levels (low-income, middle-income, and high-income countries); (c) a variety of legal traditions of the world; and (d) a range of inclusiveness of sexual and gender minorities (from less inclusive to more inclusive)—all with the goal of presenting a diverse and holistic picture of these issues in the countries analyzed.

The EQOSOGI report measures aspects of six indicator sets to identify differences in the legal treatment of sexual and gender minorities (figure ES.1). The six indicator sets, which are not exhaustive, give a sense of the challenges experienced by sexual and gender minorities. The study highlights the protections and rights embedded in the legal and regulatory framework in these six broad areas concerning the treatment of sexual and gender minorities in the analyzed countries. The methodology also allows comparisons with the best performer in each indicator set (termed *distance to frontier*). Although some of the 16 countries provide broader protections to sexual and gender minorities than others, no country has fully eliminated discriminatory laws.

Starting with the fundamental question of whether a country treats sexual and gender minority identities as "legal" or not, the study finds that some countries continue to criminalize sexual and gender minorities, either by banning same-sex intimacy or by associating transgender expression with criminalized behaviors contrary to public morals.

FIGURE ES.1

What the EQOSOGI Indicator Sets Measure

Criminalization and SOGI	Examines the level of criminalization of same-sex behavior and legal inclusion of sexual and gender minorities
Access to inclusive education	Examines the ability of LGBTI individuals to equally access public education
Access to the labor market	Identifies gender identity–motivated or sexual orientation–motivated restrictions in accessing the job market and the existence of workplace protections against such discrimination
Access to public services and social protection	Examines the ability of LGBTI individuals to equally access public services and social protection
Civil and political inclusion	Examines the degree of participation by sexual and gender minorities and civil society actors in the political process, as well as the freedom of nongovernmental organizations to operate freely; also analyzes different aspects related to family law and laws related to same-sex marriage and partnership
Protection from hate crimes	Examines the existence of laws and mechanisms that criminalize hate crimes and provide protection for sexual and gender minorities or those perceived as sexual and gender minorities

Source: World Bank Group, Equality of Opportunity project.
Note: EQOSOGI = Equality of Opportunity for Sexual and Gender Minorities; LGBTI = lesbian, gay, bisexual, transgender, and intersex; SOGI = sexual orientation and gender identity.

The study findings also demonstrate that sexual and gender minorities can face many barriers in accessing inclusive public services,[2] education, and employment that are essential to develop human capital and generate livelihoods. Students belonging to sexual and gender minorities experience discrimination in education in many forms—from challenges enrolling in public or private schools to falling victim to bullying and harassment. Schools in most analyzed countries also fail to provide inclusive sex education curricula and SOGI-inclusive language in textbooks, and teachers lack appropriate antidiscrimination training. The resulting lower levels of education for these students lead to reduced skills and diminished capacity to secure employment. As adults, sexual and gender minorities frequently face barriers to accessing the labor market when applying or interviewing for jobs. Even after securing employment, sexual and gender minorities are often confronted with discrimination and harassment by colleagues or managers, unequal remuneration, and lack of equal benefits for their partners, as well as dismissal based on their perceived or actual SOGI.

Equal participation in society requires that people be treated equally under the law. However, equality is often not a reality for sexual and gender minorities. For example, many countries prohibit same-sex couples from entering into civil unions, partnerships, marriages, and/or adopting children. Similarly, transgender and gender nonconforming people are not always provided with the appropriate legal framework to change their gender markers in official documents without pathologizing requirements.[3] Sexual and gender minorities also often face discrimination when obtaining identity documents. The legal prohibition of invasive gender-affirming surgeries on intersex infants and children is almost nonexistent. Conversion therapy and a lack of protections for sexual and gender minorities remain a reality in many countries.

The study also reveals that access to political and civic spaces is more limited for sexual and gender minorities. Nongovernmental organizations (NGOs) advocating for sexual and gender minorities' rights can face legal and financial barriers to the provision of relevant services.[4] In some countries, these organizations face legal and bureaucratic hurdles to registration and often operate in fear of persecution. Living as an equal citizen also includes the right to freely exercise one's political rights by participating in politics while being open about one's SOGI. However, politicians who are sexual or gender minorities are open about their own SOGI in very few countries analyzed in this study.

Several of the countries analyzed in the report inadequately address hate crimes. A majority of the countries do not consider crimes based on a person's SOGI to be aggravating circumstances under the law, nor do they require the monitoring and collection of hate crime–related data and training of professionals. A minority of analyzed countries provide services for victims of hate crimes, including legal assistance, shelter or housing, forensic or medical examinations, and medical certificates.

Laws do matter but they are not enough. Implementation varies across countries and a key factor is the ability to report discrimination through the legal mechanisms of the state. The report looks at the presence of national equality bodies or national human rights institutions responsible for handling SOGI-based discrimination claims and the existence of national action plans that specifically address sexual orientation and gender identity issues. While the existence of such plans, bodies, and laws may not always translate into a better environment for sexual and gender minorities, they are nonetheless critical elements of an enabling environment for improved SOGI inclusion.

This very uneven legal and regulatory framework across the 16 countries probably has had important ramifications for how sexual and gender minorities in each country have been able to cope with the COVID-19 pandemic. Challenges in accessing health care or other critical public services due to restrictions or lack of health insurance for partners has made sexual and gender minorities more vulnerable to the impacts of COVID-19 and will also make the recovery more difficult and drawn out. Looking ahead, having data on the legal and regulatory framework will be critical to building resilience among sexual and gender minorities to future shocks.

This report offers numerous good practice policy actions to address discriminatory measures. It also aims to inspire countries to review their legal frameworks and ensure equal opportunities for all citizens. EQOSOGI's ultimate goal is to encourage governments to reform laws that hold sexual and gender minorities back from working and actively participating in society. The following good practice policy actions are advised for consideration by countries to improve the equality of opportunity for sexual and gender minorities (a more comprehensive set of actions can be found at the end of each section of the report):

- Repeal laws, constitutional provisions, and regulations that criminalize people based on their sexual orientation, gender identity, gender expression, and sex characteristics.

- Introduce progressive legislation and effective legal protections to combat discrimination, bullying, cyberbullying, and harassment in educational settings and to create more inclusive educational systems for students and teachers who are sexual and gender minorities.

- Amend existing laws or create more inclusive and protective legal frameworks in the workplace to explicitly protect people from discrimination on the basis of sexual orientation, gender identity and expression, and sex characteristics.

- Establish a comprehensive legal framework to regulate nondiscriminatory access to public services.

- Introduce legislation or amend current laws or regulations to allow sexual and gender minority organizations to register and operate freely and ensure that activists can advocate for sexual and gender minority equality.

- Enact or amend laws to specifically prohibit hate crimes against sexual and gender minorities.

In this first 16-country report, the drivers behind specific laws and policies in different countries are not explored, nor are the implications of discriminatory legislation on economic performance. It will be important to expand this analysis to a larger set of countries to be able to do this more detailed analysis to better understand the key factors that drive reform and to fully assess the impact of SOGI-related discrimination on economic performance. Yet, to date, investment in data collection on institutional discrimination has been limited. The International Labour Organization (ILO) reports that ". . . data [on discrimination] are typically collected through ad hoc research or situation tests, but seldom in a systematic way" (ILO 2011). Only 5 percent of global funding for sexual and gender minority issues supports research (World Bank and UNDP 2016). EQOSOGI provides a useful methodology to effectively analyze the impact of SOGI exclusion on inclusive growth.

Notes

1. For more information, see the World Bank's Sexual Orientation and Gender Identity website at https://www.worldbank.org/en/topic/sexual-orientation-and-gender-identity.
2. These public services can include health care, social housing, public transportation, electricity, water supply, waste disposal, microcredits, health insurance, social pensions, unemployment insurance, and child benefits, among others.
3. Pathologizing requirements can include sterilization, sex-affirming surgeries, psychiatric diagnosis, and divorce, among others.
4. These services include access to vaccinations, sanitation, transportation, family planning, health services, HIV prevention services, information on vulnerable sexual practices, antiretrovirals, medication for gender-reassignment surgery, and support for transgender individuals during and after gender reassignment survey, among others.

References

ILO (International Labour Organization). 2011. "Equality at Work: The Continuing Challenge—Global Report under the Follow-Up to the ILO Declaration on Fundamental Principles and Rights at Work." Geneva: International Labour Office. http://www.ilo.org/wcmsp5/groups/public/---ed_norm/---declaration/documents/publication/wcms_166583.pdf.

World Bank and UNDP (United Nations Development Programme). 2016. "Investing in a Research Revolution for LGBTI Inclusion." World Bank, Washington, DC. https://openknowledge.worldbank.org/handle/10986/25376.

Abbreviations

CCMA	Commission for Conciliation, Mediation and Arbitration (South Africa)
CMU	Country Management Unit
CONAPRED	National Council to Prevent Discrimination (Mexico)
CSO	civil society organization
EQOSOGI	Equality of Opportunity for Sexual and Gender Minorities
ESF	Environmental and Social Framework
GDP	gross domestic product
ILGA World	International Lesbian, Gay, Bisexual, Trans and Intersex Association
ILO	International Labour Organization
JAMAKON	National Human Rights Commission of Bangladesh
LAU	Lebanese American University
LGBT	lesbian, gay, bisexual, transgender
LGBTI	lesbian, gay, bisexual, transgender, and intersex
NGO	nongovernmental organization
NHRIs	national human rights institutions
OAPA	Offences Against the Person Act (Jamaica)
OHCHR	United Nations Office of the High Commissioner for Human Rights
PEPUDA	Promotion of Equality and the Prevention of Unfair Discrimination Act (South Africa)
SOGI	sexual orientation and gender identity
SOGIESC	sexual orientation, gender identity, gender expression, and sex characteristics
UNDP	United Nations Development Programme
USAID	United States Agency for International Development
WBL	Women, Business and the Law
WHO	World Health Organization

The World Bank uses the acronym SOGI as short-hand when referring to the issues related to sexual orientation, gender identity, gender expression, and sex characteristics (SOGIESC). When referring to people, the World Bank sometimes uses the acronym LGBTI (lesbian, gay, bisexual, transgender, intersex) or LGBTI+ to represent the full spectrum of people of diverse sexual orientation and gender identity/gender expression/sex characteristics; and it sometimes uses the term "sexual and gender minorities" when referring to country or local contexts in which it is not common for sexual and gender minorities to use LGBTI+ or in which they are more likely to use local, culturally specific terms instead.

Introduction

Background

At the core of the World Bank Group's development mandate is a commitment to protect those who are most vulnerable so that everyone—regardless of their gender, race, religion, ethnicity, age, sexual orientation, or disability status—can access the benefits of development. Discrimination creates an uneven playing field and entails substantial economic and social costs. Nonetheless, discrimination against minorities—including sexual and gender minorities—is a global reality and is frequently enshrined in the law. This report, entitled *Equality of Opportunity for Sexual and Gender Minorities*, examines legal discrimination against sexual and gender minorities (lesbian, gay, bisexual, transgender, and intersex—LGBTI—people) by reviewing laws regulating sexual and gender minorities and by comparing laws related to sexual and gender minorities to laws applicable to the heterosexual and cisgender community.

The study finds that sexual and gender minorities often face discriminatory legal and regulatory barriers in accessing opportunities related to the markets, services, and spaces required for the development of their productive potential and earning capacity. These include barriers to accessing education, labor markets, social protection, and public services. In addition, sexual and gender minorities often experience discrimination when forming organizations, expressing their identities, seeking political participation, applying for a change in their gender marker, entering into civil partnerships or marriages, adopting children with their partners, and applying for asylum. In many countries, sexual and gender minorities are victims of hate crimes and hate speech; in others, they are criminalized. Sexual minorities might also experience discrimination—even persecution—particularly in countries where same-sex relationships are illegal.

When such injustices are institutionalized and enshrined in the law, opportunities for sexual and gender minorities to participate in and contribute to economic growth are limited, thereby constraining a country's overall development. A study in India found that discrimination against sexual and gender minorities cost the country up to 1.7 percent of gross domestic product (GDP), the equivalent of US$32 billion (Badgett 2014).[1] Similarly, the Williams Institute finds a positive correlation between GDP per capita and the existence of legal protections for sexual and gender minorities.[2] Other research shows that discrimination—for instance, in the labor sector—negatively affects productivity and opportunity (Fredman 2013). A World Bank study reveals that LGBTI people in Thailand may experience significant levels of discrimination and exclusion (World Bank 2018b).[3] Other World Bank research shows that taking action to promote the inclusion of sexual and gender minorities will not only ensure that all people's rights are protected, respected, and fulfilled, but that such measures will bring benefits to societies, countries, and regions at-large (World Bank 2018c).

The report is intended to be the first in a series of studies analyzing laws and regulations affecting sexual and gender minorities' economic opportunities in countries worldwide. The study provides a comprehensive overview of legislation and policies that discriminate against sexual and gender minorities or do not provide appropriate protective measures against discrimination. It provides countries and the development community with methodological guidelines to monitor the legal framework regulating marginalized groups' access to markets, services, and public spaces. The aim is to promote a snapshot of the legal hurdles facing sexual and gender minorities to encourage reforms that lead to more inclusive growth. There is a dearth of comparable data on the legal and regulatory framework impacting sexual and gender minorities, and this report is an important step by the World Bank to help fill the data gap.

Methodology and Scoring

The *Equality of Opportunity for Sexual and Gender Minorities* (EQOSOGI) report identifies laws that impact sexual and gender minorities' access to markets, services, and spaces in a country and examines how those laws either enable or inhibit the inclusion of sexual and gender minorities (World Bank 2013). The methodology consists of a data set of laws and policies based on a survey of experts as well as desk research and information retrieved from databases. It relies on approaches from previous World Bank initiatives, including Equality of Opportunity in Global Prosperity (Panter and others 2017) and Women, Business and the Law.[4]

These initiatives have produced global objective quantitative indicators for business regulation and gender discrimination. The data set collected for this study presents laws and policies in the following areas:

- Laws giving rise to discriminatory treatment on the basis of sexual orientation, gender identity, gender expression, and/or sex characteristics

- Laws prohibiting discrimination against sexual and gender minorities

- Policies and other enforcement mechanisms that implement existing antidiscrimination laws

Data Sources and Country Selection

Three sources were used to collect relevant data: (a) a standardized questionnaire answered by lawyers, ombudsman institutions, judges, academics, and civil society organizations (CSOs); (b) public government records identifying national laws and regulations, as well as relevant data from international legal databases and human rights organizations; and (c) desk research.

Sixteen countries were selected (table I.1 and map I.1) to represent several key characteristics: (a) diversity of geographies (representing all World Bank regions and a high-income country grouping);[5] (b) income levels (representing low-income, middle-income, and high-income countries); (c) various legal traditions of the world; and (d) inclusiveness of sexual and gender minorities (those less inclusive to those more inclusive), ensuring a diverse and holistic picture of these issues.

TABLE I.1

EQOSOGI Coverage, by Region

Region or grouping	Number of countries	Countries
East Asia and the Pacific	1	Indonesia
Europe and Central Asia	2	Kosovo, Ukraine
Latin America and the Caribbean	4	Costa Rica, Jamaica, Mexico, Uruguay
Middle East and North Africa	2	Lebanon, Tunisia
OECD high income	2	Canada, Japan
South Asia	2	Bangladesh, India
Sub-Saharan Africa	3	Mozambique, Nigeria, South Africa

Source: World Bank Group, Equality of Opportunity project.

Note: These countries were selected to represent the various regions and legal traditions of the world. They range from low- to high-income countries, and all contain segments of the population that are considered minorities and that face discrimination. EQOSOGI = Equality of Opportunity for Sexual and Gender Minorities; OECD = Organisation for Economic Co-operation and Development.

MAP I.1

Countries Covered by EQOSOGI, 2021

IBRD 45503 |
JANUARY 2021

Source: World Bank Group, Equality of Opportunity project.

Indicator Sets

The report developed six indicator sets to measure discriminatory legislation on the basis of sexual orientation, gender identity and expression, and sex characteristics. For consistency purposes, where relevant, EQOSOGI adopted indicator language from A Set of Proposed Indicators for the LGBTI Inclusion Index. This index was developed under the leadership of the World Bank and the United Nations Development Programme (UNDP) with LGBTI CSOs and other stakeholders; it was intended to be the indicators that will populate the LGBTI Inclusion Index, a UNDP initiative. The six EQOSOGI indicator sets are as follows:

1. Criminalization and SOGI

2. Access to inclusive education

3. Access to the labor market

4. Access to public services and social protection

5. Civil and political inclusion

6. Protection from hate crimes

The indicator set on *criminalization and SOGI* examines the level of criminalization of same-sex behavior between consenting adults and the outlawing of sexual and gender minorities. It also looks at whether sexual and gender minorities are indirectly discriminated against through vagrancy, public nuisance, or public morals laws. The indicator set on *access to inclusive education* examines the ability of sexual and gender minorities to have equal access to public education of a consistent quality across the entire population. The indicator set reviews whether laws and policies exist to combat the bullying of sexual and gender minority students. Similarly, the indicator set on *access to the labor market* identifies antidiscrimination laws and regulations to protect sexual and gender minorities from discrimination during the recruitment process in public and private sector workplaces. The indicator set on *access to public services and social protection* mechanisms is especially important to sexual and gender minorities because it analyzes access to health care, HIV preventive services, and gender reassignment surgery. The *civil and political inclusion* indicator set examines the level of political participation by sexual and gender minorities and civil society actors, as well as the ability of nongovernmental organizations (NGOs) to operate without fear of persecution. Finally, the indicator set on *protection from hate crimes* examines the existence of laws and mechanisms that criminalize hate crimes and provide protections for sexual and gender minorities or those perceived to be sexual and gender minorities.

The EQOSOGI indicator sets were constructed using codified sources of national law—constitutions, education laws and regulations, labor codes, family laws, and criminal codes, as well as public moral, nuisance, and vagrancy laws. The study relies on responses from country practitioners with expertise in the areas covered. Laws and policies that are understood to include sexual and gender minorities but do not explicitly mention them were not included, unless interpreted so by the courts.

The EQOSOGI methodology offers several advantages. It is transparent and uses factual information derived directly from laws and regulations. Because standard assumptions are used when collecting data for the six areas covered, comparisons are valid across countries. For example, it was assumed that sexual and gender minorities reside in each country's largest business city. The study's focus on written legislation does not disregard the often-substantial gap between the law and actual practice. It recognizes that sexual and gender minorities do not always have access to the equality to which they are entitled by law. Still, the data on formal legal differentiation provide a first step to identify potential challenges for sexual and gender minorities in the six areas studied. Finally, the data identify both obstacles to sexual and gender minority participation and legislation that could be amended based on this information.

More than 160 professionals worldwide assisted in providing the data for the EQOSOGI indicators. Respondents were selected based on their expertise in the applicable legal and regulatory fields. They were identified through desk research on CSOs, law firms specializing in the areas covered by the study, judges, academics in the relevant fields, practitioners, and activists, among others. Contributors were also identified with the help of the International Lesbian, Gay, Bisexual, Trans and Intersex Association (ILGA World) and through referrals from other experts in each country. Experts are central to the EQOSOGI initiative, and the team allocated significant time and resources to ensure the quality of the experts consulted. The local experts that supported this initiative did so on a pro bono basis.

The lawyers on the EQOSOGI team corroborated the data points that contributed to the EQOSOGI indicator sets by analyzing the relevant laws and regulations. The role of contributors is mainly advisory. EQOSOGI has a team of experts on the topics measured by the study (lawyers familiar with different legal systems who specialize in different areas of law such as labor, human rights, and criminal law). They analyzed the information provided by country-based contributors and cross-checked the responses against relevant laws and regulations. For example, the EQOSOGI team examined the relevant criminal code to determine whether the country criminalizes same-sex relations between consenting adults.

The standardized questionnaire was the first point of contact with the local experts. After receiving the questionnaires, the EQOSOGI team followed up by phone or email with the local experts to conduct additional research and reconcile possible discrepancies in responses. When the team encountered conflicting responses, it attempted to clarify the answer through desk research or entries from public legal international databases and local CSOs. In addition, the team reverted to the contributors that submitted conflicting answers and requested clarifications. The most common reason for conflicting answers is the interpretation of the law or the law's practical application.

Limitations of the Methodology and Data

There are limitations with the data and this initiative does not cover many important policy areas. The collected data refer to the formal legal and regulatory environment (de jure) for six indicator sets. The practice or implementation of the law (de facto) is covered only tangentially by identifying policies and other enforcement mechanisms seen as proxies of implementation. For example, the study excludes political party laws, which are an important factor in determining minority representation in political parties. The crime of genocide, which may be regarded as a crime inherently motivated by hate or bias, is also not discussed. This omission was intentional because the study concerns only individually motivated crimes and not mass atrocities that constitute international crimes. In addition, the study focuses only on laws governing the formal economy. Although many sexual and gender minorities may work in the informal economy, one of the study's main goals is to define features of the formal economy that prevent sexual and gender minorities from making the transition from informal to formal employment. Finally, the study does not cover customary or religious laws because of their often-uncodified status and the resulting difficulties in defining the rules.

Future editions of this study will cover additional countries and refine the indicator sets. In the interim, the six indicator sets will be monitored to capture progress regarding laws and regulations related to sexual and gender minorities' inclusion under the law in the current list of countries. This initial 16-country report presents the factual data as collected. It does not attempt to analyze the drivers behind the existence or lack of specific laws and policies. Future editions will contain more details on legal changes and the processes associated with those changes.

Currently, the sample of countries in this report is small (16) and does not allow for economic analysis, simple or sophisticated. In future reports, when more countries are included, a simple correlation analysis would allow a comparison of this initiative's findings with measures of economic growth and prosperity and would facilitate an examination of connections. For example, a positive correlation between EQOSOGI scores and GDP per capita would suggest that countries with more inclusive environments for sexual and gender minorities are more economically advanced. Similar correlations could be established with openness indicators, such as the Worldwide Governance Indicators and the Freedom House Index.[6] Human development indicators, such as the Human Development Index and the Human Capital Index,[7] could also offer unique insights. Lastly, a comparison between the EQOSOGI data and the data produced by the World Bank's Women, Business and the Law initiative would offer insight into the interconnection between equality under the law for sexual and gender minorities and equality under the law for women. Box I.1 provides a general example of the basic type of analysis that could be carried out with a larger sample size.

Data presented in *Equality of Opportunity for Sexual and Gender Minorities* are current as of February 28, 2020 (see table I.2 for the indicator questions).

BOX I.1 Opportunities for Further Analysis

An example of possible future correlation analysis

There is a positive and very strong correlation between the Women, Business and the Law scores and the *Equality of Opportunity for Sexual and Gender Minorities* (EQOSOGI) scores (Spearman r = 0.8948*; Pearson r = 0.8326*) (figure BI.1.1). Women, Business and the Law analyzes laws and regulations affecting women's economic inclusion. Sexual orientation and gender identity (SOGI) inclusion has been paralleled with gender equality, and indicators of women's economic autonomy are often used as proxies for the economic inclusion of lesbian, gay, bisexual, transgender, and intersex (LGBTI) people (Badgett and Sell 2018). The strong positive correlation between the Women, Business and the Law scores and the EQOSOGI scores further supports the hypothesis that countries with laws that empower women tend to also have inclusive laws toward sexual and gender minorities and that countries with inclusive SOGI laws tend also to empower women.

FIGURE BI.1.1

Correlation between EQOSOGI and Women, Business and the Law Scores

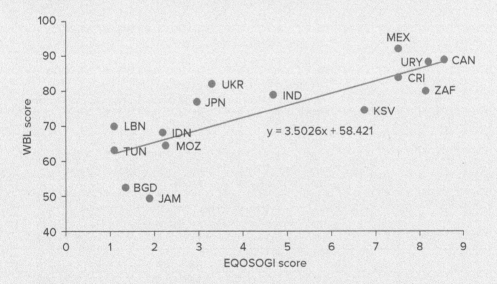

Source: World Bank Group, Equality of Opportunity database.

Note: EQOSOGI = Equality of Opportunity for Sexual and Gender Minorities (scores range from 0 to 10); WBL = Women, Business and the Law (scores range from 0 to 100). BGD = Bangladesh; CAN = Canada; CRI = Costa Rica; IDN = Indonesia; IND = India; JAM = Jamaica; JPN = Japan; KSV = Kosovo; LBN = Lebanon; MEX = Mexico; MOZ = Mozambique; NGA = Nigeria; TUN = Tunisia; UKR = Ukraine; URY = Uruguay; ZAF = South Africa.

TABLE I.2

Equality of Opportunity for Sexual and Gender Minorities Indicator Sets

Indicator	Scoring	Question
Criminalization and SOGI		
1.	If no: +2.5	Are there any laws, constitutional provisions, and/or regulations that criminalize people based on sexual orientation, gender identity, gender expression, and sex characteristics (SOGIESC)?
2.	If no: +2.5	Does your country criminalize same-sex relations between consenting adults?
3.	+2.5	Is the legal age for consensual sex the same for heterosexuals as for sexual and gender minorities?
4.	If no: +2.5	Are sexual and gender minorities targeted with other laws such as vagrancy, public nuisance, or public morals?
Access to inclusive education		
1.	+2	Are there any laws, constitutional provisions, and/or regulations that prohibit discrimination against students and/or teachers in educational settings based on sexual orientation, gender identity, gender expression, and sex characteristics?
2.	+1.2	Are there any laws and/or regulations that prohibit discrimination in school admission based on sexual orientation and gender identity (SOGI)?
3.	+2	Are there any laws and/or regulations preventing and addressing bullying and harassment against students and/or teachers in the educational system that include students based on actual or perceived SOGI?
4.	+1.2	Are there any laws and/or regulations that mandate the revision of national textbooks/national curricula in primary and secondary education to eliminate discriminatory language (homophobic or transphobic language, for example)?
5.	+1.2	Are there any laws and/or regulations that mandate training of schoolteachers and other school staff in primary and secondary education on antidiscrimination of students who are sexual and gender minorities, or those perceived as such?
6.	+1.2	Are there any laws and/or regulations that mandate the creation of courses on sex education in a SOGI-inclusive manner in secondary and tertiary education?
7.	+1.2	Are there any concrete mechanisms (national or local) for reporting cases of SOGI-related discrimination, violence, and bullying toward students, including incidents perpetrated by representatives of the education sector such as teachers and other school staff?

TABLE I.2 *continued*

Indicator	Scoring	Question
		Access to the labor market
1.	+1.5	Are there any laws, constitutional provisions, and/or regulations prohibiting discrimination based on sexual orientation, gender identity, gender expression, and sex characteristics (SOGIESC) in public and private sector workplaces at the national level?
2.	+0.75	Are there any laws and/or regulations prohibiting discrimination in recruitment in the public sector based on SOGI?
3.	+0.75	Are there any laws and/or regulations prohibiting discrimination in recruitment in the private sector based on SOGI?
4.	If no: +0.75	Are there any laws and/or regulations prohibiting sexual and gender minorities from obtaining employment in specific industries?
5.	+0.75	Are there any laws and/or regulations prohibiting an employer from asking an individual's SOGI and/or marital status during the recruitment process?
6.	+0.75	Are there any laws, constitutional provisions, and/or regulations prescribing equal remuneration for work of equal value for sexual and gender minorities?
7.	+1	Are there any laws and/or regulations prohibiting the dismissal of employees on the basis of their perceived or actual SOGI?
8.	+0.75	Are there any laws and/or regulations that allow an employee to bring a claim for employment discrimination on SOGI grounds in the public sector?
9.	+0.75	Are there any laws and/or regulations that allow an employee to bring a claim for employment discrimination on SOGI grounds in the private sector?
10.	+0.75	Do victims of employment discrimination based on SOGI grounds have a right to free or reduced legal assistance (if proven they do not have the necessary means to cover the cost of the claim)?
11.	+0.75	Is there a national equality body or national human rights institution responsible for handling charges of employment discrimination related to SOGI?
12.	+0.75	Does the pension system for civil servants provide the same benefits to same-sex partners provided to different-sex spouses?
		Access to public services and social protection
1.	If 1: +2.5 If 2-4: +5 If 5-12: +7.5	Are there any laws, constitutional provisions, and/or regulations that prohibit discrimination based on sexual orientation, gender identity, gender expression, and sex characteristics in accessing health care, social housing, public transportation, electricity, water supply, waste disposal services, microcredits, subsidized health insurance, social pensions, unemployment insurance, child benefits, other social services, and so on?

TABLE I.2 *continued*

Indicator	Scoring	Question
1.1		In health care?
1.2		In social housing?
1.3		In public transportation?
1.4		In electricity?
1.5		In water supply?
1.6		In waste disposal services?
1.7		In microcredits?
1.8		In subsidized health insurance?
1.9		In social pensions?
1.10		In unemployment insurance?
1.11		In child benefits?
1.12		In other services?
2.	Not scored	Are there any laws and/or regulations that allow civil society organizations (CSOs) to provide social services specifically to sexual and gender minorities? (for example, vaccinations, sanitation, transportation, family planning, health services—psychological, physiological, and sexual and reproductive; HIV preventive services [for example, condoms, lubricants, pre-exposure prophylaxis, and so on]; and information on vulnerable sexual practices, antiretrovirals, medication for gender-reassignment surgery, and support for transgender people during/after gender reassignment surgery)
2.1		Vaccinations?
2.2		Sanitation?
2.3		Transportation?
2.4		Family planning?
2.5		Health services (psychological)?
2.6		Health services (physiological)?
2.7		Health services (sexual and reproductive)?
2.8		HIV prevention services and information on vulnerable sexual practices?
2.9		Antiretrovirals?
2.10		Medication for gender-reassignment surgery?
2.11		Support for transgender individuals during/after gender reassignment surgery?
2.12		Other

TABLE I.2 *continued*

Indicator	Scoring	Question
3.	If no: +1.25	Are there any laws and/or regulations imposing funding limitations on civil society organizations on the provision of such services?
4.	+1.25	Is there a national equality body or national human rights institution responsible for handling charges of SOGI-based discrimination in public services?
Civil and political inclusion		
1.	+0.5	Are there laws and/or regulations that establish national human rights institutions that include sexual orientation, gender identity, gender expression and sex characteristics (SOGIESC) within their mandate and/or specific institutions with expertise on and a mandate to deal with sexual and gender minority rights and inclusion?
2.	+1	Are organizations (NGOs—nongovernmental organizations—and so on) related to (a) sexual minority rights, (b) transgender rights, and (c) intersex rights permitted under the law?
2.1		Sexual minority rights
2.2		Transgender rights
2.3		Intersex rights
2.4		If yes, are the NGOs subject to limitation by the state on the basis of national security, public order, morality, or other grounds?
3.	Not scored	How many members of parliament or other national, elected representative body openly self-identify as a sexual or gender minority?
4.	+0.5	Does the law mandate quotas for sexual and gender minorities in parliament?
5.	+0.5	Are there national action plans on SOGI?
6.	If no: +1	Are there any laws and/or regulations that restrict expression, civic participation, or association related to SOGI?
7.	+1	Are there any centralized protocols for updating sex/gender in official certifications without pathologizing requirements?
8.	+1	Can same-sex couples enter into a registered partnership or civil union?
9.	+0.5	Can same-sex couples get legally married?
10.	+0.5	Is second parent and/or joint adoption by same-sex partner(s) legally possible?
11.	If no: +0.5	Do laws and/or regulations relating to any of these categories differ between sexual and gender minorities and the rest of the population?
11.1		Obtaining citizenship?
11.2		Obtaining a passport?

TABLE I.2 *continued*

Indicator	Scoring	Question
11.3		Obtaining an ID card?
12.	If no: +0.5	When applying for a passport or ID cards, are there only two options for "male or female"?
12.1		Passports
12.2		ID cards
13.	+0.5	Are there any laws and/or regulations that require the assigned gender on the passport and/or ID card to match the expression of one's gender?
14.	If no: +0.5	Are there any laws and/or regulations that require gender-reassignment surgery for intersex children in order to receive a birth certificate?
15.	+0.5	Are there any laws and/or regulations prohibiting/banning/protecting against sexual orientation and gender identity "conversion therapy"?
16.	+0.5	Are there any laws and/or regulations that allow an individual to obtain a new ID card or passport after gender reassignment?
17.	+0.5	Does your country recognize persecution based on SOGI as one of the grounds for asylum?
Protection from hate crimes		
1.	+2	Are there any laws, constitutional provisions, and/or regulations that criminalize hate crimes based on sexual orientation, gender identity, gender expression, and sex characteristics?
2.	+1.6	Are there any laws and/or regulations that require government agencies to collect data on hate crimes committed against sexual and gender minorities or those perceived to be sexual or gender minorities?
3.	+1.6	Are there mechanisms in your country for monitoring and reporting hate-motivated acts of violence against sexual and gender minorities?
4.	+1.6	Are crimes committed against someone based on that person's SOGI considered as aggravating circumstances by the law?
5.	+1.6 If 1: +0.8 If 2-6: +0.16	Are there any laws and/or regulations that mandate training of the following professionals on recognizing and identifying hate crimes? (for example, police officers, prosecutors, judges, social workers, and paramedics/doctors)
5.1		Police officers?
5.2		Prosecutors?
5.3		Judges?
5.4		Social workers?
5.5		Paramedics/doctors?

TABLE I.2 *continued*

Indicator	Scoring	Question
5.6		Other?
6.	+1.6 If 1: +0.8 If 2-6: +0.16	Are there any laws and/or regulations that mandate the provision of any of the following services to victims of hate crimes? (for example, legal assistance [including asylum applications and completing court forms], shelter/housing, forensic or medical examinations, and medical certificates)
6.1		Legal assistance (including asylum applications and completing court forms)?
6.2		Shelter/housing?
6.3		Forensics or medical examinations?
6.4		Medical certificates?
6.5		Other?

Source: World Bank Group, Equality of Opportunity project.

Scoring

The *Equality of Opportunity for Sexual and Gender Minorities* report seeks to identify a country's approach to sexual and gender minorities' inclusion by scoring its performance on a survey divided into six indicator sets (table I.2). Within each indicator set, a question is assigned a score based on its importance in relation to the other questions within that indicator set. The maximum potential score per indicator set is 10 (a higher score is better). Negative scores are not awarded. Questions are scored based on Yes/No answers. Indicator set–specific scores are calculated out of 10 (for example, Kosovo's score in the access to inclusive education indicator set is 5.2 out of 10). High scores do not necessarily imply poor overall legal and social environments and vice versa because the focus is on legislation relevant for equality of opportunity for sexual and gender minorities.

Each question's base score is determined by dividing the total points available in the indicator set by the number of questions in the indicator set. All six indicator sets are equally weighted (each set is equally important). Within each indicator set, some questions are considered more important or more encompassing than others—the scoring for those questions is weighted more heavily. For example, for an indicator set with seven questions, the 10 available points are divided by 7, resulting in a base score of 1.43 per question for that indicator set. The weighted questions each receive an enhanced score of 2. The remaining points are divided equally between the remaining questions. Assuming that two weighted questions each receive the same weighted score of 2, then 2 + 2 = 4 and 10 − 4 = 6, representing the remaining available score. Therefore, the five remaining questions share the remaining 6 points, with a resulting score of 1.2 per non-weighted question.

Per World Bank methodology,[8] a distance to frontier score is calculated to assess the absolute level of performance over time compared with the best practice currently in existence. While the distance to frontier measure is a relative one, when compared across years, it shows how much a country has changed over time, as opposed to the absolute score, which indicates how much the country has changed relative to other countries. The score measures each country's distance to the "frontier," which represents the best performance observed on each of the indicator sets across all countries in the survey (table I.3). There is a possibility that a new frontier will emerge with the addition of more countries. One can see both the gap between a particular country's performance and the best performance at any point in time and assess the absolute change in the country's regulatory environment over time as measured by the *Equality of Opportunity for Sexual and Gender Minorities* report. A country's distance to frontier is reflected on a scale of 0 to 100 percent, where 0 percent represents the lowest performance and 100 percent represents the frontier (percent = country score/frontier). The distance to frontier approach is helpful when comparing results over time. For example, a score of 75 percent in 2020 means that the country was 25 percentage points away from the frontier constructed from the best performances across all countries and across time. A score of 80 percent in 2021 (with the frontier unchanged) would indicate the country is improving.[9]

TABLE I.3

Distance to Frontier Scores

Criminalization and SOGI		
Country	Score (out of 10)	Distance to frontier (%)
Canada	10	100.0
Costa Rica	10	100.0
Japan	10	100.0
Kosovo	10	100.0
Mexico	10	100.0
Mozambique	10	100.0
South Africa	10	100.0
Ukraine	10	100.0
Uruguay	10	100.0
India	7.5	75.0
Indonesia	7.5	75.0
Bangladesh	2.5	25.0
Jamaica	2.5	25.0
Lebanon	2.5	25.0
Nigeria	2.5	25.0
Tunisia	2.5	25.0

TABLE I.3 *continued*

Access to inclusive education

Country	Score (out of 10)	Distance to frontier (%)
Canada	8.8	100.0
Costa Rica	8.8	100.0
South Africa	7.6	86.4
India	7.6	86.4
Uruguay	7.6	72.7
Kosovo	5.2	59.1
Mexico	4.4	50.0
Japan	1.2	13.6
Bangladesh	0	0.0
Indonesia	0	0.0
Jamaica	0	0.0
Lebanon	0	0.0
Mozambique	0	0.0
Nigeria	0	0.0
Tunisia	0	0.0
Ukraine	0	0.0

Access to the labor market

Country	Score (out of 10)	Distance to frontier (%)
South Africa	8.5	100.0
Canada	8.25	97.1
Costa Rica	7.75	91.2
Kosovo	7.75	91.2
Mexico	7.5	88.2
India	6.75	79.4
Uruguay	6.75	79.4
Ukraine	6	70.6
Jamaica	4.5	52.9

TABLE I.3 *continued*

Country	Score (out of 10)	Distance to frontier (%)
Mozambique	3	35.3
Bangladesh	0.75	8.8
Indonesia	0.75	8.8
Japan	0.75	8.8
Lebanon	0.75	8.8
Nigeria	0.75	8.8
Tunisia	0.75	8.8

Access to public services and social protection

Country	Score (out of 10)	Distance to frontier (%)
Canada	10	100.0
Mexico	10	100.0
South Africa	10	100.0
Uruguay	10	100.0
Costa Rica	8.75	87.5
Kosovo	8.75	87.5
India	5	50.0
Bangladesh	1.25	12.5
Indonesia	1.25	12.5
Jamaica	1.25	12.5
Japan	1.25	12.5
Lebanon	1.25	12.5
Mozambique	1.25	12.5
Tunisia	1.25	12.5
Ukraine	1.25	12.5
Nigeria	0	0.0

TABLE I.3 *continued*

Civil and political inclusion		
Country	Score (out of 10)	Distance to frontier (%)
Costa Rica	8	100.0
Canada	7.5	93.8
Mexico	7.5	93.8
South Africa	7	87.5
Uruguay	7	87.5
India	5.5	68.8
Bangladesh	4	50.0
Japan	4	50.0
Kosovo	4	50.0
Indonesia	3.5	43.8
Jamaica	3	37.5
Ukraine	3	37.5
Lebanon	2	25.0
Mozambique	2	25.0
Tunisia	2	25.0
Nigeria	1	12.5

Protection from hate crimes		
Country	Score (out of 10)	Distance to frontier (%)
Uruguay	8.4	100.0
Canada	6.8	81.0
Mexico	6.4	76.2
Kosovo	5.2	61.9
South Africa	5.2	61.9
Costa Rica	3.2	38.1
India	1.6	19.0
Bangladesh	0	0.0
Indonesia	0	0.0

TABLE I.3 *continued*		
Country	Score (out of 10)	Distance to frontier (%)
Jamaica	0	0.0
Japan	0	0.0
Lebanon	0	0.0
Mozambique	0	0.0
Nigeria	0	0.0
Tunisia	0	0.0
Ukraine	0	0.0

Source: World Bank Group, Equality of Opportunity database.

Notes

1. India has decriminalized homosexuality since the Badgett research.
2. See, for example, Badgett (2014); Badgett, Waaldijk, and van der Meulen Rodgers (2019); Flores and Park (2018).
3. Because the acronym LGBTI is centered on Western cultures and may not encompass concepts around the world that have long preceded this acronym, the study uses the term *sexual and gender minorities* interchangeably. Furthermore, the World Bank uses the acronym SOGI as shorthand when referring to the issues related to sexual orientation, gender identity, gender expression, and sex characteristics (SOGIESC).
4. Information about Women, Business and the Law is available at https://wbl.worldbank.org/en/wbl.
5. The World Bank Group regions are East Asia and Pacific, Europe and Central Asia, Latin America and the Caribbean, Middle East and North Africa, South Asia, and Sub-Saharan Africa.
6. Information about the Worldwide Governance Indicators project can be found at https://info.worldbank .org/governance/wgi/; information about the Freedom House Index is available at https://freedomhouse .org/countries/freedom-world/scores.
7. Details about the UNDP's Human Development Index can be found at http://hdr.undp.org/en /content/human-development-index-hdi; details about the World Bank's Human Capital Project are available at https://www.worldbank.org/en/publication/human-capital.
8. For more information on the Women, Business and the Law methodology, see https://wbl.worldbank .org/en/methodology. Also see the chapter on distance to frontier and ease of doing business ranking in *Doing Business 2018*, available from https://www.doingbusiness.org/content/dam/doingBusiness /media/Annual-Reports/English/DB18-Chapters/DB18-DTF-and-DBRankings.pdf.
9. For a discussion of the distance to the frontier, see the World Bank's 2018 *Doing Business* report (World Bank 2018a, 12–13).

References

Badgett, M.V. Lee. 2014. "The Economic Cost of Stigma and the Exclusion of LGBT People: A Case Study of India (English)." World Bank, Washington, DC.

Badgett, M.V. Lee, and Randall Sell. 2018. "A Set of Proposed Indicators for the LGBTI Inclusion Index (English)." World Bank, Washington, DC. http://documents.worldbank.org/curated /en/608921536847788293/A-Set-of-Proposed-Indicators-for-the-LGBTI-Inclusion-Index.

Badgett, M.V. Lee, Kees Waaldijk, and Yana van der Meulen Rodgers. 2019. "The Relationship between LGBT Inclusion and Economic Development: Macro-Level Evidence." *World Development* 120: 1–14. https://www.sciencedirect.com/science/article/pii/S0305750X19300695.

Berggren, Niclas, and Mikael Elinder. 2012. "Is Tolerance Good or Bad for Growth?" *Public Choice* 150: 283–308. https://doi.org/10.1007/s11127-010-9702-x.

Flores, Andrew Ryan, and Andrew Park. 2018. *Examining the Relationship between Social Acceptance of LGBT People and Legal Inclusion of Sexual Minorities.* The Williams Institute, UCLA School of Law. https://www.researchgate.net/publication/332060888_Examining_the_relationship_between_social _acceptance_of_LGBT_people_and_legal_inclusion_of_sexual_minorities.

Fredman, Sandra. 2013. "Anti-Discrimination Laws and Work in the Developing World: A Thematic Overview." World Development Report Background Papers. World Bank, Washington, DC.

Panter, Elaine, Tanya Primiani, Tazeen Hasan, and Eduardo Calderon Pontaza. 2017. "Antidiscrimination Law and Shared Prosperity: An Analysis of the Legal Framework of Six Economies and Their Impact on the Equality of Opportunities of Ethnic, Religious, and Sexual Minorities." Policy Research Working Paper No. 7992. World Bank, Washington, DC. https://openknowledge.worldbank.org/handle/10986/26242.

World Bank. 2013. *Inclusion Matters: The Foundation for Shared Prosperity.* Washington, DC: World Bank. https://openknowledge.worldbank.org/handle/10986/16195.

World Bank. 2018a. *Doing Business: Reforming to Create Jobs.* Washington, DC: World Bank. https://www .doingbusiness.org/content/dam/doingBusiness/media/Annual-Reports/English/DB18-print-report.pdf.

World Bank. 2018b. *Economic Inclusion of LGBTI Groups in Thailand (Vol. 2): Main Report (English).* Washington, DC: World Bank Group. https://openknowledge.worldbank.org/handle/10986/29632.

World Bank. 2018c. *Life on the Margins: Survey Results of the Experiences of LGBTI People in Southeastern Europe (English).* Washington, DC: World Bank. http://documents.worldbank.org/curated/en/123651538514203449 /Life-on-the-Margins-Survey-Results-of-the-Experiences-of-LGBTI-People-in-Southeastern-Europe.

Additional Readings

Aghion, Philippe, Eve Caroli, and Cecilia García-Peñalosa. 1999. "Inequality and Economic Growth: The Perspective of the New Growth Theories." *Journal of Economic Literature* 37 (4): 1615–60.

Bénabou, Roland. 1996. "Inequality and Growth." *NBER Macroeconomics Annual 1996* (11): 11–92.

Bertola, Giuseppe, Reto Foellmi, and Josef Zweimüller. 2005. *Income Distribution in Macroeconomic Models.* Princeton, NJ, and Woodstock, Oxfordshire, UK: Princeton University Press.

Bourguignon, Francois. 2004. "The Poverty-Growth-Inequality Triangle." Presented at Indian Council for Research on International Economic Relations, New Delhi, February 4. http://documents.worldbank .org/curated/en/449711468762020101/pdf/28102.pdf.

Ehrhart, Christophe. 2009. "The Effects of Inequality on Growth: A Survey of the Theoretical and Empirical Literature." Working Paper 107, ECINEQ, Society for the Study of Economic Inequality.

World Bank. 2006. *World Development Report 2006: Equity and Development.* Washington, DC: World Bank.

1
Criminalization and SOGI

KEY FINDINGS

Canada, Costa Rica, Japan, Kosovo, Mexico, Mozambique, South Africa, Ukraine, and Uruguay do not criminalize same-sex relations. They also do not use laws on vagrancy, public nuisance, or public morals to target sexual and gender minorities.

Five of the 16 countries measured by the report do criminalize conduct based on the individual's sexual orientation.

All sample countries have the same legal age for consensual sex for opposite sex and same-sex relations.

Almost one-half of the countries analyzed use vagrancy, public nuisance, or public moral laws to target sexual and gender minorities.

It is advised that countries repeal laws, constitutional provisions, and regulations that criminalize people based on their sexual orientation, gender identity, gender expression, and sex characteristics.

Importance of the Decriminalization of Same-Sex Behavior Indicator Set

Around the globe, sexual and gender minorities are criminalized for who they love, how they dress and express their gender, and ultimately for who they are (ILGA 2019). Diverse cultures, traditions, religions, and outlooks explain such laws. To live openly and honestly without fear represents one of the most basic human freedoms.

> As of December 2019, 70 states continue to criminalize same-sex consensual activity, and six United Nations Member States still impose the death penalty on consensual same-sex sexual acts. Furthermore, in 26 countries, the maximum penalty can vary between 10 years to life imprisonment for same-sex consensual activity.
>
> — *ILGA (2019)*

Respect for the right to privacy and freedom from discrimination are critical to minority and other excluded groups in every society. The criminalization of consensual same-sex relations violates these rights by devaluing people based on their human characteristics. Hiding one's identity and being fearful of openly communicating ideas, views, and needs can lead to isolation and frustrate the basic desire to belong to a community.

Changing society's attitudes toward sexual and gender minorities is often viewed as a path toward decriminalization. Still, it is often the legalization of same-sex sexual activity that improves attitudes toward sexual and gender minorities (Kenny and Patel 2012). Decriminalization not only encourages more open and inclusive laws, but also it creates more friendly and accepting communities for sexual and gender minorities. Repealing laws that criminalize same-sex conduct and punish sexual and gender minorities is an important step toward combating prejudice and protecting lives (Flores and Park 2018). Nevertheless, removing legal obstacles does not always or immediately translate into improvements for sexual and gender minorities.

> Decriminalization of gender and sexual minorities is often the first legal obstacle and window of opportunity for greater inclusion.
>
> —*United Nations (2016)*

Globally, sexual and gender minorities frequently fear for their lives (Mendos 2019). Such constant fear shapes all aspects of their existence and can negatively affect their physical and mental health. Consequently, individuals cannot fully contribute to their communities and society overall, which can result in diminished economic development (Badgett and others 2014). Deeply rooted homophobia, biphobia, transphobia, and interphobia—coupled with laws that criminalize people based on their sexual orientation, gender identity, gender expression, or sex characteristics—leave sexual and gender minorities vulnerable to discrimination and violence. Particular rights, such as access to health care or education, are fundamental to a person's sense of self-worth; however, the effort becomes impossible if the self-identities of sexual and gender minorities remain criminalized.[1]

The United Nations Office of the High Commissioner for Human Rights (OHCHR) has made decriminalization based on sexual orientation and gender identity a core issue in its fight against discrimination.[2] By decriminalizing identities and behavior related to sexual orientation and gender identity (SOGI), the fight for other rights within the sexual and gender minority community becomes more feasible. Decriminalization of sexual and gender minorities can also positively impact economic development (Badgett and others 2014). Increasing evidence shows that criminalizing homosexuality reduces productivity and economic growth. Studies have identified the economic costs of exclusion based on SOGI, such as lost labor and productivity and underinvestment in human capital. Badgett and others (2014) report a positive correlation between legal rights for sexual and gender minorities and gross domestic product (GDP) per capita. Discriminatory practices have real, tangible economic costs that should be considered. Furthermore, in an increasingly globalized and connected world, businesses can face public pressure if they invest in countries that criminalize sexual and gender minorities. Investment in these countries can be negatively affected as a result (Human Dignity Trust 2015).

The criminalization and SOGI indicator set examines a country's degree of SOGI criminalization. It also considers the level of criminalization of same-sex relations between consenting adults and whether there is a discrepancy between the legal age for consensual sex for heterosexuals and same-sex partners. The indicators also measure the existence of public morality, public nuisance, or vagrancy laws that specifically target sexual and gender minorities.

> As soon as Nigeria's Same-Sex Marriage Prohibition Act was passed in 2013, Nigerian authorities arrested several people perceived as gay men and held them in isolation, without access to a lawyer. The Prohibition Act punishes any public show of affection, even a kiss, between two people of the same sex with 10 years' imprisonment.
>
> —*Kamara (2014)*

Criminalization and Age of Consent

Freedom is a basic element of inclusion and a core pillar of fair and just societies. However, many sexual and gender minorities worldwide cannot exercise this basic right because of factors beyond their control—their sexual orientation, gender identity, gender expression, and sex characteristics. This is particularly true for consensual same-sex relations, which are illegal in many countries.[3] Moreover, the criminalization of same-sex activity is often used to target transgender people as well.[4]

The criminalization of what is essentially a private matter threatens the core existence of sexual and gender minorities. Sexual and gender minorities experience isolation in personal and public spheres, including education, health care, and the economy. This exclusion further translates into a lack of opportunities, inability to access basic services (such as health care and education), abuse and over-incarceration, and a general mistrust and fear of authorities (Mallory and others 2017). Sexual and gender minorities often lack basic means to formally report violence and abuse. At the same time, criminalization based on SOGI makes sexual and gender minorities more vulnerable and more prone to being targeted by the police (Hanssens and others 2014). Criminalization directly undermines equality and inclusion of sexual and gender minorities, and countries should urgently address existing shortcomings. Doing so can have far-reaching economic and social benefits.

Most of the 16 countries analyzed do not criminalize people based on their sexual orientation. Those countries that prohibit same-sex acts are Bangladesh, Jamaica, Lebanon, Nigeria, and Tunisia. Countries that criminalize same-sex acts are more likely to target men than women. In Bangladesh, for example, the law penalizes individuals who have sexual relations "against the order of nature." If found guilty, the accused can be imprisoned for life or face a fine and imprisonment of up to 10 years.[5] Sexual and gender minorities have also been targeted under Section 290 of the Penal Code for "unsocial activities."[6] Similarly, in Lebanon, any sexual activity contrary to "the order of nature" can lead to imprisonment for up to a year.[7] Lebanon also criminalizes gender expression by making it an offense for a man to "disguise himself as a woman." The penalty for this offense is up to six years' imprisonment.[8] Tunisia's criminal code criminalizes same-sex conduct between consenting adults with imprisonment of up to three years for private acts of sodomy.[9] Jamaica still applies the Offences Against the Person Act (OAPA) of 1864, which criminalizes sodomy and same-sex sexual conduct among males only. Punishment includes imprisonment with or without hard labor.[10] In Nigeria, the country's criminal code criminalizes same-sex acts between consenting men, whether in public or private. The legislation also prohibits the procurement or the attempt to procure same-sex acts, and the violation carries a prison sentence of three years.[11] In addition, Nigeria's Same Sex Marriage Prohibition Act of 2013 punishes anyone who enters into a same-sex marriage contract or civil union with 14 years' imprisonment. The Prohibition Act also penalizes anyone who administers, witnesses, abets, or aids the solemnization of a same-sex marriage or civil union, or supports the registration, operation, and sustenance of gay clubs, societies, organizations, processions, or meetings with 14 years' imprisonment.[12] Furthermore, in Nigeria's 12 northern states, Sharia law criminalizes same-sex intimacy between both men and women. These laws put sexual and gender minorities at extremely high risk of imprisonment or death and deny their access to public spaces and services (map 1.1).

MAP 1.1

EQOSOGI Countries That Criminalize Same-Sex Relations between Consenting Adults, 2021

IBRD 45504 |
JANUARY 2021

COUNTRIES THAT CRIMINALIZE SAME-SEX
RELATIONS BETWEEN CONSENTING ADULTS

■ YES ■ NO ▨ Non-EQOSOGI countries

Source: World Bank Group, Equality of Opportunity database.

Note: In Indonesia, however, some local governments apply Islamic-based laws to criminalize homosexuality, although the country overall does not. EQOSOGI = equality of opportunity for sexual and gender minorities.

Indonesia is something of an outlier in this category because its laws do not specifically criminalize same-sex relations. However, some local governments apply Islamic-based laws to criminalize homosexuality. Bylaws that criminalize consensual same-sex sexual acts, for example, were passed in Aceh province and the city of Palembang. Aceh was given autonomy to implement Sharia law and to run its own Islamic Sharia court system. The Aceh regulation on criminal offenses, introduced in 2014, imposes an interpretation of Sharia law under which same-sex sexual activity is punished with a penalty of 100 lashes and imprisonment of up to eight years. Article 63 prohibits male penetration, while Article 64 prohibits same-sex sexual activity.[13] The city of Padang Panjang in West Sumatra, for example, criminalizes same-sex sexual activity and punishes it with up to three months' imprisonment or a fine of up to 10 million rupiah (approximately US$700) (Badgett, Hasenbush, and Luhur 2017).[14]

In India, by contrast, the Supreme Court decriminalized homosexuality in September 2018 by declaring Section 377 of the Indian Penal Code unconstitutional.[15]

None of the analyzed countries have a different legal age of consent for heterosexuals and sexual and gender minorities. Canada previously prohibited anal sex before the age of 18, with the general age of consent for vaginal intercourse being 16. But on June 21, 2019, Canada officially made 16 the age of consent, regardless of the partners' sex/gender and the type of sexual act.[16] The five countries (Bangladesh, Jamaica, Lebanon, Nigeria, and Tunisia) that criminalize same-sex relations do not differentiate age of consent based on opposite-sex or same-sex relations because same-sex relations are illegal.

> Despite the growing number of countries worldwide that have abolished laws criminalizing people based on SOGI, **lesbian, gay, bisexual, transgender, and intersex (LGBTI) people continue to fear for their lives based on their identity alone.**
>
> —*Mendos (2019)*

It is advised that countries adopt the following good practice policy actions:

- Repeal laws, constitutional provisions, and regulations that criminalize people based on their sexual orientation, gender identity, gender expression, and sex characteristics.

- Repeal laws, constitutional provisions, and regulations that criminalize sodomy, same-sex attraction, or same-sex sexual activity that can be used to target sexual and gender minorities.

- Repeal laws that ban sexual and gender minorities from showing affection in public or private spaces.

- Repeal laws that distinguish between heterosexuals and sexual and gender minorities regarding the legal age of consensual sex, including provisions that set different ages of consent for different sexual acts such as vaginal, anal, or oral sex.

Vagrancy, Public Nuisance, or Public Morals Laws

In addition to specific laws criminalizing sexual and gender minorities directly, countries also indirectly target this community through vagrancy, public nuisance, or public morals laws.[17] These laws might go unnoticed by the general public. Still, they have real-life consequences for sexual and gender minorities, often preventing them from accessing basic services and job opportunities and forcing them into the informal sector, which leaves them vulnerable to abuse (Badgett and others 2014). These indirect ways of criminalizing sexual and gender minorities lead to exclusion. They prevent sexual and gender minorities from living freely and from contributing to and engaging in society. Seen as "immoral" or as a "public disturbance," sexual and gender minorities often live on the fringes of society (Human Dignity Trust 2016).

FIGURE 1.1

Use of Vagrancy, Public Nuisance, or Public Morals Laws to Target Sexual and Gender Minorities in Seven of the Analyzed Countries, 2021

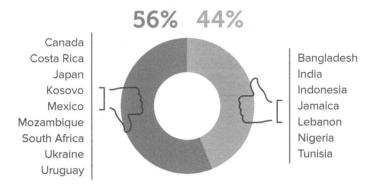

56%   44%

Canada
Costa Rica
Japan
Kosovo
Mexico
Mozambique
South Africa
Ukraine
Uruguay

Bangladesh
India
Indonesia
Jamaica
Lebanon
Nigeria
Tunisia

Source: World Bank Group, Equality of Opportunity database.

These laws target gender minorities (transgender or gender nonconforming people) in particular. They are often prosecuted on public moral grounds for the way they express their gender (including through clothing choice) when this is perceived to be at odds with their birth sex.[18]

Using indirect measures to target sexual and gender minorities is not the norm among the reviewed countries. However, 7 of the 16 countries analyzed make use of vagrancy, public nuisance, or public morals laws against sexual and gender minorities (figure 1.1). Bangladesh criminalizes "nuisance" in public places without precisely defining what this constitutes.[19] According to this study's expert contributors, this provision is arbitrarily and unfairly used to categorize and criminalize as public nuisance certain activities that transgender people traditionally rely on to survive, such as sex work and begging. Similarly, India uses public obscenity and nuisance laws that criminalize begging and regulate sex work against *hijras* (third gender).[20] Lebanon's Penal Code criminalizes gender expression by making it an offense for a man to "disguise himself as a woman."[21] It also criminalizes behavior that offends public morals and prohibits the possession, making, or distribution of materials that may incite others to immorality, thus posing barriers to freedom of expression.[22]

Although many of these laws do not explicitly target sexual and gender minorities, they are arbitrarily used against them and pose a significant threat to their social and economic well-being. In Indonesia, the Penal Code's provisions for offenses against decency and the law against pornography are open to interpretation and have been used to persecute sexual and gender minorities.[23] Those found guilty of offending decency can face up to 32 months in jail or a fine.[24] The authorities have used this law to criminalize transgender and gender-diverse people.[25] Similarly, the Tunisian Criminal Code criminalizes any act contrary to public decency and morality.[26] In Jamaica, the Offences Against the Person Act criminalizes sexual minorities and also prohibits any act of "gross indecency."[27] In Nigeria, the Same-Sex Marriage Prohibition Act of 2013 punishes any person who makes a public showing of a same-sex amorous relationship with 10 years' imprisonment.[28] Also, the Criminal Code of Nigeria prohibits acts of "gross indecency" between men with a penalty of three years' imprisonment.[29]

More countries target sexual and gender minorities indirectly than directly. Even in countries where such laws do not exist, contributors report cases in which sexual and gender minorities' moral standing is questioned. For example, experts in Canada state that sexual and gender minorities (transgender people, in particular) face increased policing in public spaces. Such measures prevent sexual and gender minorities from fully participating economically, socially, and politically in public spaces. They remain a major obstacle in the advancement of equality for sexual and gender minorities worldwide.

It is advised that countries adopt the following good practice policy actions:

- Repeal laws, constitutional provisions, and regulations that explicitly or implicitly target sexual and gender minorities on vagrancy, public nuisance, or public moral grounds.

- Enact new laws or regulations to protect sexual and gender minorities from being criminalized in the name of public nuisance or public morals.

Notes

1. For more information, see https://www.amnesty.org/en/what-we-do/discrimination/lgbti-rights.
2. For more on the United Nation's efforts to combat discrimination on the basis of sexual orientation and gender identity, see the United Nations Office of the High Commissioner for Human Rights website at https://www.ohchr.org/EN/Issues/Discrimination/Pages/LGBT.aspx.
3. Questions asked for this indicator set include: Are there any laws, constitutional provisions, and/or regulations that criminalize people based on sexual orientation, gender identity, gender expression, and sex characteristics? Does your country criminalize same-sex relations between consenting adults? Is the legal age for consensual sex the same for heterosexuals as for sexual and gender minorities?
4. See the Human Dignity Trust's map of countries that criminalize lesbian, gay, bisexual, and transgender (LGBT) people, available at https://www.humandignitytrust.org/lgbt-the-law/map-of -criminalisation/?type_filter=crim_gender_exp.
5. Bangladesh, Penal Code. 1860. Article 377: "Whoever voluntarily has carnal intercourse against the order of nature with any man, woman or animal, shall be punished with [imprisonment] for life, or with imprisonment of either description for a term which may extend to 10 years, and shall also be liable to fine. Explanation. Penetration is sufficient to constitute the carnal intercourse necessary to the offence described in this section."
6. A lesbian couple from the Jhalakati District of Bangladesh was arrested and jailed and subjected to a "gender test." A case was filed against them under Section 290 of the Penal Code for unsocial activities. This followed reports in June 2013 that two women in Bangladesh were arrested for marrying in secret (see the Human Dignity Trust at https://www.humandignitytrust.org/country-profile/bangladesh/). Section 290 of the Penal Code of 1860 provides: "Whoever commits a public nuisance in any case not otherwise punishable by this Code, shall be punished with fine which may extend to two hundred takas."

7. Lebanon, Penal Code. 1943. Article 534: "Any sexual intercourse contrary to the order of nature is punishable by up to one year in prison."

8. Lebanon, Penal Code. 1943. Article 521: "Any man who disguises himself as a woman and enters a place specifically for women only or a place in which anyone aside from women are prohibited from entering may be jailed for no more than six months."

9. Tunisia, Criminal Code. 1913. Article 230: "La sodomie, si elle ne rentre dans aucun des cas prevus aux articles precedents, est punie de l'emprisonnement pendant trois ans."

10. Jamaica, Offences Against the Person Act. 1861. Article 76: "Whosoever shall be convicted of the abominable crime of buggery, committed either with mankind or with any animal, shall be liable to be imprisoned & kept to hard labor for a term not exceeding 10 years."

11. Nigeria, Criminal Code Act. 1990. Article 217: "Any male person who, whether in public or private, commits any act of gross indecency with another male person, or procures another male person to commit any act of gross indecency with him, or attempts to procure the commission of any such act by any male person with himself or with another male person, whether in public or private, is guilty of a felony, and is liable to imprisonment for three years." Article 214: "Any person who (1) has carnal knowledge of any person against the order of nature; or (2) has carnal knowledge of an animal; or (3) permits a male person to have carnal knowledge of him or her against the order of nature is guilty of a felony, and is liable to imprisonment for 14 years." Article 352: "Any person who assaults another with intent to have carnal knowledge of him or her against the order of nature is guilty of a felony and is liable to imprisonment for 14 years."

12. Nigeria, Same Sex Marriage Prohibition Act. 2013. Article 1: "A marriage contract or civil union entered into between persons of same sex is prohibited in Nigeria and shall not be recognized as entitled to the benefits of a valid marriage." Section 5: "A person who enters into a same sex marriage contract or civil union commits an offence and is liable on conviction to a term of 14 years imprisonment."

13. Indonesia, Law No. 18/2001 on Special Autonomy for Special Region of Aceh province as Nanggroe Aceh Darussalam Province. Aceh Regulation (No. 6/2014), Articles 63 and 64.

14. For further examples of regional anti-LGBTI (lesbian, gay, bisexual, transgender, and intersex) laws, see UNDP and USAID 2014.

15. Article 377 of the Penal Code was abolished by Navtej Singh Johar v. Union of India WP (Criminal) No. 76 of 2016. Article 377 of the Penal Code of India stated that "anyone who voluntarily has carnal intercourse against the order of nature with any man, woman or animal."

16. Section 159 of the Criminal Code of Canada prohibited anal sex prior to the age of 18. This prohibition was found unconstitutional by a number of courts. This prohibition was finally repealed by Bill C-75, which passed into law on June 21, 2019.

17. The relevant question for this indicator set is: Are sexual and gender minorities targeted with other laws such as vagrancy, public nuisance, or public morals?

18. See the Human Dignity Trust's map of countries that criminalize LGBT people, available at https://www.humandignitytrust.org/lgbt-the-law/map-of-criminalisation/?type_filter=crim_gender_exp.

19. Bangladesh, Penal Code. 1860. Article 290: "Whoever commits a public nuisance in any case not otherwise punishable by this Code, shall be punished with fine which may extend to two hundred taka." Article 294: "Whoever, to the annoyance of others, (a) does any obscene act in any public place, or (b) sings, recites or utters any obscene songs, ballad or words, in or near any public place, shall be punished with imprisonment of either description for a term which may extend to three months, or with fine, or with both."

20. India, Penal Code. 1860. Section 268 provides with respect to public nuisance: "A person is guilty of a public nuisance who does any act or is guilty of an illegal omission which causes any common injury, danger or annoyance to the public or to the people in general who dwell or occupy property in the vicinity, or which must necessarily cause injury, obstruction, danger or annoyance to persons who may have occasion to use any public right." Section 294: "Obscene acts and songs. Whoever, to

the annoyance of others, (a) does any obscene act in any public place, or (b) sings, recites or utters any obscene song, ballad or words, in or near any public place, shall be punished with imprisonment of either description for a term which may extend to three months, or with fine, or with both." See also the Immoral Traffic (Prevention) Act. 1956. Section 4(1): "Any person over the age of 18 years who knowingly lives, wholly or in part, on the earnings of the prostitution of any other person shall be punishable with imprisonment for a term which may extend to two years, or with fine which may extend to 1,000 rupees, or with both and where such earnings relate to the prostitution of a child or a minor, shall be punishable with imprisonment for a term of not less than seven years and not more than 10 years." Certain state laws are also used against transgender persons who engage in begging or sex work; for instance, the Telangana Eunuchs Act, 1919, and the Karnataka Police Act, 1963.

21. Lebanon, Penal Code. Article 521: "Any man who disguises himself as a woman and enters a place specifically for women only or a place in which anyone aside from women are prohibited from entering may be jailed for no more than six months."

22. Lebanon, Penal Code. 1943. Article 532: "The exposing of public morals by any of the ways mentioned in paragraphs 2 or 3 of Article 209 shall be punished with imprisonment from one month to one year and a fine from 20,000 Lira to 100,000 Lira." Article 209: "The making or possession, importing or attempts to import for trade, distribution, for payment, copying, exhibition or display or attempts to display to the public, or for selling or attempts to sell, or distribution or engaged in the distribution of each publication, an editor or a drawing or a declaration or pictures or paintings or photographs, or the origin of the image or its template or produced anything in breach of modesty shall be punished with imprisonment from one month to one year and a fine from 20,000 Lira to 100,000 Lira."

23. Indonesia, Law No. 44 (Pornography Act). 2008. Article 1: "Dalam Undang-Undang ini yang dimaksud dengan: 1. Pornografi adalah gambar, sketsa, ilustrasi, foto, tulisan, suara, bunyi, gambar bergerak, animasi, kartun, percakapan, gerak tubuh, atau bentuk pesan lainnya melalui berbagai bentuk media komunikasi dan/atau pertunjukan di muka umum, yang memuat kecabulan atau eksploitasi seksual yang melanggar norma kesusilaan dalam masyarakat." Article 3: "Undang-Undang ini bertujuan: a. mewujudkan dan memelihara tatanan kehidupan masyarakat yang beretika, berkepribadian luhur, menjunjung tinggi nilai-nilai Ketuhanan Yang Maha Esa, serta menghormati harkat dan martabat kemanusiaan; b. menghormati, melindungi, dan melestarikan nilai seni dan budaya, adat istiadat, dan ritual keagamaan masyarakat Indonesia yang majemuk; c. memberikan pembinaan dan pendidikan terhadap moral dan akhlak masyarakat; d. memberikan kepastian hukum dan perlindungan bagi warga negara dari pornografi, terutama bagi anak dan perempuan; dan e. mencegah berkembangnya pornografi dan komersialisasi seks di masyarakat." Article 4: "(1) Setiap orang dilarang memproduksi, membuat, memperbanyak, menggandakan, menyebarluaskan, menyiarkan, mengimpor, mengekspor, menawarkan, memperjualbelikan, menyewakan, atau menyediakan pornografi yang secara eksplisit memuat: a. persenggamaan, termasuk persenggamaan yang menyimpang; b. kekerasan seksual; c. masturbasi atau onani; d. ketelanjangan atau tampilan yang mengesankan ketelanjangan; e. alat kelamin; atau f. pornografi anak."

24. Indonesia, Penal Code 1999. Article 281: "By a maximum imprisonment of two years and eight months or a maximum fine of 3,000 rupiahs shall be punished: 1st, any person who with deliberate intent publicly offends against decency; 2nd-ly, the people who with deliberate intent offend against decency whereby another person is present in spite of himself."

25. See the Human Dignity Trust's Indonesia website at https://www.humandignitytrust.org/country-profile/indonesia/.

26. Tunisia, Criminal Code. 1913. Article 226: "Est puni de six mois d'emprisonnement et de quarantehuit dinars d'amende, quiconque se sera, sciemment, rendu coupable d'outrage public à la pudeur." Article 226 bis: "Est puni de six mois d'emprisonnement et d'une amende de mille dinars quiconque porte publiquement atteinte aux bonnes mœurs ou à la morale publique par le geste ou la parole ou gène intentionnellement autrui d'une façon qui porte atteinte à la pudeur. Est passible

des mêmes peines prévues au paragraphe précédent quiconque attire publiquement l'attention sur une occasion de commettre la débauche, par des écrits, des enregistrements, des messages audio ou visuels, électroniques ou optiques."

27. Jamaica, Offences Against the Person Act. 1861. Article 79: "Any male person who, in public or private, commits, or is a party to the commission of, or procures or attempts to procure the commission by any male person of, any act of gross indecency with another male person, shall be guilty of a misdemeanor, and being convicted thereof shall be liable at the discretion of the court to be imprisoned for a term not exceeding two years, with or without hard labor."

28. Nigeria, Same-Sex Marriage Prohibition Act (Article 5 (2)). 2013: "A person who registers, operates or participates in gay clubs, societies and organisation, or directly or indirectly makes public show of same sex amorous relationship in Nigeria commits an offence and is liable on conviction to a term of 10 years imprisonment."

29. Nigeria, Criminal Code Act (Section 217): "Any male person who, whether in public or private, commits any act of gross indecency with another male person, or procures another male person to commit any act of gross indecency with him, or attempts to procure the commission of any such act by any male person with himself or with another male person, whether in public or private, is guilty of a felony and is liable to imprisonment for three years."

References

Badgett, M.V. Lee, Amira Hasenbush, and Winston Ekaprasetia Luhur. 2017. "LGBT Exclusion in Indonesia and Its Economic Effects." USAID and the Williams Institute. https://williamsinstitute.law.ucla.edu/wp-content/uploads/LGBT-Exclusion-in-Indonesia-and-Its-Economic-Effects-March-2017.pdf.

Badgett, M.V. Lee, Sheila Nezhad, Kees Waaldijk, and Yana van der Meulen Rodgers. 2014. "The Relationship between LGBT Inclusion and Economic Development: An Analysis of Emerging Economies." The Williams Institute, UCLA School of Law, Los Angeles. https://williamsinstitute.law.ucla.edu/wp-content/uploads/lgbt-inclusion-and-development-november-2014.pdf.

Flores, Andrew, and Andrew Park. 2018. "Examining the Relationship between Social Acceptance of LGBT People and Legal Inclusion of Sexual Minorities." The Williams Institute, UCLA School of Law, Los Angeles. https://williamsinstitute.law.ucla.edu/wp-content/uploads/LGBT-Acceptance-Legal-Inclusion-Mar-2018.pdf.

Hanssens, Catherine, Aisha C. Moodie-Mills, Andrea J. Ritchie, Dean Spade, and Urvashi Vaid. 2014. "A Roadmap for Change: Federal Policy Recommendations for Addressing the Criminalization of LGBT People and People Living with HIV." New York, New York: Center for Gender and Sexuality Law at Columbia Law School. https://web.law.columbia.edu/sites/default/files/microsites/gender-sexuality/files/roadmap_for_change_full_report.pdf.

Human Dignity Trust. 2015. *Criminalising Homosexuality and International Business: The Economic and Business Cases for Decriminalisation.* https://www.humandignitytrust.org/wp-content/uploads/resources/4.-Criminalisation-the-Role-of-Business.pdf.

Human Dignity Trust. 2016. *Breaking the Silence: Criminalisation of Lesbians and Bisexual Women and its Impacts.* https://www.humandignitytrust.org/wp-content/uploads/resources/Breaking-the-Silence-Criminalisation-of-LB-Women-and-its-Impacts-FINAL.pdf.

ILGA (International Lesbian, Gay, Bisexual, Trans and Intersex Association). 2019. *State-Sponsored Homophobia Report.* Geneva: ILGA World. https://ilga.org/downloads/ILGA_State_Sponsored_Homophobia_2019.pdf.

Kamara, Makmid. 2014. "Happening Now: LGBT Nigerians Jailed after Passage of New Anti-Gay Law." Amnesty International. https://www.amnestyusa.org/happening-now -lgbt-nigerians-jailed-after-passage-of-new-anti-gay-law/.

Kenny, Charles, and Dev Patel. 2012. "Norms and Reform: Legalizing Homosexuality Improves Attitudes." Working Paper 465, Center for Global Development. https://www.cgdev.org/sites/default/files/norms -and-reform-legalizing-homosexuality-improves-attitudes.pdf.

Mallory, Christy, Taylor N.T. Brown, Stephen Russell, and Brad Sears. 2017. "The Impact of Stigma and Discrimination against LGBT People in Texas." The Williams Institute, UCLA School of Law, Los Angeles. https://williamsinstitute.law.ucla.edu/wp-content/uploads/Impact-LGBT-Discrimination -TX-Apr-2017.pdf.

Mendos, Ramón Lucas. 2019. *State-Sponsored Homophobia 2019: Global Legislation Overview Update.* Geneva: ILGA World.

UNDP and USAID (United Nations Development Programme and United States Agency for International Development). 2014. *Being LGBT in Asia: Indonesia Country Report.* Bangkok: United Nations.

United Nations. 2016. *Living Free & Equal: What States Are Doing to Tackle Violence and Discrimination Against Lesbian, Gay, Bisexual, Transgender and Intersex People.* New York and Geneva: United Nations. https://www.ohchr.org/Documents/Publications/LivingFreeAndEqual.pdf.

2
Access to Inclusive Education

KEY FINDINGS

Canada and Costa Rica are the countries that have come the furthest in prohibiting discrimination, bullying, cyberbullying, and harassment based on sexual orientation and gender identity (SOGI) in educational settings and school admissions.

Countries tend to have more inclusive laws related to broader forms of discrimination, such as bullying, in educational settings than nondiscrimination prevention and training.

Only Canada, Japan, and Uruguay have laws or regulations that explicitly mandate the revision of national textbooks/national curricula to eliminate discriminatory language in educational settings.

Five countries provide concrete mechanisms for reporting cases of SOGI-related discrimination, violence, and bullying against students.

Five countries mandate training of primary and secondary school teachers and staff on antidiscrimination against students who are sexual and gender minorities, or those perceived as such.

It is advised that countries introduce progressive legislation and effective legal protections to combat discrimination, bullying, cyberbullying, and harassment in educational settings and create more inclusive educational systems for students.

Importance of the Access to Inclusive Education Indicator Set

Education is one of the most critical factors in determining a society's progress. It can break the cycle of poverty, reduce income inequality, and drive sustainable development by improving people's quality of life and enabling them to develop innovative solutions to the world's greatest problems.[1]

> If LGBTI people are prevented or hindered by discrimination from pursuing formal education or by lower returns to human capital investments, then economic losses from lost human capital investments are very likely.
>
> —*Badgett (2014)*

Education allows people to acquire the skills, knowledge, and abilities to prosper in life and compete with their peers, driving productivity and economic growth.[2] By enriching one's understanding of the world, education also allows people to build confidence, self-esteem, and a greater understanding of themselves and their societies. Equal access and a higher level of education are also linked to reduced crime rates (Moretti 2005). Moreover, education promotes entrepreneurial and technological advances. Education is one of the most powerful tools in lifting socially excluded children and adults out of poverty (UNESCO 2018b). Equal access to quality education plays a crucial role in advancing economic and social progress, improving income distribution, and enhancing economic growth (Ozturk 2001).

> The UN Sustainable Development Goal 4 aims to "ensure inclusive and equitable quality education and promote lifelong learning opportunities for all."
>
> —*UNESCO (https://en.unesco.org/themes/education)*

Depriving people of education based on their SOGI can have substantial negative effects on sustainable development and economic growth (Badgett, Waaldijk, and van der Meulen Rodgers 2019). Exclusion due to SOGI-related discrimination can also have negative personal effects across all ages and translate into broader societal problems. Moreover, exclusion may cause children and adolescents to suffer disproportionately, especially as this is the age of self-discovery in terms of personality and identity. Sexual and gender minorities facing discrimination, bullying, or stigmatization are statistically more likely than their non-LGBTI (lesbian, gay, bisexual, transgender, and intersex) peers to drop out of school, reducing their level of education.[3] Similarly, sexual and gender minorities often cut back on class participation and school attendance due to discriminatory practices, resulting in lower learning levels in school and absenteeism.[4] In sum, the exclusion of sexual and gender minorities from educational facilities and opportunities diminishes their human capital—and subsequently their productivity and contribution to the economy—resulting in stunted economic growth.[5]

> Providing every child with access to education and the skills needed to participate fully in society would boost GDP by an average 28 percent per year in lower-income countries and 16 percent per year in high-income countries for the next 80 years.
>
> *—OECD, Hanushek, and Woessmann (2015)*

The access to the inclusive education indicator set examines the existence of national laws, constitutional provisions, and/or regulations that protect sexual and gender minorities from discrimination in education based on sexual orientation, gender identity, gender expression, or sex characteristics. It measures several aspects of discrimination in schools—from laws or regulations in school admissions in both private and public schools to laws or regulations preventing and addressing bullying and harassment against students and/or teachers in the educational system. The indicator set also explores the existence of SOGI-inclusive sex education in schools and SOGI-inclusive language in textbooks. Finally, it attempts to identify laws or regulations that mandate antidiscrimination training of schoolteachers and other school staff, as well as the existence of concrete mechanisms for reporting cases of SOGI-related discrimination, violence, and bullying. Access to inclusive education during times of crisis, such as the COVID-19 pandemic, have been shown to be crucial (box 2.1).

> A 22-year-old student in her final year was expelled from a Nigerian university for committing "lesbianism." The university argued that the student's sexual orientation was disturbing and could ruin the school's reputation.
>
> *—Okanlawon (2017)*

BOX 2.1   Links between Access to Inclusive Education Data and COVID-19

Schools and teachers provide critical structure to children's lives during times of crisis, including the COVID-19 pandemic. Children and youth who are (or are perceived to be) sexual and gender minorities are at higher risk for victimization, bullying, and attempting suicide than their heterosexual classmates. Isolation can significantly increase these risks. Educators are uniquely positioned to provide support and resources to students who are (or are perceived to be) sexual and gender minorities. Furthermore, supportive teachers; the existence of inclusive textbooks/national curricula; sexual orientation and gender identity (SOGI)-inclusive sex education courses; the availability of training for schoolteachers; and reporting mechanisms for SOGI-related discrimination, violence, and bullying toward students are a lifeline.[a] Strengthening these aspects is more important than ever during this period of emergency online learning and can ensure a safer transition back to in-person classes. However, it is difficult for advocates, policy makers, and researchers to fully understand the education-related challenges facing sexual and gender minorities during the pandemic without reliable data.

Discriminatory teaching materials tend to perpetuate negative stereotypes and contribute to homophobic and transphobic violence. The effects of discriminatory teaching materials during online learning can contribute to cyberbullying. The *Equality of Opportunity for Sexual and Gender Minorities* (EQOSOGI) report found that only 2 of the 16 countries measured have laws or regulations that mandate sex education courses in a manner inclusive of sexual and gender minorities. Only three countries have laws that explicitly require the revision of national textbooks/national curricula to eliminate discriminatory language in education settings.

Educators, schoolteachers, and counselors can signal support in many ways to sexual and gender minority students who may be in unaccepting environments during the pandemic. Schools need to provide training to schoolteachers and staff on discrimination against sexual and gender minorities or those perceived as such, including cyberbullying; find ways to support students to combat feelings of social isolation or isolation from accepting communities; practice empathy and listen without judgment in an online environment; foster the creation of safe, accepting online learning environments; and share helpful health and self-care resources with students. During the pandemic, countries should also provide concrete mechanisms for reporting cases of SOGI-related discrimination, violence, bullying, and cyberbullying against sexual and gender minority students or those perceived as such.

The EQOSOGI report found that only five countries provide concrete mechanisms for reporting cases of SOGI-related discrimination, violence, and bullying against students. Just four countries mandate training of schoolteachers and staff on discrimination against students who are or are perceived to be sexual and gender minorities.

a.   See details about the Trevor project, which provides resources to lesbian, gay, bisexual, transgender, and intersex (LGBTI) youth who may have nowhere else to turn, at https://www.thetrevorproject.org/.

Discrimination in Education and Lack of Reporting Mechanisms

Equal and anti-discriminatory access to education fosters an inclusive and welcoming environment where students can reach their full potential.[6] Students and teachers are not targeted because of their sexual orientation or gender identity because everyone is treated equally. Conversely, homophobic, transphobic, and interphobic environments lead to violence against students and educational staff. Such violence occurs in classrooms, toilets, changing rooms, on playgrounds, the way to and from school, and online.[7] Students experiencing discrimination, bullying, and stigmatization might drop out of school, limiting their ability to enter higher education institutions, which can later affect their ability to find work or limit their options to lower-skilled professions. This exclusion can thus curtail a country's human capital, directly affecting economic growth (Badgett 2014).

Most countries covered by this study do not prohibit SOGI-related discrimination in educational settings or school admissions. Only Canada, Costa Rica, India, Kosovo, Mexico, South Africa, and Uruguay prohibit SOGI-related discrimination in educational settings and school admissions (figure 2.1). Of these seven countries, only six (Canada, Costa Rica, India, Kosovo, South Africa, and Uruguay) offer sexual and gender minorities additional protections from bullying and harassment. Kosovo prohibits all forms of discrimination, bullying, and harassment that might endanger students' equal access to education.[8] India's progress in recent years is also noteworthy. The new Transgender Persons (Protection of Rights) Act provides for an inclusive education without discrimination and harassment against transgender and intersex students.[9] In 2015, the India's Central Board of Secondary Education, a national-level board of education for public and private schools, issued "Guidelines for Prevention of Bullying and Ragging in both Primary and Secondary Education Schools." The guidelines provide for measures to be taken by schools to prevent bullying.[10] And in 2016, the Indian University Grants Commission amended the Anti-Ragging Regulation, which now prohibits physical or mental abuse (including bullying and exclusion) based on SOGI.[11]

Even fewer countries—Canada, Costa Rica, India, Kosovo, and Uruguay—explicitly protect gender identity in education. South Africa and Mexico do not have such a provision. However, legal protections against discrimination based on sexual orientation do not always translate into application in practice.[12] For example, although Costa Rica's Ministry of Education has taken steps to protect students and teachers from discrimination based on SOGI, several contributors reported that influential conservative groups still prevent de facto application. Similarly, the Indian Constitution prohibits discrimination (albeit without specific reference to SOGI grounds) in access to education, but only in state-run schools (private schools are exempted).[13] However, progress has been made. For example, in 2014, the Indian Supreme Court ruled that sexual orientation and gender identity are protected grounds under the category of "sex."[14] Additionally, the recently adopted Transgender Persons (Protection of Rights) Act in India explicitly bans discrimination against transgender and intersex people in both public and private educational institutions.[15] Furthermore, the Right to Education Act—which does not explicitly refer to sexual orientation, gender identity and expression, or sex characteristics—has inspired several Indian states to issue government notifications incorporating transgender and gender nonconforming children into the category of "disadvantaged groups," which, according to the Act, are entitled to 25 percent of available spots in private schools.[16]

Discrimination, bullying, and harassment in educational settings affect both the concerned individuals and the relevant country, but only a minority of countries studied for this report specifically prohibit such conduct. Most countries generally prohibit discrimination on the basis of sex, race, gender, and religion, but sexual and gender minorities are left vulnerable. Bangladesh, where the public does not generally recognize the concept of "sexual orientation," is making some progress in this regard. The Ministry of Law, Justice and Parliamentary Affairs is reviewing a draft Anti-Discrimination Law prepared by the National Human Rights Commission of Bangladesh (Sarwar 2017). This draft law includes protections for the "third gender of *hijra*" and "gender identity" as prohibited grounds for discrimination.[17]

Bangladesh's approach is uncommon. In Indonesia, some religious and coeducational schools routinely impose restrictive admission requirements on students who are sexual and gender minorities and deny them access. In 2016, Indonesia's Minister of Technology, Research and Higher Education stated that sexual and gender minorities should be barred from university campuses (Maketab 2016). Subsequently, in 2017, Andalas University in West Sumatra attempted to introduce policies to deny admission to students who identified as sexual and gender minorities (Eaton 2017). In Lebanon, the constitution states that access to education should be free to everyone as long as it is not contrary to public order and morals, and it does not affect the dignity of any of the recognized religions or sects.[18] However, no law specifically prohibits discrimination against students and staff who are sexual and gender minorities.

To address this gap, some institutions have taken matters into their own hands.[19] For example, the Lebanese American University (LAU) independently launched a Discrimination, Harassment, and Sexual Misconduct Prevention Policy that prohibits discrimination based on sexual orientation and gender identity, applying it equally to LAU staff, faculty, and students. The policy also includes procedures to notify LAU of infringements and prohibits retaliation against persons notifying LAU of prohibited acts (LAU 2019). In addition, contributors from Nigeria underscored that the Same-Sex Marriage Prohibition Act indirectly allows discrimination against students based on their SOGI.[20] Finally, none of the countries analyzed explicitly prohibit discrimination on the grounds of sex characteristics, thus leaving intersex people legally unprotected (figure 2.1).

Reporting mechanisms are important to ensuring equal and inclusive access to education. Such mechanisms ensure a safe and dynamic learning environment in which all students can thrive. The existence of such measures is scarce among the analyzed countries—only Canada, Costa Rica, India, Mexico, and South Africa provide concrete mechanisms for reporting cases of discrimination, violence, and bullying on the basis of SOGI (figure 2.2).

The approaches taken by the studied countries are diverse. For example, Costa Rica and Mexico prohibit teachers and educational institutions from discriminating against students based on SOGI, and disciplinary procedures for violators are in place.[21,22] In India, victims

FIGURE 2.1

Analyzed Countries with Legal Protections against SOGI-Related Discrimination in Education, 2021

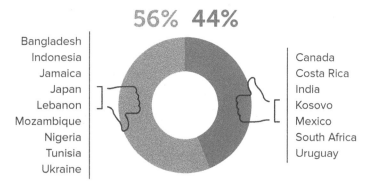

Source: World Bank Group, Equality of Opportunity database.

Note: SOGI = sexual orientation and gender identity.

FIGURE 2.2

Number of Analyzed Countries with a Reporting Mechanism for SOGI-Related Discrimination, 2021

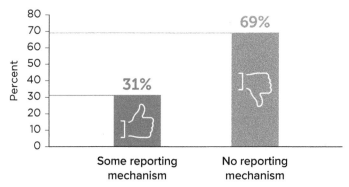

Source: World Bank Group, Equality of Opportunity database.

Note: SOGI = sexual orientation and gender identity.

of discrimination and harassment can submit their claims with the National Human Rights Commission, a statutory body established under the Protection of Human Rights Act 1993,[23] which has set up a core group to protect the rights of sexual and gender minorities. India also established a toll-free national anti-ragging helpline following a 2009 Supreme Court judgment. In 2017, an anti-ragging mobile application was developed by the University Grant Commission for filing complaints and maintaining a database.[24] In addition, the 2015 Central Board of Secondary Education mandates the creation of anti-bullying committees in schools to respond to such forms of harassment.[25] Finally, the recently adopted Transgender Persons (Protection of Rights) Act mandates the designation of compliance officers in order for transgender and intersex people to be able to lodge their complaints.[26] Following a similar mandate, the South African Human Rights Commission is authorized to enforce the provisions of the constitution, including its antidiscrimination protections, as they relate to SOGI.[27] In Ontario, Canada, teachers and other school staff receive training and information on how to address bullying and harassment of students on the basis of sexual orientation, gender identity, and expression.[28]

It is advised that countries adopt the following good practice policy actions:

- Introduce progressive legislation and effective legal protections to combat discrimination, bullying, cyberbullying, and harassment in educational settings and create more inclusive educational systems for students and teachers who are sexual and gender minorities.

- Amend existing sexual orientation laws to protect gender identity and expression and sex characteristics from discrimination in educational settings.

- Introduce antidiscrimination training for teachers and school staff to recognize SOGI issues and implement more inclusive practices for classrooms and schools.

- Carry out studies in the area of discrimination, bullying, cyberbullying, and harassment against students and teachers who are sexual and gender minorities, and their adverse socioemotional effects and risks.

- Raise awareness among school staff, teachers, students, and parents, and provide awareness training opportunities, particularly for students, to prevent peer-to-peer bullying, cyberbullying, and social exclusion.

Homophobic and Transphobic Textbooks and Curricula

In schools worldwide, students experience violence and abuse because of their actual or perceived SOGI (Human Rights Watch 2016). When students feel unsafe at school, they tend to be absent more often, perform worse, and eventually drop out of school, negatively impacting their education, employment prospects, and general well-being (UNESCO 2018a). The education sector is responsible for providing a safe and inclusive environment that allows all young people access to quality education (UNESCO 2016). As mentioned above, protection against exclusion from education and harassment in the school setting is paramount for students who are sexual and gender minorities to reap the benefits of education.

In addition to an inclusive learning environment, teaching materials should be nondiscriminatory.[29] Authorities should eliminate discriminatory teaching materials from curricula, particularly discriminatory language in textbooks, which tend to perpetuate negative stereotypes and contribute to homophobic and transphobic violence in many countries (UNESCO 2016). For example, in Kosovo, same-sex relations are equated with "... disorders, [and] criminal behavior ..." and are described as "deviant behavior" in some secondary-level textbooks (Binaku and others 2017).[30] The elimination of discriminatory language in textbooks and curricula can be achieved only through robust national legal and policy frameworks. Strong legislation is necessary for curriculum reform to address and eliminate discriminatory language in instructional materials (UNESCO 2014).

Most of the examined countries lack laws or regulations requiring the revision of national textbooks/national curricula in primary and secondary education to eliminate discriminatory language or create new textbooks that promote the inclusion of SOGI students. Only Canada, Japan, and Uruguay have laws or regulations that mandate the revision of national textbooks/national curricula to ensure that nondiscriminatory language is barred and inclusion of SOGI issues is promoted in primary and secondary education. In Canada, federal legislation does not require schools to eliminate discriminatory language. However, Ontario supports "equity and inclusive education" through textbooks depicting sexual and gender minorities.[31]

Japanese schools have also included SOGI issues in textbooks, which introduce a nonbinary approach to sexual orientation and gender identity. In 2016, the Japanese Ministry of Education issued a *Guidebook for Teachers* advising educators on how to address the issues and needs of sexual and gender minority students in schools (Japan, Ministry of Education 2016). In March 2017, the Japanese Ministry of Education announced a revised national bullying prevention policy that includes students who are sexual and gender minorities (*Migalhas International* 2018). Uruguay's laws provide for the inclusion of sexual and gender minorities in all aspects of social life, including education. Specifically, the Law on Education (Ley General de Educación) regulates the elimination of sexual orientation stereotypes in education;[32] the Law on Transgender

---

FIGURE 2.3

Number of Analyzed Countries That Legally Mandate Revisions to Textbooks/Curricula to Exclude Discriminatory Language, 2021

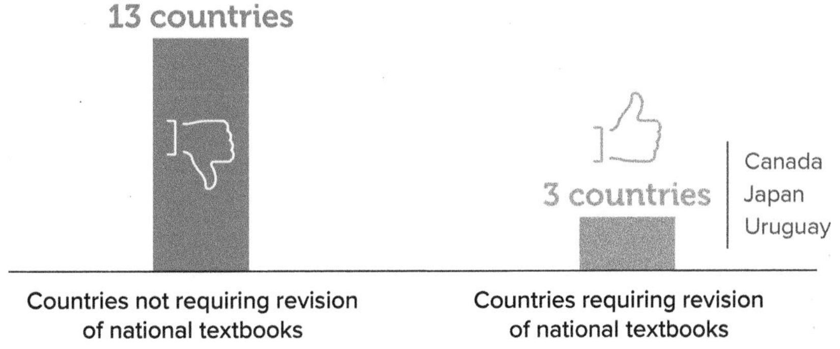

13 countries

3 countries | Canada Japan Uruguay

Countries not requiring revision of national textbooks

Countries requiring revision of national textbooks

Source: World Bank Group, Equality of Opportunity database.

People (Ley Integral Para Personas Trans) protects students who are gender minorities from discrimination based on gender identity or expression.[33]

The other 13 countries (Bangladesh, Costa Rica, India, Indonesia, Jamaica, Kosovo, Lebanon, Mexico, Mozambique, Nigeria, Tunisia, South Africa, and Ukraine) lack laws requiring the elimination of discriminatory language from national textbooks (figure 2.3). In South Africa, discrimination on the basis of sexual orientation is prohibited by the constitution and the Promotion of Equality and Prevention of Unfair Discrimination Act, but the South African Schools Act forbids only the practice of racial discrimination in the implementation of the standard of language policy in public schools.[34] Similarly, in Ukraine, the Ministry of Education issued a Ministerial Order and established a commission to analyze state-sponsored textbooks to address antidiscrimination specifically. However, the list of protected characteristics in the Ministerial Order fails to mention SOGI explicitly. Instead, it follows the list of grounds provided in the antidiscrimination law, which does not cover SOGI.[35] India's draft National Education Policy of 2019 includes a section on the education of transgender children. The draft policy states that the authorities will reorient curriculum and textbooks to address issues related to transgender children and their concerns, and to offer approaches to help meet their learning needs. In addition, teachers will be sensitized to the issues related to transgender children and their concerns and learning needs (India, Ministry of Human Resources Development 2018).

It is advised that countries adopt the following good practice policy actions:

- Introduce laws or regulations to establish inclusion-supportive curricula.

- Mandate the revision of national textbooks to eliminate discriminatory language and provide adequate learning and teaching materials.

- Promote universal language for inclusion and nondiscrimination in national textbooks.

- Ensure that curricula and learning materials convey positive messages about sexual and gender minorities and include sexual orientation, gender identity, and expression in national textbooks.

Training Educators to Recognize Discrimination in Schools

School teachers and school staff often lack adequate training to understand and address the harms of homophobic and transphobic violence, bullying, and discrimination. Some countries have invested in training educational staff to tackle this problem, but many have not.[36] Countries that have attempted to provide resources to educators have often done so on a small scale, even though such training would create a safer environment for all students (UNESCO 2016).

Only 5 of the 16 countries analyzed (Canada, Costa Rica, India, South Africa, and Uruguay) require training of primary and secondary school teachers and staff on antidiscrimination against students who are sexual and gender minorities (or those perceived as such). The remaining three-quarters do not provide such training (figure 2.4).

In Canada, the Accepting Schools Act ("Bill 13") was enacted in 2012 to amend the Education Act to address bullying actively.[37] Bill 13 instructs schools to create a positive and safe environment that is inclusive and accepting, "regardless of race . . . sex, sexual orientation, gender identity, gender expression . . . [and/or] disability." Bill 13 specifically advocates for more equitable and inclusive communities and schools, especially toward sexual and gender minorities. Annual professional development programs are established under the bill to educate schoolteachers and staff about bullying prevention and about promoting a positive school environment. In Uruguay, the country's antidiscrimination law promotes the design of educational campaigns inclusive of social, cultural, or religious differences, as well as sexual orientation and gender identity. The law also prohibits racist, xenophobic, or discriminatory behavior.[38]

In 2008, the Costa Rican Ministry of Education introduced a protocol to address SOGI-based discrimination and the bullying of students perceived as sexual and gender minorities. The protocol established guidelines and good practices for school staff and teachers aimed at combatting discrimination in schools (Costa Rica, Ministry of Public Education 2018). In South Africa, the Department of Basic Education developed a "school charter against homophobic bullying" in 2015, encouraging schools to design their own Codes of Conduct for students facing bullying, including on SOGI grounds (South Africa, Department of Basic Education 2016; UNESCO 2016). On September 25, 2020, the Ministry of Social Justice and Empowerment of India issued the Transgender Persons (Protection of Rights) Rules of 2020, which provide for the sensitization of educational institutions, teachers, and faculty in schools and colleges to foster respect for equality and gender diversity.[39]

Mexico has not introduced mandates and guidelines in this area. However, the country's Education Law (Ley General de Educación) generally stipulates that education services should

FIGURE 2.4

Number of Analyzed Countries That Do Not Provide Training to Educational Staff on SOGI-Related Discrimination in Primary and Secondary Education, 2021

Source: World Bank Group, Equality of Opportunity database.

Note: SOGI = sexual orientation and gender identity.

be provided with equity and excellence; it includes measures addressing minority groups, including students discriminated against based on their sexual orientation.[40]

It is advised that countries adopt the following good practice policy actions:

■ Introduce laws or regulations that mandate training of primary and secondary school teachers and staff on antidiscrimination related to students who are sexual and gender minorities or those perceived as such.

■ Raise awareness of the importance of equal access to education by training teachers and other school staff to identify, prevent, and address homophobic and transphobic violence, bullying, and cyberbullying in educational settings.

■ Provide pre-services and in-services, as well as continuous professional training and development, to equip educational staff with the right tools to create a discrimination-free environment and establish mechanisms for students to report homophobic and transphobic incidents (UNESCO 2012).

Sex Education about Sexual Orientation and Gender Identity in Schools

Sex education is an important factor in protecting the health and well-being of young people. However, sex education courses often lack information or materials on SOGI issues.[41] Instead, sex education literature usually uses a binary approach to discuss sexual orientation and gender identity, thereby inadequately representing students who are gender minorities. Creating sex education courses that show a nonbinary approach to sexual orientation and gender identity would ensure the inclusion and equality of all students (Slater 2013). Inclusive sex education in schools can also reduce uneducated, risky behaviors and support positive sexual health outcomes, such as reducing the rate of teen pregnancy and sexually transmitted infections (Advocates for Youth, Answer, GLSEN, Human Rights Campaign, Planned Parenthood 2015).

Despite the importance of inclusive sex education for sexual and gender minorities, only Costa Rica and Uruguay have laws or regulations that mandate inclusive sex education courses in secondary and tertiary education (figure 2.5). For example, Costa Rica introduced SOGI-inclusive courses and good practices as part of its integral sexuality protocol. The protocol provides guidance on educating students on SOGI issues in primary and secondary educational institutions (Costa Rica, Ministry of Public Education 2017). The Education Law (Ley General de Educación) in Uruguay also mandates that sex education include teaching on sexual orientation,[42] while the country's Law for Transgender People (Ley Integral Para Personas Trans) mandates the inclusion of gender identity teaching in educational settings.[43]

In contrast, the Education Ministry in Ontario, Canada, recently nullified an inclusive sex education curriculum, eliminating the requirement for teachers to teach students about sexual orientation and gender identity. This departure was the result of a widespread public protest against a SOGI-inclusive curriculum. In 2015, the Constitutional Courts in Indonesia rejected an application submitted by the Indonesian Family Planning Group to include sex education in the curriculum (*Jakarta Post* 2015).

Excluding SOGI issues from sex education in schools ignores the self-identities of students who are sexual and gender minorities. The resulting environment—in which educators, school staff, and students lack access to much-needed information—can be unsafe and result in discrimination due to the lack of representation in the curriculum and learning materials.

It is advised that countries adopt the following good practice policy actions:

■ Enact laws that promote courses on sex education in the national curriculum and establish sex education materials that include SOGI issues.

■ Eliminate inaccurate and discriminatory information and language concerning sexual and gender minorities that could make students susceptible to discrimination, violence, bullying, and cyberbullying.

FIGURE 2.5

Analyzed Countries That Require Sex Education Courses to Include Sexual and Gender Minorities: Costa Rica and Uruguay, 2021

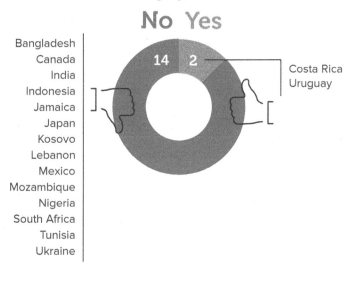

Source: World Bank Group, Equality of Opportunity database.

Notes

1. For more information, see the United Nations Sustainable Development Goals website for "Quality Education" at https://www.un.org/sustainabledevelopment/education.

2. Psacharopolous and Patrinos (2018, abstract) find that the average global rate of return to one extra year of schooling is about 9 percent a year for the individual. Moreover, social returns to schooling are above 10 percent at the secondary and higher education levels. The paper states that ". . . investing in education has a quantifiable and high pay-off, both for the individual and society."

3. According to the United Nations, between one-half and two-thirds of LGBTI youth experience bullying in childhood, forcing one of every three to skip or even drop out of school. For more information, see the website of the United Nations Free and Equal Campaign: End Bullying at https://www.unfe.org/end-bullying.

4. See the United Nations Free and Equal Campaign, Bullying and Violence in Schools, available at https://www.unfe.org/wp-content/uploads/2017/05/Bullying-and-Violence-in-School.pdf.

5. See the United Nations Free and Equal Campaign: End Bullying, available at https://www.unfe.org/end-bullying. See also https://www.unfe.org/learn-more/.

6. Questions addressing discrimination in education and lack of reporting mechanisms in this indicator set are: Are there any laws, constitutional provisions, and/or regulations that prohibit discrimination against students and/or teachers in educational settings based on sexual orientation, gender identity, gender expression, and sex characteristics? Are there any laws and/or regulations that prohibit discrimination in school admission based on SOGI? Are there any laws and/or regulations preventing and addressing bullying and harassment against students and/or teachers in the educational system that include students based on actual or perceived SOGI? Are there any concrete mechanisms (national or local) for reporting cases of SOGI-related discrimination, violence, and bullying toward students, including incidents perpetrated by representatives of the education sector such as teachers and other school staff?

7. The United Nations has established a campaign to end such bullying and violence; see the United Nations Free and Equal Campaign: End Bullying, available at https://www.unfe.org/end-bullying/.

8. Kosovo, Law No.05/L-021 on Protection from Discrimination. 2015. Article 1 provides that "[t]he purpose of this law is to establish a general framework for prevention and combating discrimination based on nationality, or in relation to any community, social origin, race, ethnicity, color, birth, origin, sex, gender, gender identity, sexual orientation, language, citizenship, religion and religious belief, political affiliation, political or other opinion, social or personal status, age, family or marital status, pregnancy, maternity, wealth, health status, disability, genetic inheritance or any other grounds, in order to implement the principle of equal treatment." Article 2 adds that "[t]his law applies to all acts or omissions, of all state and local institutions, natural and legal persons, public and private sector, who violate, violated or may violate the rights of any person or natural and legal entities in all areas of life." Article 24 of the Constitution states that "[n]o one shall be discriminated against on grounds of race, color, gender, language, religion, political or other opinion, national or social origin, relation to any community, property, economic and social condition, sexual orientation, birth, disability or other personal status."

9. India, Transgender Persons (Protection of Rights) Act. No 40 of 2019 (entered into force on December 5, 2019). Section 2: "In this Act, unless the context otherwise requires, … (d) 'inclusive education' means a system of education wherein transgender students learn together with other students without fear of discrimination, neglect, harassment or intimidation and the system of teaching and learning is suitably adapted to meet the learning needs of such students; … (k) 'transgender person' means a person whose gender does not match with the gender assigned to that person at birth and includes trans-man or trans-woman (whether or not such person has undergone Sex Reassignment Surgery or

hormone therapy or laser therapy or such other therapy), person with intersex variations, genderqueer and person having such socio-cultural identities as kinner, hijra, aravani, and jogta."

10. India, Guidelines for Prevention of Bullying and Ragging in Schools, Reg: (D.O. No. 12-19/2012 -RMSA-I). 2015. Available at http://cbseacademic.nic.in/web_material/Circulars/2015/17_Prevention%20 of%20Bullying%20&%20Ragging%20in%20Schools.pdf.

11. India, University Grants Commission. UGC Regulation on Curbing the Menace of Ragging in Higher Educational Institutions (Third Amendment). 2016. Article 3 (j): "Any act of physical or mental abuse (including bullying and exclusion) targeted at another student (fresher or otherwise) on the ground of color, race, religion, caste, ethnicity, gender (including transgender), sexual orientation, appearance, nationality, regional origins, linguistic identity, place of birth, place of residence, or economic background." Available at https://www.ugc.ac.in/pdfnews/7823260_Anti-Ragging-3rd-Amendment.pdf.

12. This information comes from contributors to the Equality of Opportunity for Sexual and Gender Minorities survey in those countries.

13. India, Constitution of India. 2007. Article 15 (1) of the Constitution: "The State shall not discriminate against any citizen on grounds only of religion, race, caste, sex, place of birth or any of them." Article 21A states that "[t]he State shall provide free and compulsory education to all children of the age of 6 to 14 years in such manner as the State may, by law, determine." Article 29 (2) provides that "no citizen shall be denied admission into any educational institution maintained by the State or receiving aid out of State funds on grounds only of religion, race, caste, language or any of them."

14. National Legal Services Authority v. Union of India, WP (Civil) No. 400 of 2012. In 2014, the Supreme Court of India directed the central government and state governments to ensure treatment of "hijras"/ "eunuchs" (transgenders) as a third gender as opposed to male or female so as to afford them the same protections of fundamental rights, including those under Article 14 (Right to Equality) and Article 15 (Prohibition of Discrimination). Justice K. S. Puttaswamy (Retd.) and Anr. v. Union Of India And Ors., WP (Civil) No 494 of 2012. In 2017, the Supreme Court of India declared that the sexual autonomy is inherent in the Right to Privacy protected under Article 21 of the Constitution of India ("Right to Life and Liberty"). Therefore, the protection of the rights and interests of the people belonging to the LGBTI community is ensured by the constitution. Navtej Singh Johar v. Union of India, WP (Crl.) No 76 of 2016, affirmed the principles upheld earlier, the court in a 2018 judgment stated that the word "sex" under Article 15 (Prohibition of Discrimination) and Article 16 (Equality of Opportunities) of the Constitution has to be read widely to include gender and sexual minorities.

15. India, Transgender Persons (Protection of Rights) Act. 2019. Section 2: "In this Act, unless the context otherwise requires, … (e) 'institution' means an institution, whether public or private, for the reception, care, protection, education, training or any other service of transgender persons; … (k) 'transgender person' means a person whose gender does not match with the gender assigned to that person at birth and includes trans-man or trans-woman (whether or not such person has undergone Sex Reassignment Surgery or hormone therapy or laser therapy or such other therapy), person with intersex variations, genderqueer and person having such socio-cultural identities as kinner, hijra, aravani and jogta." Section 3: "No person or establishment shall discriminate against a transgender person on any of the following grounds, namely: (a) the denial, or discontinuation of, or unfair treatment in, educational establishments and services thereof." Section 13: "Every educational institution funded or recognised by the appropriate Government shall provide inclusive education and opportunities for sports, recreation and leisure activities to transgender persons without discrimination on an equal basis with others."

16. India, Right of Children to Free and Compulsory Education Act. 2009. Article 2: "In this Act, unless the context otherwise requires, (n) 'school' means any recognised school imparting elementary education and includes (ii) an aided school receiving aid or grants to meet whole or part of its expenses from the appropriate Government or the local authority; (iii) a school belonging to specified category; and (iv) an unaided school not receiving any kind of aid or grants to meet its expenses from the appropriate Government or the local authority." Article 12: "(1) For the purposes of this Act, a school, (b) specified

in sub-clause (ii) of clause (n) of section 2 shall provide free and compulsory elementary education to such proportion of children admitted therein as its annual recurring aid or grants so received bears to its annual recurring expenses, subject to a minimum of 25 percent; (c) specified in sub-clauses (iii) and (iv) of clause (n) of section 2 shall admit in class I, to the extent of at least 25 percent of the strength of that class, children belonging to weaker section and disadvantaged group in the neighborhood and provide free and compulsory elementary education till its completion." See also https://indianexpress .com/article/cities/delhi/reserved-seats-for-transgender-children-in-schools/, http://14.139.60.153 /bitstream/123456789/10222/1/TEACHER%20RELATED%20GOVERNMENT%20ORDER%20 TAMIL%20NADU_D-14674.pdf.

17. Bangladesh, Draft of Proposed Anti-Discrimination Act. 2014. http://www.nhrc.org.bd/site /notices/12c79873-4144-47fa-9885-bd7b86f3a090/Draft-of-proposed-Anti-Discrimination-Act.

18. Constitution of Lebanon 1926 (amended 1995). Article 10 of the Constitution provides that ". . . education shall be free insofar as it is not contrary to public order and morals and does not affect the dignity of any of the religions or sects. There shall be no violation of the right of religious communities to have their own schools provided they follow the general rules issued by the state regulating public instruction."

19. See, for example, the Policies and Procedures of the Phoenicia University (https://www.pu.edu.lb /policies-and-procedures) and the American University of Beirut (https://aub.policytech.eu/dotNet /documents/?docid=1569&public=true), specifically mentioning gender identity and sexual orientation as protected grounds.

20. Nigeria, Same-Sex Marriage Prohibition Act. 2013. Section 1 of the Act: "(1) A marriage contract or civil union entered into between persons of same sex: (a) is prohibited in Nigeria; and (b) shall not be recognized as entitled to the benefits of a valid marriage." Section 5: "(1) A person who enters into a same sex marriage contract or civil union commits an offence and is liable on conviction to a term of 14 years imprisonment."

21. Costa Rica, Decreto Ejecutivo 38999. Política del Poder Ejecutivo para erradicar de sus instituciones la discriminación hacia la población LGBTI. 2015 (Amended 2017). Article 12: "1. Cuando una persona usuaria sufra de discriminación por motivos de orientación sexual o identidad de género, podrá plantear denuncia oral o escrita ante la Oficina de Gestión Institucional de Recursos Humanos o ante la Oficina de Asesoría Jurídica Institucional o aquella instancia que por vía reglamentaria haya sido designada por parte de la Institución para tales efectos. El plazo para interponer la denuncia será de un año y se computará a partir del último hecho consecuencia de la discriminación por razones de orientación sexual o identidad de género o a partir de que cesó la causa justificada que le impidió denunciar. 2. Al plantear la denuncia se le debe indicar al usuario la posibilidad hacerse representar por patrocinio letrado y por apoyo emocional o psicológico de su confianza en las diversas fases del procedimiento. 3. Además, se le indicará al usuario denunciante los plazos del procedimiento y se le solicitará un medio por el cual pueda ser contactado y recibir notificaciones." http://www.pgrweb.go.cr/scij/Busqueda/Normativa/Normas/nrm_texto_completo .aspx?param1=NRTC&nValor1=1&nValor2=79466&nValor3=108740&strTipM=TC.

Costa Rica, Decreto Ejecutivo N. 5771-E, Reglamento Autónomo de Servicios del Ministerio de Educación Pública. 2013 (Amended 2015). Article 46: "Además de lo dispuesto en el Código de Trabajo, Estatuto de Servicio Civil y su Reglamento y otras normas del presente Reglamento, queda absolutamente prohibido a los empleados: . . . r) Realizar cualquier forma de discriminación, en razón de género, etnia, credo, orientación sexual, nacionalidad, preferencia política o condición social." http:// www.pgrweb.go.cr/scij/Busqueda/Normativa/Normas/nrm_texto_completo.aspx?param1=NRTC &nValor1=1&nValor2=80623&nValor3=102375&strTipM=TC.

22. Mexico, Ley Federal para Prevenir y Eliminar la Discriminación. 2003. Article 20IX: "Investigar presuntos actos y prácticas discriminatorias, en el ámbito de su competencia."

23. India, Protection of Human Rights Act. 1993. http://nhrc.nic.in/acts-&-rules/protection-human -rights-act-1993-1. India, National Human Rights Commission, Annual Action Plan, 2019-2020. http://nhrc.nic.in/activities/annual-action-plans.

24. See https://www.antiragging.in/Site/Aboutus.aspx.

25. India, Guidelines for Prevention of Bullying and Ragging in Schools, Reg: (D.O. No. 12-19/2012 -RMSA-I). 2015. http://cbseacademic.nic.in/web_material/Circulars/2015/17_Prevention%20of%20 Bullying%20&%20Ragging%20in%20Schools.pdf.

26. India, Transgender Persons (Protection of Rights) Act. 2019. Section 2: "In this Act, unless the context otherwise requires, (k) 'transgender person' means a person whose gender does not match with the gender assigned to that person at birth and includes trans-man or trans-woman (whether or not such person has undergone Sex Reassignment Surgery or hormone therapy or laser therapy or such other therapy), person with intersex variations, genderqueer and person having such socio-cultural identities as kinner, hijra, aravani, and jogta." Section 11: "Every establishment shall designate a person to be a complaint officer to deal with the complaints relating to violation of the provisions of this Act."

27. South African, Human Rights Commission Act 54. 1994.

28. Canada, Ontario, Accepting Schools Act, S.O. 2012, c. 5 - Bill 13. 2012. https://www.ontario.ca/laws /statute/s12005.

29. The question addressing homophobic and transphobic textbooks and curricula discrimination in this indicator set is: Are there any laws and/or regulations that mandate the revision of national textbooks/ national curriculum in primary and secondary education to eliminate discriminatory language (homophobic or transphobic language, for example)?

30. See also Berisha and others (2016); Bajraktari and others (2015); and Mato and Shatri(2015).

31. See "Teaching Human Rights in Ontario – A Guide for Ontario Schools," which is available from the Ontario Human Rights Commission at http://www.ohrc.on.ca/en/book/export/html/10772.

32. Uruguay, Ley General de Educación No. 18.437. 2008. Article 3: "La educación estará orientada a la búsqueda de una vida armónica e integrada a través del trabajo, la cultura, el entretenimiento, el cuidado de la salud, el respeto al medio ambiente, y el ejercicio responsable de la ciudadanía, como factores esenciales del desarrollo sostenible, la tolerancia, la plena vigencia de los derechos humanos, la paz y la comprensión entre los pueblos y las naciones." Article 18: "El Estado brindará los apoyos específicos necesarios a aquellas personas y sectores en especial situación de vulnerabilidad, y actuará de forma de incluir a las personas y sectores discriminados cultural, económica o socialmente, a los efectos de que alcancen una real igualdad de oportunidades para el acceso, la permanencia y el logro de los aprendizajes. Asimismo, estimulará la transformación de los estereotipos discriminatorios por motivos de edad, género, raza, etnia u orientación sexual. El Estado asegurará a los educandos que cursen la enseñanza pública obligatoria, el acceso a las tecnologías de la información y la comunicación. Promoverá su máximo aprovechamiento para la educación, su uso con sentido y su apropiación por parte de los educandos."

33. Uruguay, Ley Integral Para Personas Trans. 2018. Article 15: "Sin perjuicio de lo dispuesto por los artículos 202 y 204 de la Constitución de la República, los órganos y organismos responsables de las políticas educativas de todos los niveles, en el ámbito de sus competencias, asegurarán la inclusión de las personas trans a lo largo de su vida educativa, conforme a los principios previstos en la Ley N° 18.437, de 12 de diciembre de 2008 (Ley General de Educación)."

34. South African Schools Act. 1996. Article 6 (3): "No form of racial discrimination may be practiced in implementing policy determined under this section."

35. Ukraine, Ministry of Education and Science. Order No. 713 of July 3, 2015. Provisions on Competitive Selection of Textbook Projects for 1-2 Grade Secondary Education. https://zakon.rada.gov.ua/laws /show/z0359-18/ed20180316#n27.

36. The question addressing training educators to recognize discrimination in schools in this indicator set is: Are there any laws and/or regulations that mandate training of schoolteachers and other school

staff in primary and secondary education on antidiscrimination of students who are sexual and gender minorities, or those perceived as such?

37. Canada, Ontario, Accepting Schools Act, S.O. 2012, c. 5 - Bill 13. 2012. https://www.ontario.ca/laws/statute/s12005.

38. Uruguay, Law 17817. 2004. Article 2: "A los efectos de la presente ley se entenderá por discriminación toda distinción, exclusión, restricción, preferencia o ejercicio de violencia física y moral, basada en motivos de raza, color de piel, religión, origen nacional o étnico, discapacidad, aspecto estético, género, orientación e identidad sexual, que tenga por objeto o por resultado anular o menoscabar el reconocimiento, goce o ejercicio, en condiciones de igualdad, de los derechos humanos y libertades fundamentales en las esferas política, económica, social, cultural o en cualquier otra esfera de la vida pública. Article 5: D) Diseñar e impulsar campañas educativas tendientes a la preservación del pluralismo social, cultural o religioso, a la eliminación de actitudes racistas, xenofóbicas o discriminatorias y en el respeto a la diversidad."

39. India, Ministry of Social Justice and Empowerment, Transgender Persons (Protection of Rights) Rules of 2020, Article 10 (7): "The appropriate Government shall also provide for sensitization of institutions and establishments under their purview, including: (a) sensitization of teachers and faculty in schools and colleges, changes in the educational curriculum to foster respect for equality and gender diversity."

40. Mexico, Ley General de Educación. 2019. Article 8: "El Estado está obligado a prestar servicios educativos con equidad y excelencia. Las medidas que adopte para tal efecto estarán dirigidas, de manera prioritaria, a quienes pertenezcan a grupos y regiones con mayor rezago educativo, dispersos o que enfrentan situaciones de vulnerabilidad por circunstancias específicas de carácter socioeconómico, físico, mental, de identidad cultural, origen étnico o nacional, situación migratoria o bien, relacionadas con aspectos de género, preferencia sexual o prácticas culturales."

41. The question addressing sex education about sexual orientation and gender identity in schools in this indicator set is: Are there any laws and/or regulations that mandate the creation of courses on sex education in a SOGI-inclusive manner in secondary and tertiary education?

42. Uruguay, Ley General de Educación No. 18.437. 2008. Article 40: "El Sistema Nacional de Educación, en cualesquiera de sus modalidades contemplará líneas transversales entre las cuales se encuentran: (H) La educación sexual, (I) La educación física, la recreación y el deporte, de acuerdo a los lineamientos que se especifican: (8) La educación sexual tendrá como propósito proporcionar instrumentos adecuados que promuevan en educadores y educandos, la reflexión crítica ante las relaciones de género y la sexualidad en general para un disfrute responsable de la misma."

43. Uruguay, Ley 19684 Integral Para Personas Trans. 2018. Article 15: "Sin perjuicio de lo dispuesto por los artículos 202 y 204 de la Constitución de la República, los órganos y organismos responsables de las políticas educativas de todos los niveles, en el ámbito de sus competencias, asegurarán la inclusión de las personas trans a lo largo de su vida educativa, conforme a los principios previstos en la Ley N° 18.437, de 12 de diciembre de 2008 (Ley General de Educación)."

References

Advocates for Youth, Answer, GLSEN, Human Rights Campaign, Planned Parenthood. 2015. "A Call to Action: LGBTQ Youth Need Inclusive Sex Education." https://www.hrc.org/resources/a-call-to-action-lgbtq-youth-need-inclusive-sex-education.

Badgett, M.V. Lee. 2014. "The Economic Cost of Stigma and the Exclusion of LGBT People: A Case Study of India (English)." World Bank, Washington, DC.

Badgett, M.V. Lee, Kees Waaldijk, and Yana van der Meulen Rodgers. 2019. "The Relationship Between LGBT Inclusion and Economic Development: Macro-Level Evidence." *World Development* 120 (August): 1–14. https://doi.org/10.1016/j.worlddev.2019.03.011.

Bajraktari, Ismet D., Ahmet Berisha, Fetah Halili, and Agim Gashi. 2015. *Biology 12*. 27, s. 5. Prishtina: School Textbook Publishing House (Libri Shkollor).

Berisha, Ahmet, Ismet Bajraktari, Kasamedin Abdullahu, and Agim Gashi. 2016. *Biology 10*. 136, s. 3. Prishtina: School Textbook Publishing House (Libri Shkollor).

Binaku, Trina, Vesa Deva, Bjeshka Guri, Albert Selimi, Ramadan Sokoli, Veton Sylhasi, and Marigona Shabiu. 2017. *Discriminatory Language in School Textbooks: An Analysis of Upper Secondary Level School Textbooks in Kosovo*. https://advocacy-center.org/wp-content/uploads/2018/09/Discriminatory-language-in-school-textbooks.pdf.

Costa Rica, Ministry of Public Education. 2017. Educar para una Nueva Ciudadanía: Programa de Estudio de Afectividad y Sexualidad. Government of Costa Rica: San Jose. http://cse.go.cr/sites/default/files/afectividad_y_sexualidad_integral_iii_ciclo_2017.pdf.

Costa Rica, Ministry of Public Education. 2018. *Protocolo de atención del acoso escolar contra población estudiantil LGTB inserta en los centros educativos del Ministerio de Educación Pública*. Government of Costa Rica: San Jose. https://www.mep.go.cr/sites/default/files/atencion-bullying-contra-poblacion-lgtb.pdf.

Eaton, Krisit. 2017. "Indonesian University Tries to Weed Out LGBTQ Applicants." *NBC News*, May 9, 2017. https://www.nbcnews.com/feature/nbc-out/indonesian-university-tries-weed-out-lgbtq-applicants-n756841.

Human Rights Watch. 2016. *The Education Deficit*. New York: Human Rights Watch. https://www.hrw.org/report/2016/06/09/education-deficit/failures-protect-and-fulfill-right-education-through-global.

India, Ministry of Human Resources Development. 2018. *Draft National Education Policy 2019*. Bangalore. https://mhrd.gov.in/sites/upload_files/mhrd/files/Draft_NEP_2019_EN_Revised.pdf.

Jakarta Post. 2015. "MK Rejects Petition for Sex Education on School Curriculum." November 5, 2015. https://www.thejakartapost.com/news/2015/11/05/mk-rejects-petition-sex-education-school-curriculum.html.

Japan, Ministry of Education. 2016. *Guidebook for Teachers*. https://www.mext.go.jp/b_menu/houdou/28/04/1369211.htm.

LAU (Lebanese American University). 2019. *Discrimination, Harassment and Sexual Misconduct Prevention Policy*. https://www.lau.edu.lb/about/policies/harassment_policy.pdf.

Maketab, Hanis. 2016. "Indonesia's Education Minister Faces Censure Over LGBT Comments." *SI News*, January 26, 2016. https://www.studyinternational.com/news/indonesias-education-minister-faces-censure-over-lgbt-comments.

Mato, Erlehtaand, and Bajram Shatri. 2015. *Civic education 10*. 102, s. 1. Prishtina: School Textbook Publishing House (Libri Shkollor).

Migalhas International. 2018. "Tokyo Bans LGBT Discrimination: Japan." October 8, 2018. https://www.migalhas.com/TopStories/64,MI288848,31047-Tokyo+bans+LGBT+discrimination+Japan.

Moretti, Enrico. 2005. "Social Returns to Human Capital." NBER (National Bureau of Economic Research) Reporter: Research Summary. https://www.nber.org/reporter/spring05/moretti.html.

OECD (Organisation for Economic Co-operation and Development), Eric A. Hanushek, and Ludger Woessmann. 2015. *Universal Basic Skills: What Countries Stand to Gain*. Paris: OECD Publishing. https://doi.org/10.1787/9789264234833-en.

Okanlawon, Kehinde. 2017. "Homophobic Bullying in Nigerian Schools: The Experiences of LGBT University Students." *Journal of LGBT Youth* 14 (1): 51–70.

Ozturk, Ilhan. 2001. "The Role of Education in Economic Development: A Theoretical Perspective." MPRA Paper 9023, Munich: University Library of Munich.

Psacharopoulos, George, and Harry Anthony Patrinos. 2018. "Returns to Investment in Education: A Decennial Review of the Global Literature (English)." Policy Research Working Paper 8402. World Bank, Washington, DC. http://documents.worldbank.org/curated/en/442521523465644318/Returns-to-investment-in-education-a-decennial-review-of-the-global-literature.

Sarwar, Mohammad Golam. 2017. "Analyzing the Draft Elimination of Discrimination Act." *Daily Star*, June 20. https://www.thedailystar.net/law-our-rights/law-analysis/analysing-the-draft-elimination-discrimination-act-1422682.

Slater, Hannah. 2013. "LGBT-Inclusive Sex Education Means Healthier Youth and Safer Schools." Center for American Progress. https://www.americanprogress.org/issues/lgbt/news/2013/06/21/67411 /lgbt-inclusive-sex-education-means-healthier-youth-and-safer-schools.

South Africa, Department of Basic Education. 2016. *Challenging Homophobic Bullying in Schools.* Government of the Republic of South Africa: Pretoria. https://www.education.gov.za/Portals/0/Documents/Publications /Homophobic%20Bullying%20in%20Schools.pdf?ver=2016-02-19-133822-337.

UNESCO (United Nations Educational, Scientific and Cultural Organization). 2012. *Education Sector Responses to Homophobic Bullying.* Paris: UNESCO. https://unesdoc.unesco.org/ark:/48223/pf0000216493.

UNESCO (United Nations Educational, Scientific and Cultural Organization). 2014. "Teaching Respect for All: Implementation Guide." Paris: UNESCO. https://unesdoc.unesco.org/ark:/48223/pf0000227983.

UNESCO (United Nations Educational, Scientific and Cultural Organization). 2016. *Out in the Open: Education Sector Responses to Violence Based on Sexual Orientation and Gender Identity/Expression.* Paris: UNESCO. https://www.gale.info/doc/unesco/INT-2016-UNESCO-OutInTheOpen.pdf.

UNESCO (United Nations Educational, Scientific and Cultural Organization). 2018a. "Are Education Systems LGBTI-inclusive? UNESCO Teams up With Youth Organization to Find Out." June 22, 2018. https:// en.unesco.org/news/are-education-systems-lgbti-inclusive-unesco-teams-youth-organization-find-out.

UNESCO (United Nations Educational, Scientific and Cultural Organization). 2018b. "What You Need to Know About the Right to Education." October 10, 2018. https://en.unesco.org/news /what-you-need-know-about-right-education.

Additional Readings

Paddock, Richard C., and Makita Suharto. 2019. "A Test for Foreign Teachers in Indonesia: Are You Gay?" *New York Times*, December 23, 2019. https://www.nytimes.com/2019/12/23/world/asia/indonesia -gay-teachers.html.

3

Access to the Labor Market

KEY FINDINGS

Canada, followed by Costa Rica, has the most advanced legal framework for protecting sexual and gender minorities in the labor market.

Countries tend to have better legal frameworks for protecting employees from sexual orientation and gender identity (SOGI) discrimination in employment in the public sector than in the private sector.

Only Canada and Mozambique have enacted laws that explicitly prohibit employers from discussing sexual orientation, gender identity, or marital status during the recruitment process.

Few countries offer equal benefits and pay for all employees, regardless of their SOGI. Canada and Uruguay have the most advanced reporting mechanisms for filing an employment-related discrimination claim on SOGI grounds in the public and private sectors.

It is advised that countries amend existing laws or create more inclusive and protective legal frameworks in the workplace to explicitly protect people from discrimination on the basis of sexual orientation, gender identity and expression, and sex characteristics.

Importance of the Access to the Labor Market Indicator Set

The elimination of discrimination in employment and occupation is a basic principle of the International Labour Organization's (ILO) Declaration on Fundamental Principles and Rights at Work (ILO 1998). The declaration provides that the right to work and the nondiscriminatory access to employment are universal and fundamental rights, regardless of a country's level of economic development. Equal access to the labor market and security in the workplace ensures a sense of belonging, allowing individuals to pursue their dreams and achieve their potential. Conversely, discrimination based solely on a person's identity (rather than skills or performance) decreases productivity and leads to increased unemployment (Panter and others 2017). Equality of opportunity in the labor market also allows individuals to choose their personal and professional paths. But to ensure equal access to the labor market, countries should eliminate legal barriers and adopt protective legislation. Only then will the affected population feel truly free to make economic decisions that increase labor productivity and, ultimately, economic output (Badgett 2014).

> Employment discrimination is a very real concern to lesbian, gay, bisexual, transgender, and intersex (LGBTI) people. LGBTI discrimination not only harms LGBTI citizens, but it is also bad for employers and negatively impacts human capital and economies.
>
> —Crosby (2012)

Awareness of the extent of violence and discrimination against sexual and gender minorities has risen in the past decade. Even in countries with more progressive legal frameworks, deep-rooted stigma and negative stereotypes perpetuate discrimination against sexual and gender minorities in the workplace (UN OHCHR 2017). Discrimination and fear of discrimination can negatively affect the wages, job opportunities, mental and physical health, productivity, and job satisfaction of sexual and gender minorities (Sears and Mallory 2011). Furthermore, sexual and gender minority discrimination is also bad for employers (Crosby 2012). Statistically, a diverse workforce boosts ideas and problem-solving approaches; it also increases innovation, potentially appealing to new markets (UN OHCHR 2017).

The current global situation regarding workplace inclusiveness leaves much to be desired. According to a 2017 United Nations report, of the 193 countries reviewed, only 67 had banned discrimination based on sexual orientation in the workplace (UN OHCHR 2017). Similarly, in a World Bank study conducted in Thailand, 77 percent of transgender,

49 percent of gay, and 62.5 percent of lesbian respondents reported that employers rejected their job applications because they were sexual or gender minorities (World Bank 2018). A 2016 study in the United States found that lesbian, bisexual, and transgender women were 30 percent less likely to get a call-back from potential employers after job interviews (Mishel 2016).

Countries that explicitly prohibit discrimination against sexual and gender minorities in the workplace are likely to experience higher LGBTI employee motivation and productivity. According to the theory of "anticipated discrimination," individuals who have experienced past discrimination due to their identity often expect that others will stigmatize them in the future if their identity is revealed (Ng, Schweitzer, and Lyons 2012). Sexual and gender minorities expect disparate treatment in the workplace because of their SOGI, leading to decreased confidence and self-esteem as well as to potentially diminished socioeconomic opportunities. A study of postsecondary students in Canada found that sexual and gender minorities are less likely to apply for a job, have lower career earnings expectations, and are prone to accepting less-than-ideal jobs (Ng, Schweitzer, and Lyons 2012). A lack of labor market antidiscrimination laws can result in an expectation on the part of sexual and gender minorities that they will experience discrimination in the workplace. Moreover, discriminatory workplace practices have also affected workers who are sexual and gender minorities during the COVID-19 pandemic in a way that reverberates across the community because it affects their ability to take time off work to care for family members; it also leaves them more vulnerable to job loss (box 3.1).

The indicator set on access to the labor market aims to identify the existence (or absence) of national laws, constitutional provisions, and/or regulations that prohibit discrimination based on sexual orientation, gender identity, gender expression, or sex characteristics in accessing the labor market. It examines the existence of laws or regulations prohibiting discrimination when applying for work, interviewing for jobs, and obtaining employment. The indicator set addresses equal remuneration, equal benefits in the pension system for same-sex partners, and employee dismissal based on their perceived or actual SOGI. Finally, the possibilities of redress and the existence of relevant reporting mechanisms, along with the provision of free or reduced legal aid for sexual and gender minorities, are also analyzed in the study.

A Japanese woman sued the Osaka hospital (her employer) in September 2019, alleging that her supervisor, ignoring her wishes and privacy, revealed to colleagues that she is transgender. She claims that she was later harassed by colleagues, with one telling her "it feels gross" to get changed in the same room with her.

—*Japan Times (2019)*

BOX 3.1   Links between Labor Market Access and COVID-19

Because of discriminatory unemployment compensation, as well as paid sick and leave policies that cover only unions between people of the opposite sex, sexual and gender minorities may not be able to take time off from work to care for family members. The Equality of Opportunity for Sexual and Gender Minorities (EQOSOGI) initiative collected data related to the absence or presence of laws that recognize same-sex couples (through registered partnership, civil unions, or legal marriage) and laws providing equal benefits to same-sex spouses as compared with opposite-sex spouses. Many countries leave same-sex spouses without access to health services and pension benefits that opposite-sex spouses enjoy.

The COVID-19 pandemic has triggered one of the worst employment crises in modern times. As the COVID-19 pandemic continues to spread and economies put in place lockdown and slowdown measures, people worldwide are increasingly anxious about their job security. The report found that only 3 of the 16 analyzed countries legally prohibit employers from dismissing employees on the basis of their sexual orientation, and gender identity and expression, leaving sexual and gender minorities more susceptible to job loss during the pandemic. There is a real danger that the crisis will widen inequalities, and sexual and gender minorities could become more vulnerable during the pandemic response. Inclusive laws should protect sexual and gender minorities from being dismissed from their jobs based on their SOGI.

Discrimination in Employment and the Workplace

Sexual and gender minorities face various forms of discrimination in employment.[1] They experience discrimination in recruiting procedures, are denied employment or passed over for promotions, and are often victims of harassment or homophobic and transphobic behavior in the workplace (Sears and Mallory 2014). Inclusive workplace environments allow sexual and gender minorities to access employment and improve their well-being and contribute to growth. More inclusive working environments can also benefit countries, particularly as respect and protection of minorities on a domestic level can influence how countries are perceived globally (Badgett 2014).

People identified as gay or lesbian during the initial stage of the hiring process are more vulnerable to discrimination than heterosexual applicants with comparable skills and experience. This pattern has been observed in various countries, including Austria, Canada, Cyprus, Greece, Sweden, and the United States (Ahmed, Andersson, and Hammarstedt 2013; Drydakis 2019). Discrimination in hiring based on sexual orientation has been found to be a matter of employer preference and not a result of uncertainty regarding gay and lesbian applicants' commitment. That is, non-heterosexual identity is perceived as a devalued characteristic in hiring compared with heterosexual identity (Ahmed, Andersson, and Hammarstedt 2013). An ILO study on sexual and gender minorities in Argentina, Hungary, and Thailand underscores the experience of surveyed individuals in all three countries. Applicants were refused jobs because of sexual orientation—in some cases, in an explicit manner during the job interview. Similarly, many were denied jobs because their gender expression (such as clothing, mannerism, or voice) did not "match" their legal gender identity (ILO 2012).

Protection against workplace and employment discrimination on SOGI grounds varies among the 16 countries analyzed for this *Equality of Opportunity for Sexual and Gender Minorities* (EQOSOGI) report. In general, countries tend to provide more protections in the public than they do in the private sector, with only seven countries (Canada, Costa Rica, Kosovo, Mexico, South Africa, Ukraine, and Uruguay) protecting employees from SOGI discrimination in both sectors. In Ontario, Canada, the Human Rights Code prohibits discrimination in all sectors, including the employment sector.[2] Similarly, Kosovo explicitly protects sexual and gender minorities from discrimination in employment.[3] Ukraine has a more inclusive legal framework, prohibiting all forms of discrimination in employment based on sexual orientation and gender identity.[4] Uruguay also prohibits discrimination against sexual and gender minorities in the labor market.[5] Moreover, the country's Comprehensive Law for Transgender People (Ley Integral Para Personas Trans) prohibits discrimination on the basis of gender identity.[6] The law also creates quotas (1 percent or more) for transgender people, ensuring access to public sector jobs and providing tax incentives for private sector employers to hire transgender people.

Nine countries (Canada, Costa Rica, India, Jamaica, Kosovo, Mexico, South Africa, Ukraine, and Uruguay) offer protections only in the public sector, and the same number (Canada, Costa Rica, India, Kosovo, Mexico, Mozambique, South Africa, Ukraine, and Uruguay) protect sexual and gender minorities seeking employment in the private sector (figure 3.1). Some countries are starting to apply the rules to both the private and the public sectors. For example, India's newly adopted Transgender Persons (Protection of Rights) Act also bans discrimination against transgender and intersex people in private employment.[7] Although India's Constitution

FIGURE 3.1

Analyzed Countries That Prohibit Workplace SOGI Discrimination in the Public and Private Sectors, 2021

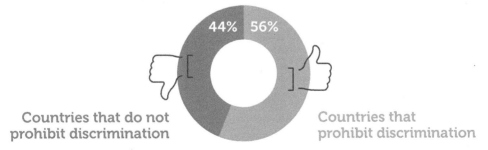

Source: World Bank Group, Equality of Opportunity database.

Note: SOGI = sexual orientation and gender identity.

prohibits discrimination in employment without referring explicitly to SOGI grounds,[8] the Indian Supreme Court has ruled that sexual orientation and gender identity are protected grounds under the category of "sex."[9]

None of the countries analyzed explicitly prohibits sexual and gender minorities from obtaining employment in specific industries. Still, three countries (Costa Rica,[10] Kosovo,[11] and South Africa[12]) prohibit employers from dismissing employees on the basis of their sexual orientation, gender identity, and/or expression. In all three countries, the law explicitly prohibits the dismissal of employees or termination of contracts on the basis of sexual orientation, gender identity, and/or expression.

More countries protect against sexual orientation discrimination than they do against gender identity discrimination. Of the 10 countries that protect employees from SOGI discrimination in public or private employment (Canada, Costa Rica, India, Jamaica, Kosovo, Mexico, Mozambique, South Africa, Ukraine, and Uruguay), only Canada, India, Kosovo, Ukraine, and Uruguay protect both sexual orientation and gender identity. The other five (Costa Rica, Jamaica, Mexico, Mozambique, and South Africa) prohibit discrimination on the basis of sexual orientation but not gender identity. Contributors from Costa Rica report that, although sexual minorities are legally protected from discrimination in employment,[13] gender minorities continue to suffer high levels of workplace discrimination given that gender identity is not included in the legally protected grounds. Similarly, two countries (Jamaica[14] and South Africa[15]) have not put in place explicit legal protections for people who experience discrimination because of their gender identity. Although the South African law does not mention gender identity, it explicitly protects intersex people under the category of "sex."[16] Mexico's legislation is inclusive of sexual minorities,[17] but contributors report that laws are not always correctly applied because the National Council to Prevent Discrimination (CONAPRED) is underfunded, and many other officials lack knowledge of recent developments pertaining to sexual and gender minorities.

Concerning the right to privacy, only Canada and Mozambique have enacted laws that explicitly prohibit employers from discussing sexual orientation, gender identity, or marital status during the recruitment process.[18] In comparison, in Indonesia, contributors report that civil service employers can ask applicants about their marital status in the recruitment process. One of the requirements to become a civil servant in Indonesia is *to be healthy both physically and spiritually*, a requirement that is open to subjective interpretation and may be used to target sexual and gender minorities (figure 3.2).

The remaining countries have employment-related protections for other groups. Bangladesh, Indonesia, Japan, Lebanon, Nigeria, and Tunisia protect employees from discrimination in employment on several grounds, including sex, race, gender, and religion. But these grounds do not protect sexual and gender minorities from discrimination: even though the laws include these categories, there are (at least) anecdotal reports of discrimination against sexual and gender minorities in those countries. Contributors from Lebanon report that companies often refrain from hiring openly sexual or gender minority candidates; transgender individuals face particular discrimination because their photo IDs usually do not match their appearance. In Indonesia,

FIGURE 3.2

Analyzed Countries That Prohibit Employers from Discussing Sexual Orientation, Gender Identity, or Marital Status during the Recruitment Process: Canada and Mozambique, 2021

Source: World Bank Group, Equality of Opportunity database.

BOX 3.2   Recent Developments in Japan

The government of Japan has recently commenced planning for the enforcement of the revised Labor Policy Comprehensive Promotion Act, including by raising awareness of the contents of the Guidelines for Preventing Power Harassment. The guidelines clarify that insulting speech and behaviors targeting diverse sexual orientation and gender identity fall under the category of power harassment in the workplace. Currently, under the Powa-Hara (Power Harassment) Prevention Act, only large corporations are required to adopt measures against power harassment; this requirement will become mandatory for small to medium-size companies as well beginning April 2022. In addition, Japan has revised NPA Rule 10-10 on prevention of sexual harassment against public sector employees and introduced a rule to ban sexual harassment on the basis of sexual orientation and gender identity. With this rule, lesbian, gay, bisexual, and transgender national public employees will be protected if they are sexually harassed.

contributors report that sexual and gender minorities serving in the military are often dishonorably discharged for immorality and accused of same-sex "adultery," which is considered a crime under the Indonesian Penal Code.[19]

Sexual and gender minorities still face discrimination in employment and the workplace in most countries, even though some governments have undertaken significant measures to ensure equality of sexual and gender minorities in the labor market. By not protecting their fundamental right to work by providing a more inclusive working environment, countries risk harming not only sexual and gender minorities but also society as a whole. Therefore, authorities must continue to expand their efforts to combat discrimination and create a more inclusive workplace for sexual and gender minorities. Sexual and gender minorities should have equal opportunities to access the labor market and participate in the workplace without facing discrimination because of their identity.

It is advised that countries adopt the following good practice policy actions:

- Amend existing laws or create more inclusive and protective legal frameworks in the workplace that explicitly protect people from discrimination on the basis of sexual orientation, gender identity and expression, and sex characteristics.

- Introduce inclusive legislation to protect the rights of sexual and gender minorities, provide more effective legal protections from discrimination in the labor market, and raise awareness of SOGI issues within the labor market.

- Amend laws prohibiting discrimination on the basis of sexual orientation to include gender identity and expression, and sex characteristics.

- Legally require employers to respect the privacy of their employees and job candidates, prohibiting questions related to sexual orientation, gender identity, or marital status.

- Encourage employers to respect the needs, wishes, and privacy of transgender employees regarding their transition by facilitating changes in internal personnel systems (such as name changes) and providing health insurance and paid leave for medical procedures.

- Introduce antidiscrimination training in the workplace to educate all employees about SOGI issues and implement antidiscrimination regulations to create a more inclusive environment for sexual and gender minorities.

- Conduct additional studies in the area of employment discrimination against sexual and gender minorities and provide adequate reporting mechanisms for sexual and gender minorities experiencing discrimination in the labor market.

Equal Pay and Benefits

Sexual and gender minorities are often paid less than their colleagues who are not sexual and gender minorities (figure 3.3).[20] These pay gaps cannot be objectively explained by factors such as differences in education, training and work experience, part-time versus full-time work, or company size, suggesting that they can be attributed to direct or implicit bias against sexual and gender minorities (Sears and Mallory 2014). In addition, sexual and gender minorities are frequently refused certain benefits—such as family-related leave and pension arrangements—usually granted to people in opposite-sex marriages (Pizer and others 2012). In countries in which same-sex civil unions or marriages are not legal, same-sex couples can experience discrimination regarding the benefits offered to different-sex spouses. This unequal treatment can have adverse effects on employees' mental and physical health, productivity, and job satisfaction, leading to economic losses for the employer.

Nine of the 16 countries reviewed condone unequal pay. Only Costa Rica, India, Kosovo, Mexico, Mozambique, South Africa, and Ukraine legally require equal remuneration for employees that belong to sexual and gender minorities. In Kosovo[21] and Costa Rica,[22] the law prohibits discrimination in working conditions, including salary. In South Africa[23] and Mexico,[24] the law prevents employers from varying the terms and conditions of employment for employees responsible for substantially the same work on the basis of their sexual orientation. While South Africa, Costa Rica, Mexico, and Mozambique prohibit pay discrimination only on the basis of sexual orientation, Ukraine and Kosovo prohibit discrimination based on both sexual orientation and gender identity.[25] India recently enacted a new law that prohibits discrimination in wages for all genders, including transgender people.[26]

Pension benefits are usually not available to sexual and gender minorities (figure 3.4). Only Canada, Costa Rica, Mexico, South Africa, and Uruguay grant civil servants' same-sex partners the same

FIGURE 3.3

Analyzed Countries That Do Not Require Equal Pay for Sexual and Gender Minorities, 2021

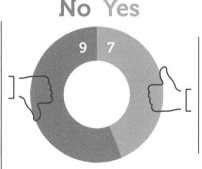

No Yes

9 7

Bangladesh
Canada
Indonesia
Jamaica
Japan
Lebanon
Nigeria
South Africa
Uruguay

Costa Rica
India
Kosovo
Mexico
Mozambique
South Africa
Ukraine

Source: World Bank Group, Equality of Opportunity database.

FIGURE 3.4

Analyzed Countries That Provide Equal Pension Benefits for Same-Sex and Different-Sex Spouses, 2021

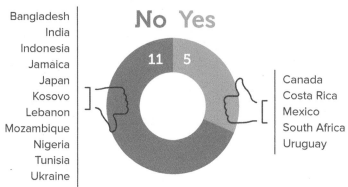

Source: World Bank Group, Equality of Opportunity database.

pension benefits as different-sex partners. In Canada, following the 1999 decision of the Supreme Court in *M. v. H.*,[27] the Canadian federal government amended the Canada Pension Plan,[28] so that it now extends survivor benefits to same-sex partners by changing the definition of "spouse" to conform to the equal rights provisions of Section 15(1) of the Canadian Charter of Rights and Freedoms.[29] In 2018, Costa Rica also instructed its National Pensions Directorate to provide identical benefits to same-sex partners.[30] In South Africa, same-sex civil unions are treated like different-sex marriages. The law prohibits discrimination with regard to pension benefits for civil servants.[31] In Mexico, same-sex civil unions and same-sex marriages are not recognized at the federal level. Most Mexican states, however, have considered legislation on these issues, and the federal law extends its antidiscrimination protections to the pension system as well.[32] However, contributors reported that same-sex couples in Mexico face hurdles in registering their spouses. In Uruguay, the marriage equality law for same-sex partners also establishes equal rights in the pension system for civil servants.[33] The remaining analyzed countries do not allow same-sex partnerships, and thus no benefits are available for these couples (figure 3.4). However, India has taken important steps in this direction. States including Kerala, Tamil Nadu, Odisha Karnataka, Andhra Pradesh, and Himachal Pradesh have introduced schemes that provide pension benefits to transgender persons (*Business Standard* 2017; ILGA 2014; Sharma 2016).

It is advised that countries adopt the following good practice policy actions:

- Establish transparent and equal benefits and pay for all employees, regardless of their SOGI.

- Facilitate the registration of same-sex partnerships to ensure that benefits are available to all individuals.

Filing Employment-Related Discrimination Complaints

Effective reporting mechanisms are necessary to provide adequate legal protections for sexual and gender minorities experiencing discrimination in the labor market.[34] Victims of SOGI discrimination should also receive free or reduced-cost legal representation if they are unable to cover the costs of an employment-related discrimination claim. Moreover, they should have access to relevant national human rights or equality institutions specializing in handling charges of employment discrimination against sexual and gender minorities. Authorities should establish a holistic redress system that encourages reporting. Reporting and remedying discrimination is as important as prohibiting discrimination, and it offers a greater scope of protection to affected minorities.

Most of the countries studied legally enforce employees' right to bring employment-related claims in the public sector. However, that number decreases in the private sector. Specifically, Canada, Costa Rica, India, Jamaica, Kosovo, Mexico, South Africa, Ukraine, and Uruguay legally protect employees' right to bring claims for employment discrimination on SOGI grounds in the public sector. However, only Canada, Costa Rica, India, Kosovo, Mexico, South Africa, Ukraine, and Uruguay also have similar provisions for discrimination claims in the private sector (figure 3.5).

Many countries offer free or reduced-cost legal aid to discrimination victims who are unable to cover legal fees. However, laws in most countries fail to explicitly identify discrimination grounds eligible for subsidized legal aid, such as sexual orientation, gender identity and expression, or sex characteristics. Only Canada and Uruguay explicitly grant victims of sexual

Analyzed Countries That Allow Employees to Bring Claims for Employment Discrimination on SOGI Grounds: Public Sector Compared with Private Sector, 2021

More countries allow employees to bring claims for employment discrimination on SOGI grounds in the public sector than in the private sector

7

9

8

8

Public sector   Private sector

Source: World Bank Group, Equality of Opportunity database.

Note: SOGI = sexual orientation and gender identity.

and gender minority employment discrimination the right to free or reduced-cost legal assistance if victims lack the means to cover the costs of claims. In Canada, access to legal aid in Ontario is governed by the Legal Aid Services Act,[35] which acknowledges the diverse legal needs of low-income individuals and disadvantaged communities in Ontario and offers legal aid in a cost-effective and efficient manner. Community legal clinics, such as Legal Aid Ontario,[36] provide services to address the needs of low-income people and communities. In Uruguay, the law on violence against women explicitly protects women from discrimination on the basis of sexual orientation and gender identity in any area of life and guarantees their right to free legal assistance (table 3.1).[37]

TABLE 3.1

Legal Methods Available to Employees Filing an Employment-Related Discrimination Claim on SOGI Grounds

Country	Allow employee claims for employment discrimination on SOGI grounds in public sector	Allow employee claims for employment discrimination on SOGI grounds in private sector	National human rights or equality institutions/bodies that handle charges of employment discrimination against sexual and gender minorities	Laws/regulations explicitly granting victims of sexual and gender minority employment discrimination the right to free or reduced-cost legal assistance
Bangladesh				
Canada	✓	✓	✓	✓
Costa Rica	✓	✓		
India	✓	✓	✓	
Indonesia				
Jamaica	✓			
Japan				
Kosovo	✓	✓	✓	
Lebanon				
Mexico	✓	✓	✓	
Mozambique				
Nigeria				
South Africa	✓	✓	✓	
Tunisia				
Ukraine	✓	✓		
Uruguay	✓	✓	✓	✓

Source: World Bank Group, Equality of Opportunity database.

Note: SOGI = sexual orientation and gender identity.

It is advised that countries adopt the following good practice policy actions:

- Establish legal frameworks allowing victims of SOGI-related employment discrimination to report discrimination and harassment cases in the public and private sectors and pursue available remedies.

- Ensure that free or reduced-cost legal aid is available to employment discrimination victims if necessary.

Notes

1. Questions addressing discrimination in employment and the workplace in the indicator set on access to the labor market include: Are there any laws, constitutional provisions, and/or regulations prohibiting discrimination based on sexual orientation, gender identity, gender expression, and sex characteristics in public and private sector workplaces at the national level? Are there any laws and/or regulations prohibiting discrimination in recruitment in the public sector based on SOGI? Are there any laws and/or regulations prohibiting discrimination in recruitment in the private sector based on SOGI? Are there any laws and/or regulations prohibiting sexual and gender minorities from obtaining employment in specific industries? Are there any laws and/or regulations prohibiting an employer from asking an individual's SOGI and/or marital status during the recruitment process? Are there any laws and/or regulations prohibiting the dismissal of employees on the basis of their perceived or actual SOGI?

2. Ontario's Human Rights Code of 1990. 2019 (amended). Article 5: "(1) Every person has a right to equal treatment with respect to employment without discrimination because of race, ancestry, place of origin, colour, ethnic origin, citizenship, creed, sex, sexual orientation, gender identity, gender expression, age, record of offences, marital status, family status or disability. (2) Every person who is an employee has a right to freedom from harassment in the workplace by the employer or agent of the employer or by another employee because of race, ancestry, place of origin, colour, ethnic origin, citizenship, creed, sexual orientation, gender identity, gender expression, age, record of offences, marital status, family status or disability."

3. Kosovo, Law No.05/L-021 on Protection from Discrimination. Article 1, Section 1: "The purpose of this law is to establish a general framework for prevention and combating discrimination based on nationality, or in relation to any community, social origin, race, ethnicity, colour, birth, origin, sex, gender, gender identity, sexual orientation, language, citizenship, religion and religious belief, political affiliation, political or other opinion, social or personal status, age, family or marital status, pregnancy, maternity, wealth, health status, disability, genetic inheritance or any other grounds, in order to implement the principle of equal treatment." Article 2, Section 1: "This law applies to all acts or omissions, of all state and local institutions, natural and legal persons, public and private sector, who violate, violated or may violate the rights of any person or natural and legal entities in all areas of life, especially related to: 1.1. conditions for access to employment, self-employment and occupation, including employment conditions and selection criteria, regardless of activity and at all levels of the professional hierarchy, including promotions; … 1.3. conditions of employment and working conditions, including discharge or termination of the contract and salary; 1.4. membership and involvement in organizations of workers or employers or any organization whose members exercise a particular profession, including the benefits provided for by such organizations."

4. Ukraine, Labor Code 1971. Article 2-1: "All forms of discrimination in the field of work are forbidden, including the violation of the principle of equality of rights and opportunities, direct or indirect restriction of the rights of workers, depending on race, color, political, religious and other beliefs, sex, sexual orientation and gender identity, ethnicity, social and foreign origin, age, health, pregnancy, disability, suspicion or presence of a HIV/AIDS, family and property status, family responsibilities, residence, membership in a trade union or other CSO's, participating in a strike, addressing or intent to apply to a court or other bodies for the protection of their rights or to provide support to other workers in the protection of their rights, in linguistic or other grounds, not related to the nature of the work or the conditions for its implementation."

5. Uruguay, Ley 17.817. Lucha contra el racismo, la xenofobia y la discriminación. 2004. Article 2: "A los efectos de la presente ley se entenderá por discriminación toda distinción, exclusión, restricción, preferencia o ejercicio de violencia física y moral, basada en motivos de raza, color de piel, religión, origen nacional o étnico, discapacidad, aspecto estético, género, orientación e identidad sexual, que tenga por objeto o por resultado anular o menoscabar el reconocimiento, goce o ejercicio, en condiciones de igualdad, de los derechos humanos y libertades fundamentales en las esferas política, económica, social, cultural o en cualquier otra esfera de la vida pública." Article 5(K): "Informar a la opinión pública sobre actitudes y conductas racistas, xenofóbicas y discriminatorias o que pudieren manifestarse en cualquier ámbito de la vida nacional, especialmente en las áreas de educación, salud, acción social y empleo; provengan ellas de autoridades públicas o entidades o personas privadas."

6. Uruguay, Ley Integral Para Personas Trans. 2018 de Uruguay. Article 3 : "La presente ley tiene como objeto asegurar el derecho de las personas trans residentes de la República a una vida libre de discriminación y estigmatización, para lo cual se establecen mecanismos, medidas y políticas integrales de prevención, atención, protección, promoción y reparación." Article 13: "Encomiéndase al Instituto Nacional de Empleo y Formación Profesional la determinación de un cupo no inferior al 1% (uno por ciento) destinado a las personas trans, en los diversos programas de capacitación y calificación que implemente."

7. India, Transgender Persons (Protection of Rights) Act. 2019. Section 2: "In this Act, unless the context otherwise requires, ... (b) 'establishment' means (i) any body or authority established by or under a Central Act or a State Act or an authority or a body owned or controlled or aided by the Government or a local authority, or a Government company as defined in section 2 of the Companies Act, 2013, and includes a Department of the Government; or (ii) any company or body corporate or association or body of individuals, firm, cooperative or other society, association, trust, agency, institution; ... (k) 'transgender person' means a person whose gender does not match with the gender assigned to that person at birth and includes trans-man or trans-woman (whether or not such person has undergone Sex Reassignment Surgery or hormone therapy or laser therapy or such other therapy), person with intersex variations, genderqueer and person having such socio-cultural identities as kinner, hijra, aravani and jogta." Section 3: "No person or establishment shall discriminate against a transgender person on any of the following grounds, namely: ... (b) the unfair treatment in, or in relation to, employment or occupation; (c) the denial of, or termination from, employment or occupation." Section 9: "No establishment shall discriminate against any transgender person in any matter relating to employment including, but not limited to, recruitment, promotion and other related issues."

8. Constitution of India. Article 15: "(1): The State shall not discriminate against any citizen on grounds only of religion, race, caste, sex, place of birth or any of them. Article 16. (1): There shall be equality of opportunity for all citizens in matters relating to employment or appointment to any office under the State. (2) No citizen shall, on grounds only of religion, race, caste, sex, descent, place of birth, residence or any of them, be ineligible for, or discriminated against in respect of, any employment or office under the State."

9. In 2014, the Supreme Court of India directed the central government and state governments to ensure treatment of "hijras"/"eunuchs" (transgenders) as third gender when opposed to male or female so as to afford them the same protections of fundamental rights, including those under Article 14

(Right to Equality) and Article 15 (Prohibition of Discrimination). In 2017, the Supreme Court of India declared that sexual autonomy is inherent in the Right to Privacy protected under Article 21 of the Constitution of India ("Right to Life and Liberty"). Therefore, the protection of the rights and interests of sexual and gender minorities is ensured by the constitution. Affirming the principles upheld earlier, the court in a 2018 judgment stated that the word "sex" under Article 15 (Prohibition of Discrimination) and Article 16 (Equality of Opportunities) of the constitution has to be read widely to include gender and sexual minorities.

10. Costa Rica, Código de Trabajo de Costa Rica. 1934 (Amended in 2016). Article 406: "Se prohíbe el despido de los trabajadores o las trabajadoras por las razones señaladas en el artículo 404." Article 404: "Se prohíbe toda discriminación en el trabajo por razones de edad, etnia, sexo, religión, raza, orientación sexual, estado civil, opinión política, ascendencia nacional, origen social, filiación, condición de salud, discapacidad, afiliación sindical, situación económica o cualquier otra forma análoga de discriminación."

11. Kosovo, Law No.05/L-021 on Protection from Discrimination: see note 3 for the applicable text.

12. South Africa, Promotion of Equality and Prevention of Unfair Discrimination Act. 2000. Article 1: "In this Act, unless the context indicates otherwise – 'prohibited grounds' are (a) race, gender, sex, pregnancy, marital status, ethnic or social origin, colour, sexual orientation, age, disability, religion, conscience, belief, culture, language and birth; 'sex' includes intersex." Section 29: "Illustrative list of unfair practices in certain sectors, 1. 'Labour and employment: (a) Creating artificial barriers to equal access to employment opportunities by using certain recruitment and selection procedures. (b) Applying human resource utilisation, development, promotion and retention practices which unfairly discriminate against persons from groups identified by the prohibited grounds. (c) Failing to respect the principle of equal pay for equal work. (d) Perpetuating disproportionate income differentials deriving from past unfair discrimination."

13. Costa Rica, Código de Trabajo. 1934 (Amended in 2016). Article 404: "Se prohíbe toda discriminación en el trabajo por razones de edad, etnia, sexo, religión, raza, orientación sexual, estado civil, opinión política, ascendencia nacional, origen social, filiación, condición de salud, discapacidad, afiliación sindical, situación económica o cualquier otra forma análoga de discriminación."

14. Jamaica, Public Sector Staff Orders. 2004. Article 13(1): "Employees shall be treated fairly and equitably without discrimination based on any of the following grounds: 1. Age 2. Gender 3. National Origin. 4. Race 5. Colour 6. Religious Beliefs 7. Political Affiliation 8. Disability 9. Sexual Orientation."

15. South Africa, Employment Equity Act 55. 1998. Article 6 (1): "No person may unfairly discriminate, directly or indirectly, against an employee in any employment policy or practice, on one or more grounds, including race, gender, sex, pregnancy, marital status, family responsibility, ethnic or social origin, colour, sexual orientation, age, disability, religion, HIV status, conscience, belief, political opinion, culture, language and birth." South Africa, Promotion of Equality and Prevention of Unfair Discrimination Act. 2000. Article 1: "In this Act, unless the context indicates otherwise - 'prohibited grounds' are (a) race, gender, sex, pregnancy, marital status, ethnic or social origin, colour, sexual orientation, age, disability, religion, conscience, belief, culture, language and birth; 'sex' includes intersex." Section 29 provides an illustrative list of unfair practices in certain sectors: 1. "Labour and employment: (a) Creating artificial barriers to equal access to employment opportunities by using certain recruitment and selection procedures. (b) Applying human resource utilisation, development, promotion and retention practices which unfairly discriminate against persons from groups identified by the prohibited grounds. (c) Failing to respect the principle of equal pay for equal work. (d) Perpetuating disproportionate income differentials deriving from past unfair discrimination."

16. South Africa, Employment Equity Act 55. 1998.

17. Mexico, Constitución Política de los Estados Unidos Mexicanos. 1917. Article 1: "Queda prohibida toda discriminación motivada por origen étnico o nacional, el género, la edad, las discapacidades, la condición social, las condiciones de salud, la religión, las opiniones, las preferencias sexuales, el estado civil o cualquier otra que atente contra la dignidad humana y tenga por objeto anular o menoscabar los

derechos y libertades de las personas." Mexico, Ley Federal para Prevenir y Eliminar la Discriminación. Federal Labor Law of 2003, Article 2: "Las disposiciones de esta Ley son de orden público y de interés social. El objeto de la misma es prevenir y eliminar todas las formas de discriminación que se ejerzan contra cualquier persona en los términos del Artículo 1 de la Constitución Política de los Estados Unidos Mexicanos, así como promover la igualdad de oportunidades y de trato. Para los efectos de esta ley se entenderá por: III. Discriminación: Para los efectos de esta ley se entenderá por discriminación toda distinción, exclusión, restricción o preferencia que, por acción u omisión, con intención o sin ella, no sea objetiva, racional ni proporcional y tenga por objeto o resultado obstaculizar, restringir, impedir, menoscabar o anular el reconocimiento, goce o ejercicio de los derechos humanos y libertades, cuando se base en uno o más de los siguientes motivos: el origen étnico o nacional, el color de piel, la cultura, el sexo, el género, la edad, las discapacidades, la condición social, económica, de salud o jurídica, la religión, la apariencia física, las características genéticas, la situación migratoria, el embarazo, la lengua, las opiniones, las preferencias sexuales, la identidad o filiación política, el estado civil, la situación familiar, las responsabilidades familiares, el idioma, los antecedentes penales o cualquier otro motivo;" Article 9: " Con base en lo establecido en el artículo primero constitucional y el artículo 1, párrafo segundo, fracción III de esta Ley se consideran como discriminación, entre otras: III. Prohibir la libre elección de empleo, o restringir las oportunidades de acceso, permanencia y ascenso en el mismo."

18. Ontario's Human Rights Code. 1962. Section 5(1): "Every person has a right to equal treatment with respect to employment without discrimination because of ... sexual orientation, gender identity, gender expression." Section 23: "The right under section 5 to equal treatment with respect to employment is infringed where an invitation to apply for employment or an advertisement in connection with employment is published or displayed that directly or indirectly classifies or indicates qualifications by a prohibited ground of discrimination."
Mozambique: Article 6 Labor Law Nr. 23/2007: 1. "Employers cannot, when appointing an employee or during the course of an employment contract, require the employee to provide information about his or her private life, except where, by virtue of the law or the practices of the occupation, the particular nature of the occupational activity so demands, and provided the reasons for the requirement are stated in writing beforehand."

19. Same-sex relations are not *per se* criminalized in Indonesia. The Criminal Code (Article 284) only criminalizes adultery for both opposite-sex and same-sex relationships. See also Peraturan Kepala Staf TNI AD (Perkasad) Nomor 34/XII/2008 pada angka 10 huruf H (Indonesian Army Chief of Staff Regulation No. 34/XII/2008 No. 10 Letter H. However, in Sharia law, offenses against decency and law against pornography (Pornography Act) are often used to target sexual and gender minorities.

20. Questions addressing equal pay and benefits in this indicator set are: Are there any laws and/or regulations prescribing equal remuneration for work of equal value for sexual and gender minorities? Does the pension system for civil servants provide the same benefits to same-sex partners provided to different spouses?

21. Kosovo, Law No.05/L-021 on Protection from Discrimination; see note 3 for the applicable text.

22. Costa Rica, Código de Trabajo de Costa Rica. 1934 (Amended in 2016). Article 405: "Todas las personas trabajadoras que desempeñen en iguales condiciones subjetivas y objetivas un trabajo igual gozarán de los mismos derechos, en cuanto a jornada laboral y remuneración, sin discriminación alguna."

23. South Africa, Promotion of Equality and Prevention of Unfair Discrimination Act of South Africa. 2000. The act prohibits discrimination; section 6(4) of the Employment Equity Act No. 55, 1998, states: "A difference in terms and conditions of employment of employees with the same employer performing the same or substantially the same work or work of equal value that is directly or indirectly based on any one or more of the grounds listed in Subsection (1) is unfair discrimination." This is often referred to as the "same work, same pay" principle.

24. Mexico, Constitución Política de los Estados Unidos Mexicanos. 1917. See note 17 for the applicable text. See also Mexico, Constitución Política de los Estados Unidos Mexicanos. 1917. Article 9: "Con base en lo establecido en el artículo primero constitucional y el artículo 1, párrafo segundo, fracción III de esta Ley se consideran como discriminación, entre otras: IV. Establecer diferencias en la remuneración, las prestaciones y las condiciones laborales para trabajos iguales."

25. Ukraine, Labor Code. 1971. Article 2-1: "All forms of discrimination in the field of work are forbidden, including the violation of the principle of equality of rights and opportunities, direct or indirect restriction of the rights of workers, depending on race, color, political, religious and other beliefs, sex, sexual orientation and gender identity, ethnicity, social and foreign origin, age, health, pregnancy, disability, suspicion or presence of a HIV/AIDS, family and property status, family responsibilities, residence, membership in a trade union or other CSOs, participating in a strike, addressing or intent to apply to a court or other bodies for the protection of their rights or to provide support to other workers in the protection of their rights, in linguistic or other grounds, not related to the nature of the work or the conditions for its implementation."

26. India, Code on Wages. No 29 of 209 (enter into force on August 8, 2019). Section 2.(y): "(k). . . Provided further that for the purpose of equal wages to all genders and for the purpose of payment of wages, the emoluments specified in clauses (d), (f), (g) and (h) shall be taken for computation of wage." Section 3: "(1) There shall be no discrimination in an establishment or any unit thereof among employees on the ground of gender in matters relating to wages by the same employer, in respect of the same work or work of a similar nature done by any employee."

27. M. v. H., [1999] 2 S.C.R. 3. https://scc-csc.lexum.com/scc-csc/scc-csc/en/item/1702/index.do.

28. Details of the Canada Pension Plan, R.S.C. 1985, can be found at https://qweri.lexum.com/w/calegis /rsc-1985-c-c-8-en#!fragment//BQCwhgziBcwMYgK4DsDWszIQewE4BUBTADwBdoByCgSg BpltTCIBFRQ3AT0otojlzYANkIDCSNNACEyPoTC4EbDtypyFCAMp5SAIW4AlAKIAZI wDUAggDlRR2qTAAjaKWxxq1IA.

29. Canada, Constitution Act, Section 15(1). 1982. https://qweri.lexum.com/calegis/schedule-b-to-the -canada-act-1982-uk-1982-c-11-en#!fragment/sec15subsec1.

30. Costa Rica, Directive No. MTSS-DMT-DR-5-2018. 2018.

31. South Africa, Promotion of Equality and Prevention of Unfair Discrimination Act 2000 (PEPUDA or the Equality Act, Act No. 4 of 2000). 2000.

32. Mexico, Constitución Política de la República Mexicana. Article 1. Ley Federal para Prevenir la Discriminación Article 9, paragraphs IV and XX affirm that work conditions and pensions should not differ. Article 9, Section IV: "Establecer diferencias en la remuneración, las prestaciones y las condiciones laborales para trabajos iguales." Article 9, Section XX: "Impedir el acceso a la seguridad social y a sus beneficios o establecer limitaciones para la contratación de seguros médicos, salvo en los casos que la ley así lo disponga."

33. Uruguay. Ley número 19075 de Matrimonio Igualitario. 2013.

34. Questions related to filing employment-related discrimination complaints in this indicator set include: Are there any laws and/or regulations that allow an employee to bring a claim for employment discrimination on SOGI grounds in the public sector? Are there any laws and/or regulations that allow an employee to bring a claim for employment discrimination on SOGI grounds in the private sector? Do victims of employment discrimination based on SOGI grounds have a right to free or reduced legal assistance (if proven they do not have the necessary means to cover the cost of the claim)? Is there a national equality body or national human rights institution responsible for handling charges of employment discrimination related to SOGI?

35. Ontario Legal Aid Services Act. 1998. Article 1: "The purpose of this Act is to promote access to justice throughout Ontario for low-income individuals by means of, (a) providing consistently high quality legal aid services in a cost-effective and efficient manner to low-income individuals throughout Ontario;

(b) encouraging and facilitating flexibility and innovation in the provision of legal aid services, while recognizing the private bar as the foundation for the provision of legal aid services in the areas of criminal law and family law and clinics as the foundation for the provision of legal aid services in the area of clinic law; (c) identifying, assessing and recognizing the diverse legal needs of low-income individuals and of disadvantaged communities in Ontario; and (d) providing legal aid services to low-income individuals through a corporation that will operate independently from the Government of Ontario but within a framework of accountability to the Government of Ontario for the expenditure of public funds."

36. For details about Legal Aid Ontario, see https://www.legalaid.on.ca.

37. Uruguay, Law 19580 on Violence against Women. 2017. Article 1: "Esta ley tiene como objeto garantizar el efectivo goce del derecho de las mujeres a una vida libre de violencia basada en género. Comprende a mujeres de todas las edades, mujeres trans, de las diversas orientaciones sexuales, condición socio-económica, pertenencia territorial, creencia, origen cultural y étnico-racial o situación de discapacidad, sin distinción ni discriminación alguna. Se establecen mecanismos, medidas y políticas integrales de prevención, atención, protección, sanción y reparación." Article 7, Section G: "A recibir orientación, asesoramiento y patrocinio jurídico gratuito, dependiendo de la posición socioeconómica de la mujer. Dicha asistencia deberá ser inmediata, especializada e integral, debiendo comprender las diversas materias y procesos que requiera su situación."

References

Ahmed, Ali M., Lina Andersson, and Mats Hammarstedt. 2013. "Are Gay Men and Lesbians Discriminated Against in the Hiring Process?" *Southern Economic Journal*, 79 (August): 565–85.

Badgett, M.V. Lee. 2014. "The Economic Cost of Stigma and the Exclusion of LGBT People: A Case Study of India (English)." World Bank, Washington, DC.

Business Standard. 2017. "CM Naidu Announces Pension Scheme for State's Transgenders." *Business Standard*, November 28, 2017. https://www.business-standard.com/article/news-ani/cm-naidu-announces-pension -scheme-for-state-s-transgenders-117112800036_1.html.

Crosby, Burns. 2012. "The Costly Business of Discrimination: The Economic Costs of Discrimination and the Social Benefits of Gay and Transgender Equality in the Workplace." Center for American Progress, Washington, DC. https://www.americanprogress.org/issues/lgbtq-rights/reports/2012/03/22/11234 /the-costly-business-of-discrimination/.

Drydakis, Nick. 2019. "Sexual Orientation and Labor Market Outcomes." *IZA World of Labor* 111 (2): 111.

ILGA (International Lesbian, Gay, Bisexual, Trans and Intersex Association). 2014. "Karnataka Government Launches Pension Scheme 'Mythri' for Transgender People." February 24, 2014. https://ilga.org /karnataka-government-launches-pension-scheme-mythri-for-transgender-people.

ILO (International Labour Organization). 1998. *Declaration on Fundamental Principles and Rights at Work*. Geneva: ILO. https://www.ilo.org/wcmsp5/groups/public/---ed_norm/---declaration/documents /normativeinstrument/wcms_716594.pdf.

ILO (International Labour Organization). 2012. *Discrimination at Work on the Basis of Sexual Orientation and Gender Identity: Results of the ILO's PRIDE Project*. Geneva: ILO. https://www.ilo.org/wcmsp5 /groups/public/---dgreports/---gender/documents/briefingnote/wcms_368962.pdf.

Japan Times. 2019. "Transgender Worker Sues Osaka Hospital after Supervisor Told Colleagues She Transitioned to Female." *Japan Times*, August 30, 2019.

Mishel, Emma. 2016. "Discrimination against Queer Women in the U.S. Workforce: A Résumé Audit Study." *Socius: Sociological Research for a Dynamic World*. https://journals.sagepub.com/doi/pdf/10.1177/2378023115621316.

Ng, Eddy S. W., Linda Schweitzer, and Sean T. Lyons. 2012. "Anticipated Discrimination and a Career Choice in Nonprofit: A Study of Early Career Lesbian, Gay, Bisexual, Transgendered (LGBT) Job Seekers." *Review of Public Personnel Administration* 32 (4): 332–52. https://doi.org/10.1177/0734371X12453055.

Panter, Elaine, Tanya Primiani, Tazeen Hasan, and Eduardo Calderon Pontaza. 2017. "Antidiscrimination Law and Shared Prosperity: An Analysis of the Legal Framework of Six Economies and Their Impact on the Equality of Opportunities of Ethnic, Religious, and Sexual Minorities (English)." Policy Research Working Paper WPS 7992, Knowledge for Change Program (KCP), World Bank, Washington, DC.

Pizer, Jennifer C., Brad Sears, Christy Mallory, and Nan D. Hunter. 2012. "Evidence of Persistent and Pervasive Workplace Discrimination Against LGBT People: The Need for Federal Legislation Prohibiting Discrimination and Providing for Equal Employment Benefits." *Loyola of Los Angeles Law Review* 45: 715.

Sears, Brad, and Christy Mallory. 2011. "Documented Evidence of Employment Discrimination & Its Effects on LGBT People." The Williams Institute, UCLA School of Law, Los Angeles. https://escholarship.org/uc/item/03m1g5sg.

Sears, Brad, and Christy Mallory. 2014. "Employment Discrimination against LGBT People: Existence and Impact." In *Gender Identity and Sexual Orientation Discrimination in the Workplace: A Practical Guide.* UCLA: The Williams Institute.

Sharma, Ashwani. 2016. "Himachal Pradesh to Bring Transgenders under Social Security Net." *Indian Express,* September 7, 2016. https://indianexpress.com/article/india/india-news-india/himachal-pradesh-to-bring-transgenders-under-social-security-net-3018937/.

UN OHCHR (United Nations, Office of the High Commissioner for Human Rights). 2017. *Tackling Discrimination Against Lesbian, Gay, Bi, Trans, & Intersex People: Standard of Conduct for Business.* New York: United Nations. https://www.unfe.org/wp-content/uploads/2017/09/UN-Standards-of-Conduct.pdf.

World Bank. 2018. *Economic Inclusion of LGBTI Groups in Thailand: Main Report (English).* Washington, DC: World Bank. http://documents.worldbank.org/curated/en/269041521819512465/main-report.

4

Access to Public Services and Social Protection

KEY FINDINGS

Mexico, South Africa, and Uruguay possess the most advanced legal frameworks that prohibit sexual orientation and gender identity (SOGI) discrimination in public services and allow civil society organizations (CSOs) to provide social services to sexual and gender minorities.

Out of the 11 services considered by the report, health care is the most protected public service; most countries explicitly prohibit discrimination in this sector, followed by subsidized health insurance and social housing.

Of the 16 countries surveyed, only Nigeria explicitly forbids the registration, sustenance, processions, and meetings of CSOs.

Most surveyed countries do not have any equality bodies or national human rights institutions that explicitly include sexual and gender minorities or SOGI within their mandates.

It is advised that countries establish a comprehensive legal framework to regulate nondiscriminatory access to public services.

Importance of the Access to Public Services and Social Protection Indicator Set

Social protection systems help individuals of all ages cope with personal and economic crises. These systems empower individuals to live healthier lifestyles, invest in education, and seek opportunities to escape poverty and economic inequality.[1] Access to public services and social protection is deeply rooted in economic and social equality, and securing access to public services is essential to reduce poverty and inequality. Public services should specifically address the needs and rights of sexual and gender minorities. An inclusive legal framework that protects all minorities, including sexual and gender minorities, can transform people's lives and create an inclusive society in which everyone prospers.

During the COVID-19 pandemic, the stigma and discrimination faced by sexual and gender minorities has been exacerbated because health care systems have been overloaded and it has proven easy to scale back care for these minorities. It is important to ensure that decisions about scaling back services be medical and data-based decisions, not decisions based on bias (box 4.1).

> "Homophobia and other forms of stigma, violence, and discrimination against LGBTI people contribute significantly to their exclusion from society, limit their access to health and social services, and hinder social and economic development."
>
> —UNDP and PGA (2017, 8)

The access to public services and social protection indicator set examines whether the existing legal framework provides equal access to public services and social protection to sexual and gender minorities. The indicators aim to determine whether national laws, constitutional provisions, and regulations protect sexual and gender minorities from discrimination on the basis of sexual orientation, gender identity, gender expression, or sex characteristics in accessing a range of public services.[2] They also attempt to capture whether laws encourage CSOs to provide similar services,[3] and whether governments impose funding limitations on the provision of such services. Finally, the indicator set measures the existence of national equality bodies or national human rights institutions responsible for handling claims of SOGI-based discrimination in public services.

> In Japan, many lesbian, gay, bisexual, and transgender (LGBT) people unable to disclose their sexual orientation or gender identity often cannot obtain necessary services. When accessing mental health support, for example, patients often feel social pressure to hide their sexual orientation or gender identity because they do not trust that their sexuality will be understood or accepted.
>
> —Amnesty International (2017)

BOX 4.1   **Links between Access to Public Services and Social Protection and COVID-19**

Sexual and gender minorities regularly experience stigma and discrimination while seeking health services, leading to disparities in health care availability, access, and quality. Laws that criminalize same-sex relations or target transgender people because of their gender identity or expression exacerbate adverse health outcomes for sexual and gender minorities. These people may avoid accessing health care services for fear of arrest or violence. With health care systems overloaded during the COVID-19 pandemic, treatment of sexual and gender minorities—including HIV treatment and testing, hormonal treatment, and gender-affirming treatments for transgender people—may be interrupted or deprioritized. Decisions about scaling back services should be medically based and data driven; they should not reflect bias against sexual and gender minorities.

Most of the countries studied do not have legal frameworks that allow civil society organizations (CSOs) to provide social services specifically to sexual and gender minorities (such as vaccinations, sanitation, health services, and HIV prevention services, or to provide information on vulnerable practices, antiretrovirals, and gender-affirming treatments). Some countries do not have laws prohibiting discrimination on the basis of sexual orientation and gender identity (SOGI) in key public services, such as health care. Sexual and gender minorities can be more vulnerable during the pandemic because of discrimination on the basis of SOGI. The contribution of CSOs is vital in the pandemic response.

Legal Framework Related to Discrimination on the Basis of SOGI

An effective legal framework that ensures equal access to public services and social protection interventions is fundamental to an inclusive and progressive society.[4] Therefore, the basis for this indicator set is the existence of a nondiscrimination regulatory framework related to public services and social protection interventions. The survey reviewed data on 11 core services: health care, social housing, public transportation, electricity, water supply, waste disposal, microcredits, subsidized health insurance, social pensions, unemployment insurance, and child benefits. With respect to health care, for example, ignorance and discrimination in the health care sector frequently force patients who are sexual and gender minorities to avoid seeking care because they fear stigmatization by health care providers (Human Rights Watch 2014). Similarly, regarding access to housing, sexual and gender minorities are disproportionately represented in the homeless population, and they may also face discrimination in access to housing as a result of unfair treatment by public and private landlords, estate agencies, and credit providers (UNGA 2019).

Nine of the 16 studied countries (Bangladesh, Indonesia, Jamaica, Japan, Lebanon, Mozambique, Nigeria, Tunisia, and Ukraine) do not explicitly prohibit discrimination on the basis of SOGI in the provision of public services. The remaining seven countries (Canada, Costa Rica, India,

Kosovo, Mexico, South Africa, and Uruguay) do protect equal access to public services (figure 4.1). Enacting laws or regulations that prohibit discrimination in broad terms is the most inclusive approach to ensuring universal access to public services. Rather than mentioning every possible public service individually, Uruguay's legislation includes broad protections from discrimination based on sexual orientation and gender identity. The country's antidiscrimination law prohibits discrimination on the basis of sexual orientation and gender identity in "the political, economic, social, cultural, and in any other sphere of public life."[5] Mexico, another example of good practice, has a comprehensive constitutional framework that covers economic and social rights. It also adopted the Federal Law to Prevent and Eliminate Discrimination (Ley Federal para Prevenir y Eliminar la Discriminaćión), which prohibits discrimination in accessing services on the basis of sexual orientation (but not gender identity or sex characteristics).[6] Furthermore, Mexican laws on particular topics, such as health and housing,[7,8] prohibit discrimination in the provision of the relevant services.

In sum, broad regulations can protect sexual and gender minorities from discrimination in the provision of public services and social protection interventions. In Ontario, Canada, sexual orientation, gender identity, and gender expression are protected grounds with respect to access to services.[9] In 2014, Costa Rica expanded its social security system to offer same-sex and heterosexual couples equal rights (*Tico Times* 2014). The Indian Supreme Court has directed the central and state governments to take proper measures to provide medical care and appropriate counseling to transgender people in hospitals, including with regard to reproductive health, HIV/sero-surveillance, access to HIV/AIDS information and therapy, and hormonal or other therapy, as well as access to free gender-reassignment treatments when desired. Government authorities were also asked to operate separate public toilets and other facilities and offer various

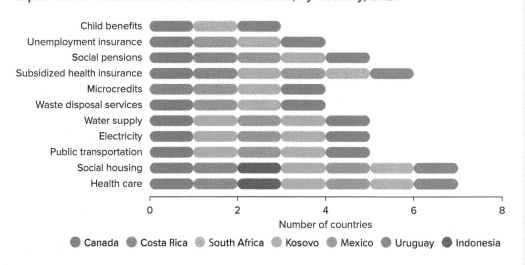

FIGURE 4.1

Equal Access Guaranteed for Different Services, by Country, 2021

Source: World Bank Group, Equality of Opportunity database.

social welfare schemes.[10] In addition, the Indian Constitution prohibits discrimination on the basis of sexual orientation and gender identity via the category of "sex"[11] in public spaces.[12] Furthermore, the country's Transgender Persons (Protection of Rights) Act protects transgender and intersex people from discrimination in access to goods, accommodation, health care, and other services. The act also provides health-related measures ranging from access to medical care facilities, counseling, and provision for medical expenses coverage through a comprehensive insurance scheme.[13] India's National AIDS Control Organization has also launched SOGI-specific HIV prevention programs (India, Ministry of Health and Family Welfare 2017).

Similarly, Kosovo's antidiscrimination law enumerates several types of services to which everyone, including sexual and gender minorities, has equal access.[14] Kosovo has also enacted a separate health care law that prohibits discrimination on the basis of sexual orientation (but not gender identity or expression).[15] South African law also prohibits discrimination in several types of services on the basis of sexual orientation (but not gender identity).[16]

It is advised that countries adopt the following good practice policy actions:

- Establish a comprehensive legal framework to regulate nondiscriminatory access to public services.

- Amend laws and regulations to prohibit SOGI-related discrimination in key public sectors, including health care, social housing, public transportation, electricity, water supply, waste disposal services, microcredits, subsidized health insurance, social pensions, unemployment insurance, and child benefits.

- Provide training for public service professionals to improve their understanding of the needs of sexual and gender minorities.

- Conduct an extensive social awareness campaign in the public sector to increase understanding of SOGI issues by public servants.

- Protect medical records and safeguard information.

Civil Society Approach to SOGI-Based Discrimination

The steady growth of CSOs that advocate for the rights of sexual and gender minorities is well-documented. However, CSOs continue to face monumental challenges in their attempts to assemble, associate, and communicate (ICNL 2016).[17] These challenges are particularly formidable when they are created by the state—that is, when they are in the form of national legislation. By imposing legal restrictions, countries not only prevent sexual and gender minorities from achieving full equality, but they also prevent CSOs from advocating on their behalf and providing social services.[18] In some countries, funding laws limit the CSOs' ability to provide basic and necessary services.

The indicator set on access to public services and social protection studies the existence of and government approach to CSOs that provide services to sexual and gender minorities. Furthermore, it measures whether governments impose funding limitations on the provision of relevant services. CSOs play an essential role in providing public services and social protections otherwise not available to sexual and gender minorities. But CSOs can fill this vacuum only if the legal framework allows it. This section evaluates whether CSOs can provide services to sexual and gender minorities in areas including vaccinations, sanitation, transportation, family planning, health services (including psychological, physiological, and sexual and reproductive services), HIV prevention services, and can provide information on vulnerable sexual practices, antiretrovirals, medication for gender-reassignment surgery, and support for transgender individuals during and after gender reassignment surgery.

Across the countries analyzed, CSOs are generally allowed to provide services to sexual and gender minorities. The one exception is Nigeria, which legally forbids CSOs from delivering social services explicitly to sexual and gender minorities.[19] Under the Same-Sex Marriage (Prohibition) Act, an individual who "registers, operates, or participates in gay clubs, societies, and organizations" commits a criminal offense subject to up to 10 years' imprisonment.[20] Even countries that criminalize same-sex relations typically do not prohibit CSOs from providing services to sexual and gender minorities. The same findings apply to funding that CSOs receive to provide services to sexual and gender minorities. The Equality of Opportunity for Sexual and Gender Minorities (EQOSOGI) team could not locate laws or regulations that explicitly prohibit funding for these purposes in any of the 16 countries studied. Therefore, absent an express prohibition, it appears that CSOs can, in principle, operate and provide important services to sexual and gender minorities as part of their operation under the principle of freedom of assembly and freedom of association. However, CSOs may still experience restrictions. As explained in the next chapter, sexual and gender minority CSOs often face legal hurdles when it comes to registration.

It is advised that countries adopt the following good practice policy actions:

■ Remove legal hurdles that restrict the ability of CSOs to register and freely operate and provide legal protections to CSOs that offer services to sexual and gender minorities.

■ Allow CSOs to receive funding to provide services to sexual and gender minorities.

Notes

1. See the World Bank's Social Protection website at https://www.worldbank.org/en/topic/socialprotection/overview.
2. *Public services* refers to, among other services, health care, social housing, public transportation, electricity, water supply, waste disposal services, microcredits, subsidized health insurance, social pensions, unemployment insurance, and child benefits.
3. These services include vaccinations, sanitation, transportation, family planning, health services, HIV prevention services, information on vulnerable sexual practices, antiretrovirals, medication for gender-reassignment surgery, and support for transgender individuals during/after gender reassignment survey.
4. Questions addressing the legal framework related to discrimination on the basis of SOGI in the indicator set on access to public services and social protection are: Are there any laws, constitutional provisions, and/or regulations that prohibit discrimination on the basis of sexual orientation, gender identity, gender expression, and sex characteristics in accessing health care, social housing, public transportation, electricity, water supply, waste disposal services, microcredits, subsidized health insurance, social pensions, unemployment insurance, child benefits, other social services, and so on?
5. Uruguay, Law No. 17817. 2004. Article 2: "A los efectos de la presente ley se entenderá por discriminación toda distinción, exclusión, restricción, preferencia o ejercicio de violencia física y moral, basada en motivos de raza, color de piel, religión, origen nacional o étnico, discapacidad, aspecto estético, género, orientación e identidad sexual, que tenga por objeto o por resultado anular o menoscabar el reconocimiento, goce o ejercicio, en condiciones de igualdad, de los derechos humanos y libertades fundamentales en las esferas política, económica, social, cultural o en cualquier otra esfera de la vida pública."
6. Mexico, Ley Federal para Prevenir y Eliminar la Discriminación. 2003. Article 9: "VII. Negar o condicionar los servicios de atención médica, o impedir la participación en las decisiones sobre su tratamiento médico o terapéutico dentro de sus posibilidades y medios; X. Impedir el ejercicio de los derechos de propiedad, administración y disposición de bienes de cualquier otro tipo ; XX. Impedir el acceso a la seguridad social y a sus beneficios o establecer limitaciones para la contratación de seguros médicos, salvo en los casos que la ley así lo disponga; XXI. Limitar el derecho a la alimentación, la vivienda, el recreo y los servicios de atención médica adecuados, en los casos que la ley así lo prevea; XXII. Impedir el acceso a cualquier servicio público o institución privada que preste servicios al público, así como limitar el acceso y libre desplazamiento en los espacios públicos; XXII. Bis. La falta de accesibilidad en el entorno físico, el transporte, la información, tecnología y comunicaciones, en servicios e instalaciones abiertos al público o de uso público; XXII. Ter. La denegación de ajustes razonables que garanticen, en igualdad de condiciones, el goce o ejercicio de los derechos de las personas con discapacidad; XXIII. Explotar o dar un trato abusivo o degradante; XXIV. Restringir la participación en actividades deportivas, recreativas o culturales; XXV. Restringir o limitar el uso de su lengua, usos, costumbres y cultura, en actividades públicas o privadas, en términos de las disposiciones aplicables; XXVI. Limitar o negar el otorgamiento de concesiones, permisos o autorizaciones para el aprovechamiento, administración o usufructo de recursos naturales, una vez satisfechos los requisitos establecidos en la legislación aplicable; XXXI. Difundir sin consentimiento de la persona agraviada información sobre su condición de salud; XXXII. Estigmatizar y negar derechos a personas con VIH/SIDA; XXXIII. Implementar o ejecutar políticas públicas, programas u otras acciones de gobierno que tengan un impacto desventajoso en los derechos de las personas."
7. Mexico, Ley General de Salud (in conjunction with Ley Federal para Prevenir y Eliminar la Discriminación, Article 9). 1984. Article 77 bis 1: "Todos los mexicanos tienen derecho a ser incorporados al Sistema de Protección Social en Salud de conformidad con el artículo cuarto de la Constitución Política de los Estados Unidos Mexicanos, sin importar su condición social. La protección social en salud es un mecanismo por el cual el Estado garantizará el acceso efectivo, oportuno, de calidad, sin desembolso

al momento de utilización y sin discriminación a los servicios médico-quirúrgicos, farmacéuticos y hospitalarios que satisfagan de manera integral las necesidades de salud, mediante la combinación de intervenciones de promoción de la salud, prevención, diagnóstico, tratamiento y de rehabilitación, seleccionadas en forma prioritaria según criterios de seguridad, eficacia, costo, efectividad, adherencia a normas éticas profesionales y aceptabilidad social. Como mínimo se deberán contemplar los servicios de consulta externa en el primer nivel de atención, así como de consulta externa y hospitalización para las especialidades básicas de: medicina interna, cirugía general, ginecoobstetricia, pediatría y geriatría, en el segundo nivel de atención."

8. Mexico, Ley de Vivienda (in conjunction with Ley Federal para Prevenir y Eliminar la Discriminación 2003, Article 9). 2006. Article 3: "Las disposiciones de esta Ley deberán aplicarse bajo principios de equidad e inclusión social de manera que toda persona, sin importar su origen étnico o nacional, el género, la edad, la discapacidad, la condición social o económica, las condiciones de salud, la religión, las opiniones, las preferencias o el estado civil pueda ejercer su derecho constitucional a la vivienda. Las políticas y programas, así como los instrumentos y apoyos a la vivienda a que se refiere este ordenamiento, se regirán bajo los principios de respeto a la legalidad y protección jurídica a la legítima tenencia, así como el combate a la invasión de predios y al crecimiento irregular de las ciudades. Las dependencias y entidades de la Administración Pública Federal que lleven a cabo u otorguen financiamiento para programas o acciones de vivienda, quedan sujetas a las disposiciones de esta Ley y demás ordenamientos que resulten aplicables. Los organismos encargados de financiar programas de vivienda para los trabajadores, conforme a la obligación prevista en el artículo 123 de la Constitución Política de los Estados Unidos Mexicanos, se regirán en los términos de las leyes que regulan su propia organización y funcionamiento y coordinarán sus lineamientos de política general y objetivos a lo que marca esta Ley y el Plan Nacional de Desarrollo. Los representantes gubernamentales en los órganos de gobierno, administración y vigilancia de dichos organismos cuidarán que sus actividades se ajusten a lo dispuesto en esta Ley."

9. Ontario's Human Rights Code (amended in 2019). 1990. Article 1: "Every person has a right to equal treatment with respect to services, goods and facilities, without discrimination because of race, ancestry, place of origin, color, ethnic origin, citizenship, creed, sex, sexual orientation, gender identity, gender expression, age, marital status, family status or disability."

10. National Legal Services Authority v. Union of India, WP (Civil) No 400. 2012.

11. In 2014, the Supreme Court of India directed the central government and state governments to ensure the treatment of "hijras"/"eunuchs" (transgenders) as third gender so as to afford them same protections of fundamental rights, including those under Article 14 (Right to Equality) and Article 15 (Prohibition of Discrimination). In 2017, the Supreme Court of India declared that sexual autonomy is inherent in the Right to Privacy protected under Article 21 of the Constitution of India ("Right to Life and Liberty"). Therefore, protection of rights and interests of sexual and gender minorities is ensured by the constitution. Affirming the principles upheld earlier, the court in a 2018 judgment stated that the word "sex" under Article 15 (Prohibition of Discrimination) and Article 16 (Equality of Opportunities) of the constitution has to be read broadly to include gender and sexual minorities.

12. Constitution of India. Article 15: "(2) No citizen shall, on grounds only of religion, race, caste, sex, place of birth or any of them, be subject to any disability, liability, restriction or condition with regard to (a) access to shops, public restaurants, hotels and places of public entertainment; or (b) the use of wells, tanks, bathing ghats, roads and places of public resort maintained wholly or partly out of State funds or dedicated to the use of the general public."

13. India, Transgender Persons (Protection of Rights) Act. 2019. Section 2: "In this Act, unless the context otherwise requires, …(k) "transgender person" means a person whose gender does not match with the gender assigned to that person at birth and includes trans-man or trans-woman (whether or not such person has undergone Sex Reassignment Surgery or hormone therapy or laser therapy or such other therapy), person with intersex variations, genderqueer and person having such socio-cultural identities

as kinner, hijra, aravani and jogta." Section 3: "No person or establishment shall discriminate against a transgender person on any of the following grounds, namely: …(d) the denial or discontinuation of, or unfair treatment in, health care services; (e) the denial or discontinuation of, or unfair treatment with regard to, access to, or provision or enjoyment or use of any goods, accommodation, service, facility, benefit, privilege or opportunity dedicated to the use of the general public or customarily available to the public; (f) the denial or discontinuation of, or unfair treatment with regard to the right of movement; (g) the denial or discontinuation of, or unfair treatment with regard to the right to reside, purchase, rent, or otherwise occupy any property." Section 15: "The appropriate Government shall take the following measures in relation to transgender persons, namely: (a) to set up separate human immunodeficiency virus Sero-surveillance Centres to conduct sero-surveillance for such persons in accordance with the guidelines issued by the National AIDS Control Organisation in this behalf; (b) to provide for medical care facility including sex reassignment surgery and hormonal therapy; (c) before and after sex reassignment surgery and hormonal therapy counselling; (d) bring out a Health Manual related to sex reassignment surgery in accordance with the World Profession Association for Transgender Health guidelines; (e) review of medical curriculum and research for doctors to address their specific health issues; (f) to facilitate access to transgender persons in hospitals and other health care institutions and centres; (g) provision for coverage of medical expenses by a comprehensive insurance scheme for Sex Reassignment Surgery, hormonal therapy, laser therapy or any other health issues of transgender persons."

14. Kosovo, Law No. 05/L-021on the Protection from Discrimination. 2015. Article 1 (1): "The purpose of this law is to establish a general framework for prevention and combating discrimination based on nationality, or in relation to any community, social origin, race, ethnicity, colour, birth, origin, sex, gender, gender identity, sexual orientation, language, citizenship, religion and religious belief, political affiliation, political or other opinion, social or personal status, age, family or marital status, pregnancy, maternity, wealth, health status, disability, genetic inheritance or any other grounds, in order to implement the principle of equal treatment." Article 2 (1): "This law applies to all acts or omissions, of all state and local institutions, natural and legal persons, public and private sector, who violate, violated or may violate the rights of any person or natural and legal entities in all areas of life, especially related to 1.5. social protection, including social assistance scheme, social security and health protection; 1.6. social advantages; 1.7. social amenities, including but not limited to humanitarian aid; 1.8. education; 1.9. access to housing, which is available to the public, and the access to other forms of property (movable and immovable); 1.10. access to and supply of goods and services which are available to the public; 1.11. fair and equal treatment in court proceedings and all other authorities administering justice; 1.12. access and participation in science, sports, art, services and cultural activities; 1.13. personal insurance; 1.14. participation in public affairs, including the right to vote and the right to be elected; 1.15. access to public places and 1.16. any other rights provided for by the legislation in force."

15. Kosovo, Law No. 04/L-125 on Health. 2013. Article 5 (1) (1.2): "Inclusiveness and nondiscrimination: equal health care for all citizens and residents by ensuring the standards during fulfilling the needs at all levels of health care as well as ensuring health care without discrimination on basis of: gender, nation, race, color, language, religion, political preferences, social status, sexual orientation, the level of physical or mental abilities, family status, or age."

16. South Africa, Promotion of Equality and Prevention of Unfair Discrimination Act 4. 2000. Schedule "Illustrative List of Unfair Practices in Certain Sectors" (Section 29): "3. Health care services and benefits (a) Subjecting persons to medical experiments without their informed consent. (b) Unfairly denying or refusing any person access to health care facilities or failing to make health care facilities accessible to any person. (c) Refusing to provide emergency medical treatment to persons of particular groups identified by one or more of the prohibited grounds. (d) Refusing to provide reasonable health services to the elderly. 4. Housing, accommodation, land and property (a) Arbitrary eviction of persons on one or more of the prohibited grounds. (b) 'Red-lining' on the grounds of race and social status.

(c) Unfair discrimination in the provision of housing bonds, loans or financial assistance on the basis of race, gender or other prohibited grounds. (d) Failing to reasonably accommodate the special needs of the elderly. 5. Insurance services (a) Unfairly refusing on one or more of the prohibited grounds to provide or to make available an insurance policy to any person. (b) Unfair discrimination in the provision of benefits, facilities and services related to insurance. (c) Unfairly disadvantaging a person or persons, including unfairly and unreasonably refusing to grant services, to persons solely on the basis of HIV/ AIDS status. 6. Pensions (a) Unfairly excluding any person from membership of a retirement fund or from receiving any benefits from the fund on one or more of the prohibited grounds. (b) Unfairly discriminating against members or beneficiaries of a retirement fund. 7. Partnerships (a) Determining in an unfair discriminatory manner who should be invited to become a partner in the partnership in question. (b) Imposing unfair and discriminatory terms or conditions under which a person is invited or admitted to become a partner. 9. Provision of goods, services and facilities (a) Unfairly refusing or failing to provide the goods or services or to make the facilities available to any person or group of persons on one or more of the prohibited grounds. (b) Imposing terms, conditions or practices that perpetuate the consequences of past unfair discrimination or exclusion regarding access to financial resources. (c) Unfairly limiting access to contractual opportunities for supplying goods and services." The same law defines "prohibited grounds" in Article 1: "Prohibited grounds are: (a) race, gender, sex, pregnancy, marital status, ethnic or social origin, color, sexual orientation, age, disability, religion, conscience, belief, culture, language and birth; or (b) any other ground where discrimination based on that other ground – (i) causes or perpetuates systemic disadvantage; (ii) undermines human dignity; or (iii) adversely affects the equal enjoyment of a person's rights and freedoms in a serious manner that is comparable to discrimination on a ground in paragraph (a)."

17. Questions addressing the civil society approach to SOGI-based discrimination in this indicator set are: Are there any laws and/or regulations that allow civil society organizations (CSOs) to provide social services specifically to sexual and gender minorities (for example, vaccinations, sanitation, transportation, family planning, health services—psychological, physiological, and sexual and reproductive); HIV prevention services [for example, condoms, lubricants, pre-exposure prophylaxis, and so on]; and information on vulnerable sexual practices, antiretrovirals, medication for gender-reassignment surgery, and support for transgender people during/after gender reassignment surgery)? Are there any laws and/or regulations imposing funding limitations on civil society organizations on the provision of such services?

18. These services can include, among others, vaccinations, sanitation, transportation, family planning, health services (psychological, physiological, sexual, and reproductive), HIV prevention services, and information on vulnerable sexual practices, antiretrovirals, medication for gender-reassignment surgery, and support for transgender individuals during and after gender-reassignment surgery.

19. Nigeria, Same-Sex Marriage Prohibition Act. 2013. Section 4: "(1) The Registration of gay clubs, societies, and organizations, their sustenance, processions, and meetings is prohibited."

20. Nigeria, Same-Sex Marriage Prohibition Act. 2013. Section 5 (2): "A person who registers, operates, or participates in gay clubs, societies, and organization, or directly or indirectly makes public show of same-sex amorous relationship in Nigeria commits an offense and is liable on conviction to a term of 10 years imprisonment."

References

Amnesty International. 2017. *Human Rights Law and Discrimination against LGBT People in Japan.* https://www.amnesty.org/en/documents/asa22/5955/2017/en/.

Human Rights Watch. 2014. *Not Safe at Home: Violence and Discrimination against LGBT People in Jamaica.* New York: Human Rights Watch.

India, Ministry of Health and Family Welfare. 2017. *National Strategic Plan for HIV/AIDS and STI 2017–2024*. New Delhi: Government of India. http://naco.gov.in/sites/default/files/Paving%20the%20Way%20 for%20an%20AIDS%2015122017.pdf.

ICNL (International Center for Not-for-Profit Law). 2016. "LGBTI Civil Society Organizations and the Rights to Peacefully Assemble and Associate." https://www.boell.de/en/2016/09/13 /lgbti-civil-society-organizations-and-rights-peacefully-assemble-and-associate.

Tico Times. 2014. "In Landmark Vote, Costa Rica Social Security System Guarantees Same-Sex Couples Same Rights as Other Couples." May 23, 2014. https://ticotimes.net/2014/05/23/in-landmark-vote -costa-rica-social-security-system-to-guarantee-same-sex-couples-same-rights-as-other-couples.

UNDP and PGA (United Nations Development Programme and Parliamentarians for Global Action). 2017. *Advancing the Human Rights and Inclusion of LGBTI People: A Handbook for Parliamentarians*. New York: UNDP and PGA.

UNGA (United Nations General Assembly). 2019. *Report of the Independent Expert on Protection against Violence and Discrimination Based on Sexual Orientation and Gender Identity*. A/74/181. New York: United Nations General Assembly. https://undocs.org/A/74/181.

5
Civil and Political Inclusion

KEY FINDINGS

Costa Rica and Canada, followed closely by Mexico, South Africa, and Uruguay, are the countries that follow many best practices in this indicator.

Six of the 16 studied countries have at least one member of parliament or a comparable national representative body who is openly a self-identified sexual or gender minority, while only four have introduced national action plans on sexual orientation and gender identity (SOGI).

Three-quarters of the sample countries prohibit same-sex couples from entering into registered partnerships, civil unions, or marriages and from legally adopting children.

While almost one-half of the analyzed countries allow people to change their gender marker in official documents, only Bangladesh, Canada, and India provide more than two gender options in passports.

Medically unnecessary surgeries on intersex children are not prohibited in any of the countries covered in the study. Only Uruguay and the south Indian state of Tamil Nadu have regulated the protection of intersex babies and children against such invasive surgeries.

It is advised that countries introduce legislation or amend current laws or regulations to allow sexual and gender minority organizations to register and operate freely and ensure that activists can advocate for sexual and gender minority equality.

Importance of the Civil and Political Inclusion Indicator Set

Discrimination based on sexual orientation and gender identity limits sexual and gender minorities' ability to participate in public discourse and influence decision-making, affecting the full spectrum of political inclusion. Governments should integrate sexual and gender minorities into the social fabric and allow them to exercise rights on an equal basis with everyone else (UNGA 2019, para. 69). Equal participation in political and civil life covers a broad range of issues, including political participation, parental equality, gender equality, ability to change gender without stigmatization, protection of intersex babies and children from invasive surgeries, and prohibition of persecution of sexual and gender minorities seeking asylum. Civil society organizations (CSOs) can play a fundamental role in promoting these principles and raising awareness of the issues faced by sexual and gender minorities. An active civil society can also be seen as a legitimate conveyor of public participation, in both public and private life. Conversely, the constriction of CSOs can amount to the "shrinking of civil society space" (Daly 2018). Despite their important role in protecting sexual and gender minorities, in many countries around the world, sexual and gender minority CSOs face legal hurdles in registering and operating. Such legal limitations, whether explicit or implicit, can hamper the effectiveness of their work.

> "In no other field do respect or stigma manifest themselves more clearly than in the political arena."
>
> —*UNGA (2019, para. 33)*

The civil and political inclusion indicator set examines issues relating to sexual and gender minorities' civil and political inclusion by analyzing the existence of SOGI-inclusive national human rights institutions (NHRIs),[1] national action plans, and the freedom of CSOs to operate without fear of persecution. The indicator set measures societal inclusiveness by reporting the number of politicians who openly self-identify as a sexual or gender minority in each country's legislature, the legality of same-sex civil unions, same-sex couples' ability to marry and adopt children, and legal protections for intersex children. The section also focuses on laws that allow changes in gender markers in official documents without pathologizing requirements and discrimination against sexual and gender minorities in obtaining identity documents. Finally, this indicator set delves into whether relevant countries have abolished conversion therapy and whether persecuted sexual and gender minorities can seek asylum under the countries' asylum laws.

> "All over the world, in instances too frequent to cite, political campaigns, referendums, policy and parliamentary debates, and public manifestations outside courthouses reveal

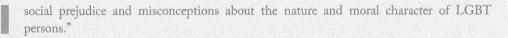

social prejudice and misconceptions about the nature and moral character of LGBT persons."

—*UNGA (2019, para. 33)*

Political Representation and National Action Plans

Civic and political participation should be equally accessible to all, regardless of sexual orientation, gender identity and expression, or sex characteristics.[2] Gaining inclusive political representation is a source of motivation for sexual and gender minorities and a fundamental step in advancing inclusion. Moreover, sexual and gender minority representation in political life can positively impact legal reform and eliminate prejudice and bias against this vulnerable group. It also allows citizens to enjoy a feeling of familiarity with their elected representatives and relate to their causes (Magni and Reynolds 2019).

Only 6 of the 16 countries reviewed (Canada, Costa Rica, Japan, Mexico, South Africa, and Uruguay) have at least one member of parliament or a comparable national representative body who openly self-identifies as a sexual or gender minority. Information from local experts suggests that none of the analyzed countries has more than 10 elected representatives who identify as sexual and gender minorities. None of the surveyed countries mandate quotas for sexual and gender minority members of parliament.

National action plans on SOGI issues are fundamental in complementing the work of the government and other relevant institutions. They help countries establish clear goals and guidelines for incorporation into their agendas. Moreover, national action plans set priorities and establish an internal control mechanism that facilitates the implementation of the defined goals. They can also inspire lawmakers to understand the guiding principles of the law.

Most of the studied countries' equality bodies, including NHRIs, lack national action plans on SOGI. Only Bangladesh, Costa Rica, India, and Uruguay have introduced such plans. The National Human Rights Commission of Bangladesh introduced a five-year strategic plan that includes sexual minorities and people living with HIV.[3] Costa Rica's National Development Plan 2019–22 introduced a strategy to develop training and awareness campaigns for public officials. These efforts are intended to improve services as well as respect for sexual and gender minority rights and ensure that sexual and gender minorities are treated with dignity.[4] India's Human Rights Commission published a National Action Plan for 2019–20 that addresses sexual and gender minorities' rights.[5] In Uruguay, the National Coordinating Council for Public Policies on Sexual Diversity, created in 2015, acts within the framework of the Ministry of Social Development. Composed of representatives of all ministries, the Mayor's Council, and CSO representatives, the council advises the executive on integrating sexual diversity in all areas of public policy (figure 5.1).[6]

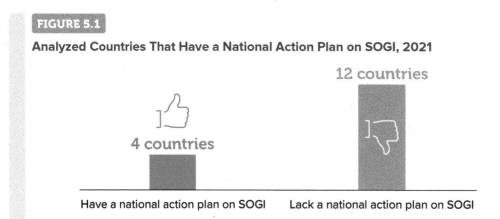

FIGURE 5.1

Analyzed Countries That Have a National Action Plan on SOGI, 2021

12 countries

4 countries

Have a national action plan on SOGI   Lack a national action plan on SOGI

Source: World Bank Group, Equality of Opportunity database.
Note: SOGI = sexual orientation and gender identity.

It is advised that countries adopt the following good practice policy actions:

- Establish inclusive legal frameworks that make it safe for sexual and gender minorities to run for political office.

- Introduce concrete national action plans on SOGI, focusing on antidiscrimination efforts and the promotion and protection of sexual and gender minorities.

Civil Society and Expression, Association, and Assembly

Freedom of expression is a crucial element of inclusion. A person's ability to exercise expression freely is fundamental.[7] Conversely, restrictions on expression, civic participation, or association directly affect an individual's very existence. Worldwide, sexual and gender minorities face restrictions based on their sexual orientation, gender identity, gender expression, and sex characteristics. In addition, some sexual and gender minority–focused organizations cannot register and operate freely because they publicly advocate for sexual and gender minority rights.[8] These restrictions endanger sexual and gender minorities and prevent them from participating freely and productively in society.

The collected data demonstrate that laws neither explicitly prohibit sexual and gender minority organizations nor specifically protect CSOs' right to register and operate freely. Consequently, although CSOs are, in principle, allowed to register and advocate for sexual and gender minorities, countries often impose legal or bureaucratic hurdles to obstruct their work. Therefore, many sexual and gender minority CSOs choose not to register as such.

Of the 16 countries analyzed, only Bangladesh, Lebanon, Nigeria, and Tunisia restrict expression, civic participation, or association related to SOGI (figure 5.2). Nigeria, which has the most severe stance, has banned the creation of sexual and gender minority CSOs; it explicitly forbids organizations that advocate for or promote sexual and gender minorities' rights.[9] In Bangladesh, restrictions against sexual and gender minorities are based on moral grounds that often prevent sexual and gender minorities from free expression. These limitations criminalize sexual minority status, as well as any conduct that disrupts the "public order," "decency," or "morality" of society.[10] In Tunisia, the Law on the Organization of Associations prohibits CSOs from any activities prohibited by law.[11] Therefore, CSOs do not use the terms "sexual and gender minorities" or "LGBTI" (lesbian, gay, bisexual, transgender, and intersex) in their registration statutes. Although Lebanese law does not specifically ban sexual and gender minority CSOs or SOGI-related expression, several laws indirectly restrict free expression. For example, Lebanon's Law on Associations authorizes the Ministry of Interior to reject any organization's registration application if the organization is founded on an "unlawful basis." According to study contributors, many openly sexual and gender minority organizations have been denied registration on this basis, even though the law does not explicitly prohibit registration of CSOs as "sexual and gender minority/LGBTI organizations."[12] In addition, the Lebanese Law on Public Meetings of 1911, which requires prior approval by authorities to assemble, has been used by the General Security Forces on several occasions to disrupt sexual and gender minority events in the country. Furthermore, the Lebanese Penal Code prohibits the possession, making,

FIGURE 5.2

Analyzed Countries with Laws That Restrict Expression, Civic Participation, or Association Related to SOGI, 2021

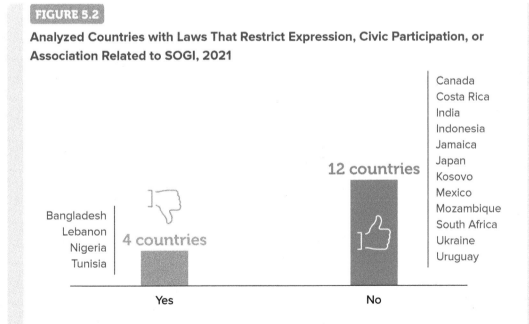

Source: World Bank Group, Equality of Opportunity database.

Note: SOGI = sexual orientation and gender identity.

or distribution of materials that may incite others to immorality; the same law also prohibits any written, visual, or verbal expressions that might be contrary to morality and ethics. This legislation is frequently used to target sexual and gender minority activists spreading awareness through public channels, such as television stations or mainstream news.[13]

It is advised that countries adopt the following good practice policy actions:

■ Introduce legislation or amend current laws or regulations to allow sexual and gender minority organizations to register and operate freely and ensure that activists can advocate for sexual and gender minority equality.

■ Abolish laws that infringe on the right of sexual and gender minorities and their advocates to speak about their identities.

Equality Bodies, Including National Human Rights Institutions

In addition to CSOs and national equality bodies (such as employment nondiscrimination bodies), NHRIs also play an important role in protecting the rights of sexual and gender minorities (UNGA 2013, para. 32 and 120 (g)).[14] Although not judicial, NHRI enforcement mechanisms are relevant to the protection of sexual and gender minority rights because they can complement the judicial system. An NHRI can even be considered "a central part of modern democracy" (Park 2015). When assessing NHRIs, a central element to consider is their compliance with the Paris Principles, "a set of minimum standards that national institutions, regardless of their structure and mandate, should respect. They are now broadly accepted as benchmarks for the accreditation of national institutions and serve as a litmus test of an institution's legitimacy" (UNGA 2013, para. 28). The Paris Principles establish six criteria for a fully functioning national ombudsman or human rights institution: (1) a broad mandate and competence; (2) autonomy from the government in their functioning and methods of operation; (3) independence, enshrined in law or the constitution; (4) pluralism through membership or cooperation; (5) adequate financial, material, and human resources; and (6) adequate powers of investigation (UNGA 2013, para. 31).

NHRIs that promote the inclusion of sexual and gender minorities perform crucial functions in some countries. In countries in which criminalization and social and cultural biases promote discrimination and even violence against sexual and gender minorities, NHRIs are often the only institutions that can advocate for promoting and protecting sexual and gender minority equality and inclusion. Such institutions demonstrate the government's willingness to monitor violations and acknowledge that such violations are undesirable. NHRIs also allow victims of discrimination to find assistance in filing claims and, more importantly, to understand their rights. The Yogyakarta Principles recommend that NHRIs integrate the promotion and protection of the human rights of persons of diverse sexual orientation or gender identities into their work.[15] In recent years, many NHRIs have implemented this recommendation.[16]

Nine of the 16 countries analyzed do not have NHRIs that include SOGI within their mandate; they also do not have special institutions with expertise in or a mandate to deal with sexual and gender minority rights and inclusion. Only Canada, Costa Rica, India, Kosovo, Mexico, South Africa, and Uruguay have legally established NHRIs authorized to promote, protect, and incorporate the inclusion of sexual and gender minorities (table 5.1). In Canada, the Ontario Human Rights Commission was established to prevent discrimination and promote and advance human rights. The grounds protected under the Human Rights Code are, among others, age, ancestry, color, race, sexual orientation, gender identity, and gender expression.[17] In May 2018, Costa Rica's government created the Commissioner's Office for LGBTI Affairs to promote sexual and gender minority rights and establish public policies on this topic.[18] In India, the National Human Rights Commission, a statutory body established under the Protection of Human Rights Act 1993,[19] established a core group to deal with sexual and gender minority issues. Kosovo's constitution sets forth the role and competences of the Ombudsperson to monitor and protect human rights and freedoms of legal and natural persons from unlawful and irregular actions or inactions

TABLE 5.1

National Equality Bodies and National Human Rights Institutions That Explicitly Deal with Sexual and Gender Minority Rights and Inclusion

Country	Institution or body	Website
Canada	Ontario's Human Rights Commission	http://ohrc.on.ca/en
Costa Rica	Commissioner Office for LGBTI Issues	—
India	National Human Rights Commission	https://nhrc.nic.in
Kosovo	Ombudsperson Institution of Kosovo	http://ennhri.org/our-members/kosovo/
Mexico	Consejo Nacional Para Prevenir la Discriminación	https://www.conapred.org.mx
South Africa	Human Rights Commission	https://www.sahrc.org.za
Uruguay	National Human Rights Institution and the Honorary Commission against Racism, Xenophobia and All Other Forms of Discrimination	https://www.gub.uy/ministerio-educacion-cultura/politicas-y-gestion/comision-honoraria-contra-racismo-xenofobia-toda-otra-forma-discriminacion

Source: World Bank Group, Equality of Opportunity database.

Note: — = not available; LGBTI = lesbian, gay, bisexual, transgender, and intersex.

by public authorities.[20] Since July 2015, under the Law on the Protection from Discrimination, the Ombudsperson Institution of Kosovo is responsible for handling discrimination claims by sexual and gender minorities.[21] Mexico's National Council to Prevent Discrimination (Consejo Nacional para Prevenir la Discriminación) is a government agency responsible for protecting all citizens from exclusion based on ethnic or national origin, sex, age, disability, social or economic status, health, pregnancy, language, religion, opinion, sexual orientation, marital status, or any other status that would prevent or defeat the recognition or exercise of rights and equality of opportunity.[22] In South Africa, the Human Rights Commission was inaugurated in 1995 under the Human Rights Commission Act 54 of 1994 as provided by the constitution.[23] The Human Rights Commission in that country is tasked with eradicating inequality and unfair discrimination on different grounds, including sexual orientation.[24] Finally, the National Institution of Human Rights and Ombudsman's Office of Uruguay also promotes human rights in accordance with the Constitution of Uruguay and international law.[25] In addition, the National Human Rights Institution and the Honorary Commission against Racism, Xenophobia and all Other Forms of Discrimination are responsible for handling SOGI-based discrimination claims.[26]

The remaining nine countries (Bangladesh, Indonesia, Jamaica, Japan, Lebanon, Mozambique, Nigeria, Tunisia, and Ukraine) do not have NHRIs that explicitly include SOGI within their mandate to deal with sexual and gender minority rights and inclusion (figure 5.3). Bangladesh, Indonesia, Mozambique, and Ukraine have an Ombudsman office or NHRI, but their mandates do not mention SOGI explicitly (APF and UNDP 2016). For example, the National Human Rights Commission of Bangladesh (JAMAKON), although not legally mandated to do so, expressly advocates for sexual and gender minority rights. JAMAKON has developed and submitted antidiscrimination legislation to the Ministry of Law, Justice and Parliamentary Affairs. It has also developed a manual for gender and sexual minorities that explains its role and work on sexual orientation and gender identity issues and encourages people to file complaints

FIGURE 5.3

Analyzed Countries with a National Body or Institution Authorized to Address SOGI-Related Employment Discrimination, 2021

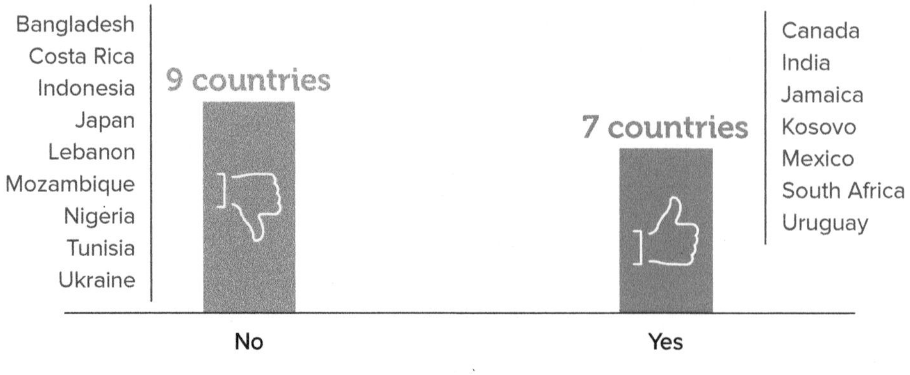

No	Yes
Bangladesh	Canada
Costa Rica	India
Indonesia	Jamaica
Japan	Kosovo
Lebanon	Mexico
Mozambique	South Africa
Nigeria	Uruguay
Tunisia	
Ukraine	

9 countries — No

7 countries — Yes

Source: World Bank Group, Equality of Opportunity database.

Note: SOGI = sexual orientation and gender identity.

if they face discrimination.[27] However, because the commission is not officially mandated to promote sexual and gender minority rights, these positive actions could be restricted by an administrative decision.

Of the 16 countries measured in the study, 7 of them (Canada, India, Jamaica, Kosovo, Mexico, South Africa, and Uruguay) provide their national equality bodies or NHRIs with a clear mandate to handle SOGI-related employment discrimination (figure 5.3). In India, victims of discrimination can bring claims before the National Human Rights Commission, which has established a core group to deal with sexual and gender minority-related issues.[28] In Kosovo, the Ombudsperson Institution is responsible for handling any charges of discrimination against sexual and gender minorities, including those related to public services and employment discrimination.[29] In South Africa, the Human Rights Commission[30] deals with cases of discrimination on SOGI grounds,[31] and the South Africa Employment Equity Act of 1998 authorizes the Commission for Conciliation, Mediation and Arbitration[32] to receive claims specifically for employment discrimination on SOGI grounds.[33] The National Human Rights Institution of Uruguay,[34] as well as the Honorary Commission Against Racism, Xenophobia and all other Forms of Discrimination, handle SOGI-based discrimination claims in the labor market and the public sector.[35] In Jamaica, the law allows public sector employees who believe they are being mistreated or denied opportunities because of their sexual orientation (but not gender identity) to file complaints with the Permanent Secretary or the head of their department.[36]

Not all NHRIs have been tasked with clear SOGI-related mandates. Of the seven countries with NHRIs that explicitly deal with sexual and gender minority rights and inclusion (Canada, Costa Rica, India, Kosovo, Mexico, South Africa, and Uruguay), only five of them (Canada, India, Mexico, South Africa, and Uruguay) provide their national equality bodies or NHRIs with a clear legal mandate to handle SOGI-based discrimination charges in public services (figure 5.4).

FIGURE 5.4

Analyzed Countries with a National Body or Institution Authorized to Address SOGI-Based Discrimination in Public Services, 2021

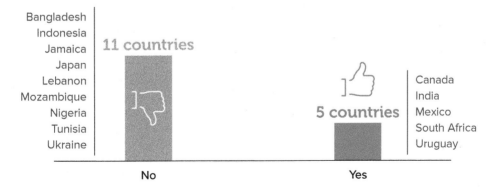

Source: World Bank Group, Equality of Opportunity database.

Note: SOGI = sexual orientation and gender identity.

It is advised that countries adopt the following good practice policy actions:

■ Ensure that equality bodies, including NHRIs, explicitly address the inclusion of sexual and gender minorities.

■ Ensure that existing equality bodies, including NHRIs, are allowed to work independently and efficiently to provide adequate protection to individuals and organizations targeted for their work with sexual and gender minorities.

■ Strengthen the institutional capacity of existing equality bodies, including NHRIs.

■ Encourage cooperation between CSOs and equality bodies, including NHRIs.

Gender in Official Certifications and Documents

Discrimination based on gender identity continues to be a major obstacle in the advancement of inclusion of gender minorities.[37] Transgender and nonbinary people face increasingly high levels of violence and exclusion from social services—even more so than sexual minorities.[38] Updating the sex/gender marker in official documents is often impossible. Moreover, even if such adjustment is legal, it can require long and invasive procedures (Chiam, Duffy, and Gil González 2017). However, transgender and nonbinary people's needs are becoming more accepted as legitimate needs around the world, and some countries are experiencing a better cultural and societal understanding of gender minorities than sexual minorities. Furthermore, some countries have taken measures to improve the rights of intersex people, particularly children, by protecting intersex children from unnecessary medical procedures.

Of the 16 countries analyzed, 4 (Bangladesh, Costa Rica, India, and Uruguay) have centralized protocols for updating sex/gender markers in official certifications without pathologizing requirements. Uruguay's process is the most straightforward. The comprehensive law for transgender people (Ley Integral Para Personas Trans) recognizes an individual's right to develop their personality according to their gender identity. The law allows transgender and nonbinary people to change their sex/gender in official certifications using a simple administrative process.[39] Previously, the law required a judicial process for such a change. In November 2013, Bangladesh's government recognized "*hijra*" as a gender marker, effectively classifying 160 million people as male, female, or *hijra*. Soon after the Cabinet declaration, a gazette was issued on January 26, 2014, to include a single sentence about the recognition: "The Government of Bangladesh has recognized the *hijra* community of Bangladesh as a *Hijra* sex" (Chiam, Duffy, and Gil González 2017).[40] Costa Rica allows sex/gender change in official certifications according to the person's perceived gender identity.[41] On April 15, 2014, India's Supreme Court ruled that transgender people have a fundamental constitutional right to change their gender without surgery, securing the ability to change one's gender judicially. The court accepted self-identification as the governing principle on gender recognition, with no additional eligibility requirements, such as gender-affirming surgeries or hormone therapy. It directed the federal and state governments to recognize these requirements. However, eligibility criteria, implementation delays, and inconsistencies across documents and agencies limit the guarantee to self-identification set out in the 2014 judgment (Chiam, Duffy, and Gil González 2017). More recently, India enacted the Transgender Persons (Protection of Rights) Act of 2019, which recognizes the right of transgender and gender nonconforming people to choose their gender and make the necessary legal changes without pathologizing requirements.[42]

Other countries analyzed in the study also offer legal frameworks for transgender and nonbinary people to change their gender marker in official documents. However, these frameworks either do not constitute centralized protocols—they form part of local or provincial laws—or contain restrictive and pathologizing requirements for the change. These requirements typically include medical procedures and surgery, sterilization, divorce, or psychiatric diagnosis. In Indonesia, there are no clear legal requirements to advise a judge on whether to recognize a change of gender marker. In practice, the court may ask family members to give evidence on whether the applicant needs the sex/gender change. Once the court grants the sex/gender change request, the applicant will include this decision, along with the transgender person's national identification (ID) card and Family Card, in the application to amend the sex details under the Population Administration Act (Chiam, Duffy, and Gil González 2017). Japan allows transgender individuals to change their legal gender marker only after receiving a diagnosis of a gender identity disorder. Furthermore, Japanese law bans people with children who are minors from changing their sex marker in the official family registry system.[43] In early 2019, Japan's Supreme Court upheld a law that effectively requires transgender people to be sterilized before they can have their gender changed on official documents (US Library of Congress 2019). In South Africa, the sex/gender marker can be changed in official certifications only after gender reassignment procedures have been completed.[44] In Ukraine, even though transgender people are allowed to change their gender marker in official documents, this change must be accompanied by pathologizing requirements, such as acknowledging "socio-psychological indications, i.e., discomfort or distress due to the discrepancy between the gender identity of the individual and the gender assigned to them at birth."[45] In Mexico, there is no uniform law. However, Mexico City modified its Civil Code in 2015 to recognize that gender identity should be understood "as the personal and internal conviction, as each person's self-perception, which may or may not correspond to the sex assigned on the first birth certificate." As such, transgender persons can change their name and gender without medical examination or judicial order. The process was also changed from a judicial procedure (and therefore at the judge's discretion) to an administrative one.[46] Similarly, even though all provinces in Canada have protocols for updating the sex/gender marker, there is no centralized protocol. In sum, although transgender individuals can change their gender marker in official certifications, in many countries that process is often extremely invasive, long, and requires a variety of court orders and medical examinations. These aggressive measures pathologize the self-identities of gender minorities.

The situation is similar when it comes to obtaining government-issued ID cards or passports. Seven out of the 16 countries analyzed (Canada, Costa Rica, Indonesia, Japan, Mexico, South

Africa, and Uruguay) allow an individual to obtain a new ID card or passport after gender reassignment. In Ontario, Canada, transgender people are allowed to change their gender marker and obtain new documents without gender reassignment surgery.[47] Under Mexican law, people can obtain a new ID card or passport only after gender reassignment and the issuance of a certification by the competent authority.[48] In Indonesia, a court order is necessary to obtain a new ID card or a passport after gender reassignment (Chiam, Duffy, and Gil González 2017).[49] Although almost half of the countries reviewed allow an individual to obtain a new ID card or passport after gender reassignment, obstacles—such as long administrative processes, court orders, and invasive psychiatric and medical examinations—often make the process costly, lengthy, and therefore inaccessible to most people. A case of a transgender person requiring legal recognition of their gender marker change in their identification documents at the Civil Registry Office is currently pending before the Constitutional Court in Kosovo, with an expectation that the ruling could positively affect the country's approach regarding legal recognition of a person's changed gender marker (Halili 2018).

None of the 16 countries distinguish between sexual and gender minorities and the rest of the population when obtaining citizenship, a passport, or an ID card. However, although almost half of the analyzed countries allow people to change their gender marker in official documentation, the gender options in these documents often remain binary (either female or male). Only Bangladesh, Canada, and India have more than two gender options when applying for a passport. In Bangladesh and India, people can mark "other" in the gender category, in addition to the options "male" and "female." This approach is partially in recognition of *hijra* communities, a term used throughout South Asia to refer to transgender and intersex people, among others, who sometimes identify as a third gender rather than male or female. In Canada, gender markers in passports include an "X" option for individuals who identify as neither male nor female (figure 5.5).[50] The fee is waived for those changing their gender marker to "X" for the first time, but the renewal charges remain the same for everyone else.

When it comes to applying for an ID card, only Bangladesh, Canada, Costa Rica, and India include another option in addition to male and female in the gender marker category. The options in Bangladesh, Canada, and India are the same as when applying for a passport. However, in Costa Rica, the sex/gender marker has been completely omitted from national ID cards, eliminating the often-complicated process of changing the gender marker on a person's national ID card. The exclusion of sex in ID cards recognizes the rights of people of all sexes and gender identities. This measure was backed by the Organic Law of the Supreme Electoral Tribunal and Civil Registry, which states that the ID card will contain the necessary information to identify the bearer. Instead of including sex, ID cards have advanced security techniques for personal identification.[51]

Despite the inclusive efforts mentioned above, people changing the sex designation on a national passport may still face issues while traveling because not all countries may accept the designation of "X" or "other" on their passports.

FIGURE 5.5

Passport Application for Canada

	Government Gouvernement	Save	Reset Form	Print Form	PROTECTED WHEN COMPLETED - **B**
	of Canada du Canada				Page 1 of 7

ADULT GENERAL PASSPORT APPLICATION
for Canadians 16 years of age or over applying in Canada or the USA

Warning: Any false or misleading statement with respect to this application and any supporting document, including the concealment of any material fact, may result in the refusal to issue a passport, the revocation of a currently valid passport, and/or the imposition of a period of refusal of passport services, and may be grounds for criminal prosecution as per subsection 57 (2) of the Criminal Code (R.C.S. 1985, C-46).

Type or print in CAPITAL LETTERS using black or dark blue ink. | Read Instructions

1 PERSONAL INFORMATION (SEE INSTRUCTIONS, SECTION I)

Surname (last name) requested to appear in the passport

Given name(s) requested to appear in the passport

All former surnames (including surname at birth if different from above. These will not appear in the passport.)

Anticipated date of travel
It is recommended that you do not finalize travel plans until you receive the requested passport.

Mother's surname at birth | Month | Day | Unknown

Place of birth
City | Country | Prov./Terr./State (if applicable)

Date of birth (YYYY-MM-DD) | Sex | F Female | M Male | X Another gender | Natural eye colour | Height (cm or in)

Current home address
Number | Street | Apt. | City | Prov./Terr./State | Postal/ZIP code

Mailing address (if different from current home address)
Number | Street | Apt. | City | Prov./Terr./State | Postal/ZIP code

Email address | Telephone (daytime) | Telephone (other)

Declaration—I solemnly declare that I am a Canadian citizen, that the photos enclosed are unaltered and a true likeness of me, that all of the statements made and the information provided in this application, as well as any supporting documents, are true. I declare that I have read and understood the **Warning** at the top of this page and the **Privacy Notice Statement** (see section N). I consent to the collection, use and disclosure of my personal information as outlined in the Privacy Notice Statement.

Sign within border

Signature (see Instructions, section I)

Date (YYYY-MM-DD) | Signed at
City | Prov./Terr./State

2 DECLARATION OF GUARANTOR (SEE INSTRUCTIONS, SECTION J)

Note: You or your guarantor can complete this section, with the exception of the four fields which **must** be completed by your guarantor.

Surname (last name) in passport | Given name(s)

Date of birth (YYYY-MM-DD) | Canadian passport number | Date of issue (YYYY-MM-DD) | Date of expiry (YYYY-MM-DD)

Relationship to the applicant | Telephone (daytime) | Telephone (other)

Current home address
Number | Street | Apt. | City | Prov./Terr./State | Postal/ZIP code

Declaration: The Guarantor must validate and sign this section—I solemnly declare that I have known the applicant identified above personally for at least **two (2)** years. **I have signed the back of one (1) of the photos** to certify that the image is a true likeness of the applicant. Where applicable, I have signed and dated a copy of each document to support the applicant's identity (see section 5) to confirm that I have seen the original(s). I declare that I have read and understood the **Warning** at the top of page 1 of this application and the **Privacy Notice Statement** in section N of the instructions. I consent to the collection, use and disclosure of my personal information as outlined in the Privacy Notice Statement.

Signature of guarantor

I have known the applicant for | Date (YYYY-MM-DD) | Signed at
Number of years | City | Prov./Terr./State

PPTC 153 (07-2021) | (DISPONIBLE EN FRANÇAIS - PPTC 154 F) | Canada

Source: Government of Canada, Adult General Passport Application, https://www.canada.ca/content/dam/ircc/migration /ircc/english/passport/forms/pdf/pptc153.pdf.

No country studied requires gender-reassignment surgery for intersex children to receive a birth certificate. However, it is considered a good practice to adopt laws to protect children from gender reassignment surgeries. For example, Uruguay protects children's and adolescents' physical integrity and bodily autonomy, providing that gender identity is based on self-determination. This position protects intersex children and adolescents from invasive medical procedures.[52] Federal law in India does not specifically protect intersex children from gender reassignment surgery. However, the south Indian state of Tamil Nadu has issued an executive order banning medically unnecessary surgeries on intersex children and infants whose sex is not clear at birth (table 5.2).[53]

TABLE 5.2

Protections for Gender Reassignment

Country	Centralized protocols for updating sex/gender markers in official certifications without pathologizing requirements	Laws or regulations that allow an individual to obtain a new ID card or passport after gender reassignment	Laws or regulations that require gender-reassignment surgery for intersex children to obtain a birth certificate
Bangladesh	✓		
Canada		✓	
Costa Rica	✓	✓	
India	✓		
Indonesia		✓	
Jamaica			
Japan		✓	
Kosovo			
Lebanon			
Mexico		✓	
Mozambique			
Nigeria			
South Africa		✓	
Tunisia			
Ukraine			
Uruguay	✓	✓	

Source: World Bank Group, Equality of Opportunity database.

It is advised that countries adopt the following good practice policy actions:

- Introduce legislation that facilitates the update of the gender marker in official certifications and documents through inclusive and nondiscriminatory centralized protocols.

- Discourage pathologizing and stigmatizing requirements, and instead relate gender marker changes to self-determination alone.

- Abolish laws or regulations stipulating discriminatory conditions for gender marker updates, such as surgery, divorce, sterilization, and psychiatric examinations.

- Ensure that gender options in passports and national ID cards are inclusive of nonbinary people.

- Abolish laws and regulations requiring gender-reassignment surgery for intersex children to receive a birth certificate and ban all unnecessary and invasive medical procedures on intersex children and adolescents.

- Introduce laws that prevent gender-reassignment surgery for intersex children at birth and adolescents, and instead allow them to choose their gender on their own when ready.

Partnership and Parental Rights

This section covers whether same-sex couples can enter into registered partnerships or civil unions, be legally married, and legally adopt children.[54] These three issues are deeply ingrained in the right to form a family and are of the highest importance in sexual and gender minorities' family life.

Fewer than one-third of the analyzed countries allow same-sex couples to enter into registered partnerships, civil unions, and/or marriages (Canada, Costa Rica, Mexico, South Africa, and Uruguay) (map 5.1). The same holds for adoption (figure 5.6).

In Canada, the Civil Marriage Act recognized same-sex marriage in 2005,[55] while joint adoption by same-sex couples is also legal in all Canadian provinces and territories.[56] Same-sex marriage became legal in Costa Rica on May 26, 2020, after an 18-month grace period given by the court's constitutional chamber expired.[57] Costa Rica was the first country in Central America to recognize same-sex marriage, effectively allowing the adoption of children (stepchild and joint). There is no federal law in Mexico on same-sex marriage, but Mexico City and other jurisdictions have enacted local laws providing for this right.[58] In May 2019, Mexico's Foreign Affairs Secretary announced that all Mexican consulates will allow citizens to marry regardless of gender (Mendos 2019). In December 2019, the Senate received a draft bill providing constitutional endorsement to same-sex marriages. However, legal reforms have

MAP 5.1

Twenty-Nine Countries with National Laws Allowing Gays and Lesbians to Marry, 2021

IBRD 45505 |
JANUARY 2021

■ ALLOW GAY MARRIAGE   ■ LEGAL IN SOME JURISDICTIONS

Source: Based on Pew Research Center analysis. Map classifications as of October 2019, https://www.pewresearch.org /fact-tank/2019/10/29/global-snapshot-same-sex-marriage/.

FIGURE 5.6

Registered Partnerships, Civil Unions, Marriages, and Adoptions, by Country, 2021

Registered partnership or civil union	Legal marriage	Second parent and/or joint adoption by same-sex partners	None allowed
Canada	Canada	Canada	Bangladesh
Mexico	Costa Rica	Costa Rica	India
South Africa	Mexico	Mexico	Indonesia
Uruguay	South Africa	South Africa	Jamaica
	Uruguay	Uruguay	Japan
			Kosovo
			Lebanon
			Mozambique
			Nigeria
			Tunisia
			Ukraine
4 countries	**5 countries**	**5 countries**	

Source: World Bank Group, Equality of Opportunity database.

been delayed owing to the COVID-19 pandemic.[59] In Mexico City, second-parent adoption is also allowed for same-sex couples.[60] In July 2020, the Minister of Justice of Kosovo announced that the new Civil Code will allow for same-sex civil partnerships (bne IntelliNews 2020). Similarly, the South African Civil Union Act of 2006 allows same-sex persons the right to marry,[61] while the Children's Act of 2005 allows joint adoption by "partners in a permanent domestic life-partnership," whether same- or opposite-sex, and stepparent adoption by a person who is the "permanent domestic life-partner" of the child's current parent.[62] Finally, Uruguay's Law on Marriage Equality redefined marriage as the union of two persons "of different or same-sex."[63] In 2009, Uruguay also became the first Latin American country to allow same-sex couples to adopt children after the Senate voted to approve a bill modifying the country's adoption statute.[64]

Japan, in contrast, does not recognize same-sex couples at the national level (Mendos 2019). However, some municipalities provide the option of a partnership oath, allowing same-sex couples the right to register as unions in their respective municipalities.[65] Some municipalities in Tokyo and other major Japanese cities use this approach, which lacks the same legal validity as a legally recognized marriage. Similarly, although India has no law on same-sex marriage, on April 10, 2019, the Madras High Court of Tamil Nadu held that a marriage solemnized between a male and a transgender woman, both professing Hindu religion, is a valid marriage in terms of Section 5 of the Hindu Marriage Act of 1955, and the Registrar of Marriages is bound to register it in Tamil Nadu.[66]

It is advised that countries adopt the following good practice policy actions:

- Enact legislation that extends the right to enter into registered partnerships, civil unions, and marriages to everyone regardless of their sexual orientation or gender identity.

- Enforce laws that allow second-parent or joint adoption for same-sex couples.

Conversion Therapy

Same-sex attraction and the self-identities of transgender people are not pathologies. They cannot, therefore, be treated or "cured." Forced treatments, such as conversion therapy, are "deeply harmful and may cause severe pain and suffering and lead to depression, anxiety, and suicidal ideation" (UNGA 2019, para. 23).[67] The Inter-American Commission on Human Rights has expressed concerns about pathologizing SOGI in cases in which "parents or other family members exert physical violence against children because they perceive them as, lesbian, gay, bisexual, or gender nonconforming, with the intent of 'correcting' the children" (IACHR 2015, 315). The Yogyakarta Principles urge states to ". . . recognize that forced, coercive and otherwise involuntary modification of a person's sex characteristics may amount to torture, or other cruel, inhuman or degrading treatment" and that states should "... prohibit any practice, and repeal any laws and policies, allowing intrusive and irreversible treatments on the basis of sexual orientation, gender identity, gender expression, or sex characteristics, including forced genital-normalizing surgery, involuntary sterilization, unethical experimentation, medical display, 'reparative' or 'conversion' therapies, when enforced or administered without the free, prior, and informed consent of the person concerned."[68]

Although most countries have not prohibited conversion therapies, some provinces in Canada and some jurisdictions in Mexico have done so.[69] However, other countries are taking steps in that direction. For example, a legislative proposal currently before the Costa Rican Congress aims to ban the practice.[70] If this proposal advances, it could be a positive example for other Latin American countries.

It is advised that countries adopt the following good practice policy actions:

- Abolish laws that impose forced treatment or conversion therapy on sexual and gender minorities.

- Enact laws banning forced treatment or conversion therapy of sexual and gender minorities.

Sexual and Gender Minority Asylum Seekers

The persecution of sexual and gender minorities continues worldwide.[71] Forced migration leaves sexual and gender minorities extremely vulnerable to abuse. Despite their vulnerable status, most countries analyzed in the study fail to explicitly recognize persecution based on SOGI as one of the grounds for asylum. Sexual and gender minority asylum seekers are often victims of human trafficking, and they experience unimaginable suffering in seeking refuge (Zappulla 2018). All human beings, regardless of their sexual orientation and gender identity, should be able to live openly, freely, and without fear of persecution. Equally, all individuals should be able to seek asylum if they have a valid fear of persecution.

Despite the urgency to provide asylum to sexual and gender minorities, only Canada, Costa Rica, Kosovo, Mexico, South Africa, and Uruguay recognize persecution based on SOGI as grounds for asylum. In Canada, while the Immigration and Refugee Protection Act does not explicitly mention SOGI as protected grounds for asylum,[72] the government has confirmed that sexual orientation is a legitimate ground for asylum because it signifies membership in a particular social group.[73] In South Africa, the Refugees Act of 1998 provides refugee status to anyone fleeing persecution based on race, religion, nationality, political opinion, or membership of a particular social group. The act defines the term "social group" as "a group of persons of a particular gender, sexual orientation, disability, class, or caste."[74] In Kosovo, SOGI is a protected ground under the country's asylum law.[75] Mexico does not explicitly recognize persecution based on SOGI as grounds for asylum; however, the term "social groups" is used to offer asylum to sexual and gender minorities.[76] SOGI is also not specifically mentioned in Uruguay's asylum law, but persecution based on SOGI falls under "life-threatening risk."[77] Historically, Uruguay has received refugees fleeing persecution on the basis of their sexual orientation or gender identity.

> "Growing up in Jamaica's Montego Bay, Glenroy enjoyed an idyllic childhood until his family discovered he was gay. They physically attacked him and threw him out of the house and eventually forced him to seek refuge thousands of miles away from his home country. Glenroy made his escape from Jamaica with the help of Rainbow Railroad, a Canadian organization that helps LGBT+ people escape danger in their home countries and find safety elsewhere."

—*Lopez (2018)*

It is advised that countries adopt the following good practice policy actions:

- Introduce legislation that specifically recognizes persecution based on SOGI as grounds for asylum.

- Offer support to sexual and gender minority organizations and groups that work with sexual and gender minority asylum seekers, while abolishing laws that ban the creation of such organizations.

- Provide SOGI-inclusive training to customs officials, police officers, and civil servants working on asylum claims.

Notes

1. See chapter 4 on access to public services and social protection.
2. Questions addressing political representation and national action plans in the indicator set on civil and political inclusion are: How many members of parliament or other national, elected representative body openly self-identify as sexual or gender minority? Are there national action plans on SOGI?
3. Bangladesh's Second Five-Year Strategic Plan (2016–20) is available at http://nhrc.portal.gov.bd/sites /default/files/files/nhrc.portal.gov.bd/page/535c363f_91a8_40b6_b58a_714954c85b4e/2nd_Five -Year_Strategic_Plan_%282016-2020%29_of_JAMAKON.pdf.

4. Costa Rica's Plan Nacional de Desarrollo y de Inversión Pública del Bicentenario 2019–22 is available at https://observatorioplanificacion.cepal.org/es/planes/plan-nacional-de-desarrollo-y-de-inversion-publica-del-bicentenario-2019-2022-de-costa-rica.

5. India's Draft Annual Action Plan for the period April 1, 2019, to March 31, 2020, is available at https://nhrc.nic.in/sites/default/files/Annal_Action_Plan_2019-2020_07052019.pdf.

6. For more information on Uruguay's National Council on Sexual Diversity, see https://latinno.net/en/case/18131.

7. The questions addressing civil society and expression, association, and assembly in this indicator set include: Are there any laws and/or regulations that restrict expression, civic participation, or association related to SOGI?

8. For a discussion of sexual and gender minority rights, see Amnesty International (2019).

9. Nigeria, Same-Sex Marriage Prohibition Act. 2013. Section 4: "(1) The Registration of gay clubs, societies and organizations, their sustenance, processions and meetings is prohibited."

10. Constitution of Bangladesh, 1972. For general constitutional provision establishing limitations, see Article 39, paragraph 2 a): "Subject to any reasonable restrictions imposed by law in the interests of the security of the State, friendly relations with foreign states, public order, decency or morality, or in relation to contempt of court, defamation or incitement to an offence - a) the right of every citizen of freedom of speech and expression."

11. Tunisia, Law No. 59-154 on the Organization of Associations. 1959. Article 2: "La cause et l'objectif de cette convention ne doivent, en aucun cas, être contraires aux lois, aux bonnes mœurs, de nature à troubler l'ordre public ou à porter atteinte à l'intégrité du territoire national et la forme républicaine de l'Etat. Les fondateurs et dirigeants des associations ne doivent avoir encouru aucune condamnation pour crime ou délit relatif aux bonnes mœurs. Ne peuvent être dirigeants d'une association à caractère général ceux qui assument des fonctions ou des responsabilités dans les organes centraux de direction des parties politiques. Ces dispositions s'appliquent au comité directeur des associations sus-indiquées, ainsi qu'aux sections, filiales ou organisations annexes ou groupes secondaires visés à l'article 6 bis de la présente loi."

12. Lebanon, Law on Associations. 1909. Article 3: "Founding an association on any unlawful basis which violates the provisions of laws and public documents or which aims to jeopardize the comfort of the monarchy and integrity of state property, change the form of the current government, or politically discriminate between different citizens is not permitted. The attestations of such will be refused and they will be dissolved by decree issued by the Council of Ministers." Article 532 of the Penal Code: "The exposing of public morals by any of the ways mentioned in paragraphs 2 or 3 of Article 209 shall be punished with imprisonment from one month to one year and a fine from 20,000 Lira to 100,000 Lira." Article 209 of the Penal Code: "The making or possession, importing or attempts to import for trade, distribution, for payment, copying, exhibition or display or attempts to display to the public, or for selling or attempts to sell, or distribution or engaged in the distribution of each publication, an editor or a drawing or a declaration or pictures or paintings or photographs, or the origin of the image or its template or produced anything in breach of modesty shall be punished with imprisonment from one month to one year and a fine from 20,000 Lira to 100,000 Lira."

13. Lebanon, Penal Code. 1943. Article 209 is read in conjunction with Articles 531 and 532.

14. The questions addressing equality bodies, including national human rights institutions, in this indicator set include: Are there laws and/or regulations that establish national human rights institutions that include sexual orientation, gender identity, gender expression, and sex characteristics (SOGIESC) within their mandate and/or specific institutions with expertise on and a mandate to deal with sexual and gender minority rights and inclusion? Is there a national equality body or national human rights institution responsible for handling charges of employment discrimination related to SOGI? Is there a national equality body or national human rights institution responsible for handling charges of SOGI-based discrimination in public services?

15. Details about the Yogyakarta Principles are available at http://yogyakartaprinciples.org/principles-en /about-the-yogyakarta-principles/.

16. See OutRight's NHRI Scorecard at https://outrightinternational.org/content/nhri-scorecard-0.

17. Ontario's Human Rights Code. 1962. Article 29: "The functions of the Commission are to promote and advance respect for human rights in Ontario, to protect human rights in Ontario and, recognizing that it is in the public interest to do so and that it is the Commission's duty to protect the public interest, to identify and promote the elimination of discriminatory practices and, more specifically, (a) to forward the policy that the dignity and worth of every person be recognized and that equal rights and opportunities be provided without discrimination that is contrary to law; (b) to develop and conduct programs of public information and education to, (i) promote awareness and understanding of, respect for and compliance with this Act, and (ii) prevent and eliminate discriminatory practices that infringe rights under Part I; (c) to undertake, direct and encourage research into discriminatory practices and to make recommendations designed to prevent and eliminate such discriminatory practices; (d) to examine and review any statute or regulation, and any program or policy made by or under a statute, and make recommendations on any provision, program or policy that in its opinion is inconsistent with the intent of this Act; (e) to initiate reviews and inquiries into incidents of tension or conflict, or conditions that lead or may lead to incidents of tension or conflict, in a community, institution, industry or sector of the economy, and to make recommendations, and encourage and co-ordinate plans, programs and activities, to reduce or prevent such incidents or sources of tension or conflict; (f) to promote, assist and encourage public, municipal or private agencies, organizations, groups or persons to engage in programs to alleviate tensions and conflicts based upon identification by a prohibited ground of discrimination; (g) to designate programs as special programs in accordance with section 14; (h) to approve policies under section 30; (i) to make applications to the Tribunal under section 35; (j) to report to the people of Ontario on the state of human rights in Ontario and on its affairs; (k) to perform the functions assigned to the Commission under this or any other Act. 2006, c. 30, s. 4." The same code (Article 1) prohibits actions that discriminate against people based on a protected ground in a protected social area. Protected grounds are: age, ancestry, color, race, citizenship, ethnic origin, place of origin, creed, disability, family status, marital status (including single status), gender identity, gender expression, receipt of public assistance (in housing only), record of offenses (in employment only), sex (including pregnancy and breastfeeding), and sexual orientation.

18. Costa Rica, Por medio del Decreto Ejecutivo 41158-MP el 17 de mayo de 2018 se creó la figura del Comisionado de la Presidencia de la República para asuntos relacionados con las personas LGTBI, adscrito al despacho del presidente de la República. Decreto Ejecutivo 41158-MP. http://www.pgrweb.go.cr/scij/Busqueda/Normativa /Normas/nrm_texto_completo.aspx?param1=NRTC&nValor1=1&nValor2=86603&nValor3=112437&strTipM=TC.

19. India, Protection of Human Rights Act. 1993. http://nhrc.nic.in/acts-&-rules/protection-human -rights-act-1993-1. Annual Action Plan that includes LGBTI rights. The focus areas are: human dignity for all, protect rights of the people from marginalized sections of society, prison reforms, women and child rights, rights of disabled, elderly, and LGBT rights, among others. http://nhrc.nic .in/activities/annual-action-plans.

20. Constitution of Kosovo. Article 132 (1): "The Ombudsperson monitors, defends and protects the rights and freedoms of individuals from unlawful or improper acts or failures to act of public authorities."

21. Kosovo, Law No. 05/L-019. 2017 on Ombudsperson. Article 1(2): "The Ombudsperson is a mechanism of equality for promoting, monitoring and supporting equal treatment without discrimination on grounds protected by the Law on Gender Equality and the Law on the Protection from Discrimination." Article 1 (1) of the Law on the Protection from Discrimination states that the purpose of this law is to establish a "general framework for prevention and combating discrimination based on nationality, or in relation to any community, social origin, race, ethnicity, color, birth, origin, sex, gender, gender identity, sexual orientation, language, citizenship, religion and religious belief, political affiliation, political or other opinion, social or personal status, age, family or marital status, pregnancy, maternity,

wealth, health status, disability, genetic inheritance or any other groups, in order to implement the principle of equal treatment. Article 9 (1) of the Law on the Protection from Discrimination (Law No. 05/L-021) states that the Ombudsperson shall handle cases related to discrimination, and (2) The Ombudsperson has the following competences: 2.1. receives and investigates submissions of persons, gives opinions and recommendations on concrete cases of discrimination; 2.2. provides assistance to victims of discrimination during preparation of complaints from discrimination." In addition, Article 4 (1) of the Law on Gender Equality states: "It is prohibited the direct or indirect gender discrimination, including less favorable treatment of women for reasons of pregnancy and maternity, marital status, nationality, race, disability, sexual orientation, social status, religion and belief, age or any other basis defined by law or agreement and international instruments into force."

22. Mexico, Ley Federal para Prevenir y Eliminar la Discriminación. 2003. Article 17: "El Consejo tiene como objeto: I. Contribuir al desarrollo cultural, social y democrático del país; II. Llevar a cabo, las acciones conducentes para prevenir y eliminar la discriminación. Article 1: "Discriminación significa toda distinción, exclusión, restricción o preferencia que, por acción u omisión, con intención o sin ella, no sea objetiva, racional ni proporcional y tenga por objeto o resultado obstaculizar, restringir, impedir, menoscabar o anular el reconocimiento, goce o ejercicio de los derechos humanos y libertades, cuando se base en uno o más de los siguientes motivos: el origen étnico o nacional, el color de piel, la cultura, el sexo, el género, la edad, las discapacidades, la condición social, económica, de salud o jurídica, la religión, la apariencia física, las características genéticas, la situación migratoria, el embarazo, la lengua, las opiniones, las preferencias sexuales, etc."

23. South Africa, Human Rights Commission Act No. 40. 2013. The Human Rights Commission is authorized "to promote respect for human rights and a culture of human rights; to promote the protection, development and attainment of human rights; and to monitor and assess the observance of human rights in the Republic." Section 25 of the Promotion of Equality and Prevention of Unfair Discrimination, Sections 115 up to and including 118 of the Constitution of South Africa provide for the establishment of a Human Rights Commission. The Human Rights Commission is thereby charged with the mandate of enforcing the provisions in the constitution including Section 9 (3) of the constitution: "The state may not unfairly discriminate directly or indirectly against anyone on one or more grounds, including race, gender, sex, pregnancy, marital status, ethnic or social origin, colour, sexual orientation, age, disability, religion, conscience, belief, culture, language and birth."

24. South Africa, Employment Equity Act No. 55. 1998. Section 10 (2): "Any party to a dispute . . . may refer the dispute in writing to the Commission for Conciliation, Mediation and Arbitration ('CCMA') within six months after the act or omission that allegedly constitutes unfair discrimination for conciliation. Should the dispute remain unresolved following conciliation, the matter may be referred for arbitration at the CCMA, alternatively referred to the Labor Court for adjudication." Since Section 9(3) of the constitution and the Employment Equity Act No. 55 of 1998 prohibit discrimination on sexual orientation grounds, a victim of sexual and gender minority discrimination in employment is within their rights to refer the dispute to the Commission for Conciliation, Mediation and Arbitration.

25. Uruguay, Law 18806. 2011. Article 1: "The National Institution of Human Rights and Ombudsman's Office is created, as an institution of the Legislative Power, which shall have as its mission, within the scope of competencies defined by this law, the defense, promotion and protection in all its extension, of the human rights recognized by the Constitution of the Republic and International Law."

26. Uruguay, Law No. 17817 for the Fight Against Racism, Xenophobia and All Other Forms of Discrimination (Lucha contra el racismo, la xenophobia y la discriminación). Article 3: "Crease la Comisión Honoraria contra el Racismo, la Xenofobia y toda otra forma de discriminación. Article 2: A los efectos de esta ley, se entenderá por discriminación toda distinción, exclusión, restricción, preferencia o ejercicio de violencia física y moral basada en motivos de raza, color de piel, religión, origen nacional o étnico, discapacidad, aspecto estético, genero, orientación e identidad sexual, que tenga por objeto o por resultado anular o menoscabar el reconocimiento, goce o ejercicio, en condiciones de igualdad, de los

derechos humanos y libertades fundamentales en las esferas política, económica, social, cultural o en cualquier otra esfera de la vida pública."

27. Act No. 53 of 2009 that establishes the National Human Rights Commission of Bangladesh.

28. India, National Human Rights Commission. 1993. Protection of Human Rights Act, available at http://nhrc.nic.in/acts-&-rules/protection-human-rights-act-1993-1; Draft Annual Action Plan for the period April 1, 2019, to March 31, 2020, available at http://nhrc.nic.in/activities/annual-action -plans. Transgender Persons (Protection of Rights) Act of 2019.

29. Kosovo Law No. 05/L-019. 2017. Article 1(2): "The Ombudsperson is a mechanism of equality for promoting, monitoring and supporting equal treatment without discrimination on grounds protected by the Law on Gender Equality and the Anti-Discrimination Law." Article 16 (1): "The Ombudsperson has the power to investigate complaints received from any natural or legal person related to assertions for violation of human rights envisaged by the Constitution." In connection with Law on the Protection from Discrimination (Law No. 05/L-021) and Law on Gender Equality (Law No. 05/L-020).

30. South Africa, Human Rights Commission Act No. 40. 2013. The Human Rights Commission is authorized "to promote respect for human rights and a culture of human rights; to promote the protection, development and attainment of human rights; and to monitor and assess the observance of human rights in the Republic." Section 25 of the Promotion of Equality and Prevention of Unfair Discrimination, sections 115 up to and including 118 of the Constitution of South Africa provide for the establishment of a Human Rights Commission. The Human Rights Commission is thereby charged with the mandate of enforcing the provisions in the constitution including section 9 (3) of the constitution: "The state may not unfairly discriminate directly or indirectly against anyone on one or more grounds, including race, gender, sex, pregnancy, marital status, ethnic or social origin, colour, sexual orientation, age, disability, religion, conscience, belief, culture, language and birth."

31. South Africa Employment Equity Act No. 55. 1998. Section 10 (2): "Any party to a dispute . . . may refer the dispute in writing to the Commission for Conciliation, Mediation and Arbitration ('CCMA') within six months after the act or omission that allegedly constitutes unfair discrimination for conciliation. Should the dispute remain unresolved following conciliation, the matter may be referred for arbitration at the CCMA, alternatively referred to the Labor Court for adjudication." Since section 9(3) of the constitution and the Employment Equity Act No. 55 of 1998 prohibit discrimination on sexual orientation grounds, a victim of sexual and gender minority discrimination in employment is within their rights to refer the dispute to the Commission for Conciliation, Mediation and Arbitration.

32. South Africa. The Commission for Conciliation, Mediation and Arbitration (CCMA) and the Labor Court deal with disputes arising in the workplace. Section 112 of the LRA established the CCMA as the juristic person/body responsible for the resolution of employment-related disputes. The CCMA has jurisdiction in all provinces of South Africa, with at least one office within each province. Based on the area within which the dispute arose, the local CCMA office in the relevant area will have jurisdiction to hear the dispute. Should the CCMA be unable to resolve the dispute based on the alleged discrimination, the matter may be referred to the Labor Court failing which the Labor Appeal Court, and ultimately the Constitutional Court. Section 115 of the Labor Relations Act enumerates the functions of the Commission for Conciliation, Mediation and Arbitration: "The commission must attempt to resolve, through conciliation, any dispute referred to it in terms of this Act." Likewise, the Human Rights Commission under the Human Rights Commission Act No. 40, 2013 is authorized to "promote respect for human rights and a culture of human rights; to promote the protection, development, and attainment of human rights; and to monitor and assess the observance of human rights in the Republic." Section 25 of the Promotion of Equality and Prevention of Unfair Discrimination, sections 115 up to and including 118 of the Constitution of South Africa provide for the establishment of a Human Rights Commission. The Human Rights Commission is thereby charged with the mandate of enforcing the provisions in the constitution including section 9 (3) of the constitution.

33. South Africa, Employment Equity Act No. 55. 1998. Section 10 (2): "Any party to a dispute . . . may refer the dispute in writing to the Commission for Conciliation, Mediation and Arbitration ('CCMA') within six months after the act or omission that allegedly constitutes unfair discrimination for conciliation. Should the dispute remain unresolved following conciliation, the matter may be referred for arbitration at the CCMA, alternatively referred to the Labor Court for adjudication." Since section 9(3) of the constitution and the Employment Equity Act No. 55 of 1998 prohibit discrimination on sexual orientation grounds, a victim of sexual and gender minority discrimination in employment is within their rights to refer the dispute to the Commission for Conciliation, Mediation and Arbitration.

34. Uruguay, Law 18806. 2011. Article 1: "The National Institution of Human Rights and Ombudsman's Office is created, as an institution of the Legislative Power, which shall have as its mission, within the scope of competencies defined by this law, the defense, promotion and protection in all its extension, of the human rights recognized by the Constitution of the Republic and International Law."

35. Uruguay, Law 18.446. Article 4: "Establece que la Institución Nacional de Derechos Humanos y Defensoría del Pueblo tiene la competencia de conocer e investigar eventuales violaciones de derechos humanos reconocidos en las normas nacionales o internacionales, originadas exclusivamente en la responsabilidad de instituciones y organismos del Estado por acción y omisión." https://www.gub.uy /institucion-nacional-derechos-humanos-uruguay. Uruguay, Law No. 17.817, Article 5 (K): "Infomar a la opinión pública sobre actitudes y conductas racistas, xenofóbicas, y discriminatorias o que pudieran manifestarse en cualquier ámbito de la vida nacional, especialmente en las áreas de educación, salud, acción social y empleo; provengan ellas de autoridades públicas o entidades o personas privadas."

36. Jamaica, Public Sector Staff Orders. 2004. Section 13, Article 13.1: "Employees shall be treated fairly and equitably without discrimination based on any of the following grounds: 1. Age 2. Gender 3. National Origin 4. Race 5. Colour 6. Religious Beliefs 7. Political Affiliation 8. Disability 9. Sexual Orientation, Article 13.4 (i) Employees who have reason to believe they are being treated unfairly or denied opportunity on the basis of any of the grounds stated above (13.1) may file a complaint to the Permanent Secretary or Head of Department." https://jis.gov.jm/media/Staff-Orders-for-Public -Service.pdf.

37. The questions concerning gender in official certifications and documents include: Are there any centralized protocols for updating sex/gender in official certifications without pathologizing requirements? Do laws and/or regulations relating to any of these categories differ between sexual and gender minorities and the rest of the population? Are there any laws and/or regulations that require the assigned gender on the passport and/or ID card to match the expression of one's gender? Are there any laws and/or regulations that require gender reassignment surgery for intersex children to receive a birth certificate? Are there any laws and/or regulations that allow an individual to obtain a new ID card or passport after gender reassignment?

38. See the National Resource Center on Domestic Violence's website Violence Against Trans and Non-Binary People at https://vawnet.org/sc/serving-trans-and-non-binary-survivors-domestic-and-sexual-violence /violence-against-trans-and.

39. Uruguay, Ley Integral Para Personas Trans. 2018. Article 1: "Toda persona tiene derecho al libre desarrollo de su personalidad conforme a su propia identidad de género, con independencia de su sexo biológico, genético, anatómico, morfológico, hormonal, de asignación u otro. Este derecho incluye el de ser identificado de forma que se reconozca plenamente la identidad de género propia y la consonancia entre esta identidad y el nombre y sexo señalado en los documentos identificatorios de la persona." Article 6: "Any person may request the adaptation of the registration of their name, sex, or both, when it does not match their gender identity."

40. Government of the People's Republic of Bangladesh, Ministry of Social Welfare. 2014. Bangladesh Gazette, No. sokom/work-1sha/Hijra-15/2013-40 (January 26, 2014).

41. Costa Rica, Executive Order No. 41173-MP. 2018: "Regula la adecuación de trámites, documentos y registros al reconocimiento del Derecho a la Identidad Sexual y de Género." June 28, 2018. Article 5:

"La persona interesada en rectificar o adecuar su nombre, la imagen, y/o la referencia al sexo o género podrá realizar su solicitud a través de los trámites ordinarios que ya existen en las instituciones para confección por primera vez, renovación o corrección de dichos documentos, sin que se les obligue a las personas interesadas a suministrar otro tipo de información o requisitos adicionales a los ya contemplados. La persona interesada deberá haber realizado con anterioridad a la solicitud, el cambio de nombre por identidad de género, de conformidad con el procedimiento fijado en el Reglamento del Registro del Estado Civil, Título X, Capítulo Único 'Cambio de nombre por identidad de género.' Las instituciones de la Administración Pública Central estarán en la obligación de realizar la adecuación en los registros correspondientes y la expedición de los documentos solicitados, sin mayores dilaciones ni requisitos adicionales a los previstos para los trámites ordinarios."

42. India, Transgender Persons (Protection of Rights) Act. 2019. Section 2: "In this Act, unless the context otherwise requires, (k) 'transgender person' means a person whose gender does not match with the gender assigned to that person at birth and includes trans-man or trans-woman (whether or not such person has undergone Sex Reassignment Surgery or hormone therapy or laser therapy or such other therapy), person with intersex variations, genderqueer and person having such socio-cultural identities as kinner, hijra, aravani and jogta." Section 4: "(1) A transgender person shall have a right to be recognised as such, in accordance with the provisions of this Act. (2) A person recognised as transgender under sub-section (1) shall have a right to self-perceived gender identity." Section 5: "A transgender person may make an application to the District Magistrate for issuing a certificate of identity as a transgender person, in such form and manner, and accompanied with such documents, as may be prescribed: Provided that in the case of a minor child, such application shall be made by a parent or guardian of such child." Section 6: "(1) The District Magistrate shall issue to the applicant under section 5, a certificate of identity as transgender person after following such procedure and in such form and manner, within such time, as may be prescribed indicating the gender of such person as transgender. (2) The gender of transgender person shall be recorded in all official documents in accordance with certificate issued under sub-section (1). (3) A certificate issued to a person under sub-section (1) shall confer rights and be a proof of recognition of his identity as a transgender person." Section 7: "(1) After the issue of a certificate under sub-section (1) of section 6, if a transgender person undergoes surgery to change gender either as a male or female, such person may make an application, along with a certificate issued to that effect by the Medical Superintendent or Chief Medical Officer of the medical institution in which that person has undergone surgery, to the District Magistrate for revised certificate, in such form and manner as may be prescribed. (2) The District Magistrate shall, on receipt of an application along with the certificate issued by the Medical Superintendent or Chief Medical Officer, and on being satisfied with the correctness of such certificate, issue a certificate indicating change in gender in such form and manner and within such time, as may be prescribed. (3) The person who has been issued a certificate of identity under section 6 or a revised certificate under sub-section (2) shall be entitled to change the first name in the birth certificate and all other official documents relating to the identity of such person: Provided that such change in gender and the issue of revised certificate under sub-section (2) shall not affect the rights and entitlements of such person under this Act."

43. Japan, Act on Special Cases in Handling Gender Status for Persons with Gender Identity Disorder. 2003. Article 3(1): "A family court may make a ruling of a change in the recognition of the gender status of a person who is a Person with Gender Identity Disorder and who falls under all of the following items, at the request of such person: (i) is not less than 20 years of age; (ii) is not currently married; (iii) currently has no child who is a minor; (iv) has no reproductive glands or whose reproductive glands have permanently lost function; and (v) has a body which appears to have parts that resembles the genital organs of those of the Opposite Gender."

44. South Africa, Alteration of Sex Description and Sex Status Act. 2003. Section 2: "Any person whose sexual characteristics have been altered by surgical or medical treatment or by evolvement through

natural development resulting in gender reassignment, or any person who is intersexed may apply to the Director-General of the National Department of Home Affairs for the alteration of the sex description on this or her birth register."

45. Ukraine, Order No 1041 of the Ministry of Health "on establishing biomedical and psychosocial indications of change (correction) of sex and approval of the form of primary records and instructions for its completion." 2016. Article 1: "Встановити медико-біологічні та соціально-психологічні показання для зміни (корекції) статевої належності, що додаються."

46. Mexico, Código Civil para el Distrito Federal. 1928 (Last amended 2015). Article 135 Bis § 3: "Se entenderá por identidad de género la convicción personal e interna, tal como cada persona se percibe así misma, la cual puede corresponder o no, al sexo asignado en el acta primigenia. En ningún caso será requisito acreditar intervención quirúrgica alguna, terapias u otro diagnóstico y/o procedimiento para el reconocimiento de la identidad de género." Article 135 Ter: "Para realizar el levantamiento de una nueva acta de nacimiento para el reconocimiento de identidad de género, las personas interesadas deberán presentar: I. Solicitud debidamente requisitada; II. Copia certificada del acta de nacimiento primigenia para efecto de que se haga la reserva correspondiente; III. Original y copia fotostática de su identificación oficial, y IV. Comprobante de domicilio. El levantamiento se realizará en el Juzgado Central, se procederá de inmediato a hacer la anotación y la reserva correspondiente; si se hiciere en un Juzgado distinto, se dará aviso mediante escrito al Juzgado en que se encuentre el acta de nacimiento primigenia para los mismos efectos anteriormente señalados. El acta de nacimiento primigenia quedará reservada y no se publicará ni expedirá constancia alguna, salvo mandamiento judicial o petición ministerial. Una vez cumpliendo el trámite se enviarán los oficios con la información, en calidad de reservada, a la Secretaría de Gobernación, Secretaría de Finanzas, Secretaría de Educación pública, Secretaría de Salud, Secretaría de Relaciones Exteriores, Instituto Nacional Electoral, Tribunal Superior de Justicia del Distrito Federal, Procuraduría General de la República, Centro Nacional de Información del Sistema Nacional y al Consejo de la Judicatura Federal, para los efectos legales procedentes."

47. On April 11, 2012, the Human Rights Tribunal of Ontario ruled that gender confirmation surgery is no longer required for a change in registered gender on Ontario documents. In its decision, the tribunal ordered that the Ontario government "cease requiring transgender persons to have 'transsexual surgery' (sic) in order to obtain a change in sex designation on their registration of birth" and has 180 days to "revise the criteria for changing sex designation on a birth registration." https://www.canlii.org/en/on/onhrt/doc/2012/2012hrto726/2012hrto726.html.

48. Mexico, Reglamento de Pasaportes y del Documento de Identidad y Viaje. 2011. Article 16: "En el caso de reasignación para la concordancia sexo-genérica no se considerará extemporaneidad el tiempo transcurrido entre el nacimiento y el nuevo registro. Lo anterior surtirá efectos una vez que la Secretaría sea debidamente notificada por la autoridad judicial competente y el interesado acompañe el acta correspondiente."

49. Indonesia does not have specific gender recognition laws, but a district court may allow a "change of sex" under population administration provisions for registering "other important events." That court decision can be submitted as evidence to change sex details on an identification card and birth certificate. https://ilga.org/downloads/ILGA_Trans_Legal_Mapping_Report_2017_ENG.pdf.

50. For further information about the "X" option on Canadian passports, see the JusticeTrans website. http://justicetrans.org/regional-information/national/passport/.

51. Costa Rica, Article 93 of the Organic Law of the Supreme Electoral Tribunal and Civil Registry. https://www.costaricantimes.com/no-more-gender-on-costa-rica-ids/65860.

52. Uruguay, Law No. 19580 - Law of Violence Towards Women Based on Gender. 2017. Article 22: "El Ministerio de Salud Pública y todo otro órgano y organismo vinculado a las políticas de salud y las instituciones prestadoras de servicios de salud, en el ámbito de sus competencias, deben: (J) Protocolizar las intervenciones respecto de personas intersexuales, prohibiendo los procedimientos médicos innecesarios en niñas, niños y adolescentes."

53. G.O.(Ms) No. 355. 2019. Article 5: "The Government, after careful examination of all the above points and based on the opinions of the experts as forwarded by the Director of Medical Education, have decided to ban sex reassignment surgeries on intersex infants and children except on life-threatening situations and ordered accordingly."

54. The questions regarding partnership and parental rights in this indicator set are: Can same-sex couples enter into a registered partnership or civil union? Can same-sex couples get legally married? Is second parent and/or joint adoption by same-sex partner(s) legally possible?

55. Canada Civil Marriage Act. 2005. Article 4: "For greater certainty, a marriage is not void or voidable by reason only that the spouses are of the same sex."

56. In Canada, every jurisdiction has its own laws and regulations on the matter, which were enacted in various years: Alberta (2007), British Columbia (1996), Manitoba (2002), New Brunswick (2008), Newfoundland & Labrador (2003), Northwest Territories (2002), Nova Scotia (2001), Nunavut (2011), Ontario (2000), Prince Edward Island (2009), Quebec (2002), Saskatchewan (2001).

57. In 2018, the Supreme Court ruled that same-sex marriage should be legal in Costa Rica. However, the decision did not immediately come into effect; rather, the court provided a grace period for Congress to adopt appropriate legislation.

58. In Mexico, some jurisdictions have allowed same-sex marriage: Baja California Sur (2019); Campeche (2016); Coahuila (2014); Colima (2016); Hidalgo (2019); Mexico City (2009); Michoacán (2016); Morelos (2016) [constitutional amendment]; Nayarit (2015); Nuevo León (2019); Oaxaca (2019); and San Luis Potosí (2019). In Quintana Roo (2012), same-sex marriages were allowed by local authorities through a progressive construction of local regulations. Similarly, in Baja California (2018) and Chihuahua (2017), local authorities have administratively allowed same-sex marriages to be performed. In several other states, judicial decisions have ordered the recognition of same-sex marriages: Aguascalientes (2019); Chiapas (2017); Jalisco (2016); and Puebla (2017).

59. For more information, see https://www.senado.gob.mx/64/seguimiento_a_reformas_constitucionales/64/.

60. Mexico, Código Civil para el Distrito Federal de 1928, enmendado en 2015. Article 391: "Los cónyuges o concubinos podrán adoptar cuando los dos estén conformes en considerar al adoptado como hijo y aunque solo uno de ellos cumpla con el requisito de edad a que se refiere este capítulo, pero siempre y cuando la diferencia de edad entre cualquiera de los adoptantes y el adoptado sea de 17 años cuando menos. En todos los casos ambos cónyuges o concubinos deberán comparecer ante la presencia judicial en el procedimiento de adopción."

61. The decision of the Constitutional Court in the case of *Minister of Home Affairs v. Fourie* on December 1, 2005, extended the common law definition of marriage to include same-sex spouses—as the Constitution of South Africa guarantees equal protection before the law to all citizens regardless of sexual orientation. In December 2018, the Civil Union Amendment Act of 2018 repealed section 6, which allowed a marriage officer to inform the minister that they objected on the ground of conscience, religion, and belief to solemnizing a civil union between persons of the same sex. See Mendos (2019).

62. The 2002 decision of the Constitutional Court in the case of *Du Toit v. Minister of Welfare and Population Development* amended the Child Care Act of 1983 to allow both joint adoption and stepparent adoption by "permanent same-sex life partners." Children's Act 38. 2005. Article 231: "(1) A child may be adopted- (a) jointly by- (i) a husband and wife; (ii) partners in a permanent domestic life-partnership; or (iii) other persons sharing a common household and forming a permanent family unit; (b) by a widower, widow, divorced or unmarried person; (c) by a married person whose spouse is the parent of the child or by a person whose permanent domestic life-partner is the parent of the child; (d) by the biological father of a child born out of wedlock; (e) or by the foster parent of the child."

63. Uruguay, Law No. 19.075 on Marriage Equality. 2013. Article 1: "Sustitúyese el artículo 83 del Código Civil, por el siguiente: ARTÍCULO 83.- El matrimonio civil es la unión permanente, con arreglo a la ley, de dos personas de distinto o igual sexo."

64. Uruguay, Ley No. 17.823. Código de la Niñez y la Adolescencia. 2004 (Amended in 2009). Article 135: "(Adoptantes) - 1) La adopción simple se permite a toda persona mayor de veinticinco años,

cualquiera sea su estado civil, y siempre que tenga por lo menos quince años más que el adoptado, y hubiera tenido al niño o adolescente a su cargo por el mínimo de un año. 2) El tutor no puede adoptar al niño o adolescente hasta que hayan sido aprobadas judicialmente las cuentas del cargo. 3) Nadie puede ser adoptado por más de una persona, a no ser por dos cónyuges que tengan por lo menos un año de matrimonio y hubieran tenido al niño o adolescente a su cargo por un término no inferior a un año. Si no se computara el año de matrimonio, pero hubiera existido durante dicho lapso un concubinato estable que culminó en matrimonio, se incluirá a los efectos de la tenencia, el período de la unión libre. Por motivo fundado y expreso, el Tribunal podrá otorgar la adopción aun cuando alguno de los cónyuges o ambos no alcanzaren la diferencia de edad con el adoptado o adoptada, reduciéndola hasta un límite que admita razonablemente que éste pueda ser hijo de los adoptantes. Ninguno de los cónyuges puede adoptar sin el consentimiento expreso del otro, salvo que estuviere impedido de manifestar su voluntad o que exista sentencia de separación de cuerpos. 4) Se permitirá la adopción por parte del nuevo cónyuge o concubino del padre o madre del hijo habido dentro del matrimonio o habido fuera del matrimonio reconocido del otro cónyuge o concubino. 5) Realizada la adopción, la separación o divorcio ulterior de los cónyuges no los exime de sus obligaciones para con el adoptado menor de edad."

65. See, for example, the cases of municipalities in Tokyo and elsewhere in the country (Power 2018).

66. Arunkumar v. Inspector General of Registration, WP(MD) No. 4125 of 2019. https://indiankanoon .org/doc/188806075/?__cf_chl_jschl_tk__=pmd_JiTWsrIZg7VyE4FrqtXs0EKxSDwj7VXZCRww 1KGkBug-1629302516-0-gqNtZGzNAiWjcnBszQi9.

67. The question regarding conversion therapy in this indicator set is: Are there any laws and/or regulations prohibiting/banning/protecting against sexual orientation and gender identity "conversion therapy"?

68. See the Principles on the Application of International Human Rights Law in Relation to Sexual Orientation and Gender Identity (Yogyakarta Principles). 2006. http://yogyakartaprinciples.org /principles-en/about-the-yogyakarta-principles/.

69. Although there are no nationwide bans on "conversion therapy" in Canada, an increasing proportion of cities and provinces have adopted or are considering adopting such bans. This includes the provinces of Manitoba (2015), Ontario (2015), Nova Scotia (2018), the city of Vancouver (2018), and the city of St. Albert (2019). Therefore, around 46 percent of the Canadian population lives in areas with legal bans in force.

   While there are also no nationwide bans on "conversión therapies" in Mexico, Mexico City recently amended its Criminal Code to ban them. Código Penal para la Ciudad de Mexico. Artículo 190 Quarter: A quien imparta u obligue a otro a recibir una terapia de conversión se le impondrán de dos a cinco años de prisión y de cincuenta a cien horas de trabajo en favor de la comunidad. Este delito se perseguirá por querella. Se entiende por terapias de conversión, aquellas prácticas consistentes en sesiones psicológicas, psiquiátricas, métodos o tratamientos que tenga por objeto anular, obstaculizar, modificar o menoscabar la expresión o identidad de género, así como la orientación sexual de la persona, en las que se emplea violencia física, moral o psicoemocional, mediante tratos crueles, inhumanos o degradantes que atenten contra la dignidad humana.

   Si la terapia de conversión se hiciere en un menor de dieciocho años de edad o persona que no tenga capacidad para comprender el significado del hecho o persona que no tenga la capacidad de resistir la conducta, la pena se aumentará en una mitad y se perseguirá por oficio.

70. See Asamblea Legislativa, República de Costa Rica, at http://www.asamblea.go.cr/SitePages/Inicio. aspx.

71. The question regarding sexual and gender minority asylum seekers in this indicator set is: Does your country recognize persecution based on SOGI as one of the grounds for asylum?

72. Canada, Immigration and Refugee Protection Act. 2001. Article 3(2): "The objectives of this Act with respect to refugees are: (d) to offer safe haven to persons with a well-founded fear of persecution based on race, religion, nationality, political opinion or membership in a particular social group, as well as those at risk of torture or cruel and unusual treatment or punishment."

73. For more information about settling in Canada as a refugee, see the website of the government of Canada at https://www.canada.ca/en/immigration-refugees-citizenship/services/refugees/help-outside-canada .html.

74. South Africa. Refugees Act 130 (amended in 2011). 1998. Article 3(a): "[A] person qualifies for refugee status for the purposes of this Act if that person owing to a well-founded fear of being persecuted by reason of his or her race, tribe, religion, nationality, political opinion or membership of a particular social group, is outside the country of his or her nationality and is unable or unwilling to avail himself or herself of the protection of that country, or, not having a nationality and being outside the country of his or her former habitual residence is unable or, owing to such fear, unwilling to return to it."

75. Kosovo, Law No. 06/L-026 on Asylum. 2018. Article 3(1): "Terms and abbreviations used in this Law shall have the following meaning: 1.18. Refugee: a person who owing to the well-founded fear of persecution for the reasons of race, religion, nationality, political conviction or belonging to a particular social group, is outside their country of nationality and is unable or, owing to such fear, is unwilling to avail himself or herself of the protection of that country, or a stateless person, who, being outside of the country of former habitual residence for the same reasons as mentioned above, is unable or, owing to such fear, unwilling to return to that country; 1.18.4. a group shall be considered to form a particular social group where in particular: 1.18.4.2. that group has a distinct identity in the relevant country, because it is perceived as being different by the surrounding society. Depending on the circumstances in the country of origin, a particular social group might include a group based on a common characteristic of sexual orientation. Sexual orientation cannot be understood to include acts considered to be criminal in accordance with national law of the Republic of Kosovo. Gender related aspects, including gender identity, shall be given due consideration for the purposes of determining membership of a particular social group or identifying a characteristic of such a group;"

76. Mexico, Ley sobre refugiados, protección complementaria y asilo político. 2011. Article 13: "La condición de refugiado se reconocerá a todo extranjero que se encuentre en territorio nacional, bajo alguno de los siguientes supuestos: I. Que, debido a fundados temores de ser perseguido por motivos de raza, religión, nacionalidad, género, pertenencia a determinado grupo social u opiniones políticas, se encuentre fuera del país de su nacionalidad y no pueda o, a causa de dichos temores, no quiera acogerse a la protección de tal país."

77. Uruguay, Ley 18.076 Derecho al Refugio y a los Refugiados. 2006. Article 2: "Será reconocido como refugiado toda persona que: A) Debido a fundados temores de ser perseguida por motivos de pertenencia a determinado grupo étnico o social, género, raza, religión, nacionalidad, u opiniones políticas se encuentre fuera del país de su nacionalidad y no pueda o -a causa de dichos temores- no quiera acogerse a la protección de tal país, o que careciendo de nacionalidad y hallándose a consecuencia de tales acontecimientos, fuera del país donde antes tuviera su residencia habitual, no pueda o -a causa de dichos temores-, no quiera regresar a él. B) Ha huido del país de su nacionalidad o careciendo de nacionalidad, ha huido del país de residencia porque su vida, seguridad o libertad resultan amenazadas por la violencia generalizada, la agresión u ocupación extranjera, el terrorismo, los conflictos internos, la violación masiva de los Derechos Humanos o cualquier otra circunstancia que haya perturbado gravemente el orden público."

References

Amnesty International. 2019. "LGBT Rights." https://www.amnesty.org/en/what-we-do/discrimination /lgbt-rights.

APF and UNDP (Asia Pacific Forum of National Human Rights Institutions and the United Nations Development Programme). 2016. *Promoting and Protecting Human Rights in relation to Sexual Orientation, Gender Identity and Sex Characteristics: A Manual for National Human Rights Institutions.* https://www.asia-pacific.undp.org/content/rbap/en/home/library/democratic_governance/hiv_aids/promoting-and-protecting-human-rights-in-relation-to-sexual-orie.html.

bne IntelliNews. 2020. "Kosovo's New Civil Code Opens the Way for Gay Marriage." July 8, 2020. https://www.intellinews.com/kosovo-s-new-civil-code-opens-the-way-for-gay-marriage-187099/.

Chiam, Zhan, Sandra Duffy, and Matilda Gil González. 2017. "Trans Legal Mapping Report: Recognition Before the Law." International Lesbian, Gay, Bisexual, Trans and Intersex Association (ILGA), Geneva. https://ilga.org/downloads/ILGA_Trans_Legal_Mapping_Report_2017_ENG.pdf.

Daly, Felicity. 2018. "The Global State of LGBTQ Organizing: The Right to Register." *Outright International*: 14.

Halili, Dafina. 2018. "Transgender Case Taken to Kosovo's Highest Legal Institution." *Kosovo 2.0*, July 31, 2018. https://kosovotwopointzero.com/en/transgender-case-taken-to-kosovos-highest-legal-institution.

IACHR (Inter-American Commission on Human Rights). 2015. *Violence Against Lesbian, Gay, Bisexual, Trans and Intersex Persons in the Americas.* OEA/Ser.L/V/II. Doc.36/15 Rev. 2.

Lopez, Oscar. 2018. "Fleeing Persecution, LGBT+ Migrants Seek Refuge in South America." *Reuters*, December 19, 2018. https://www.reuters.com/article/us-latam-lgbt-immigration/fleeing-persecution-lgbt-migrants-seek-refuge-in-south-america-idUSKBN1OI1MV.

Magni, Gabriele, and Andrew Reynolds. 2019. "Voter Preferences and the Political Underrepresentation of Minority Groups: Lesbian, Gay, Transgender and HIV+ Candidates in Advanced Democracies." Manuscript under review. http://fbaum.unc.edu/teaching/articles/Magni_Reynolds-VoterPreferences-LGBTcandidates_Manuscript.pdf.

Mendos, Ramón Lucas. 2019. *State-Sponsored Homophobia 2019: Global Legislation Overview Update.* Geneva: ILGA World.

Park, Andrew. 2015. "U.S. Response to Forming a National Human Rights Institution." The Williams Institute, UCLA School of Law, Los Angeles. https://williamsinstitute.law.ucla.edu/publications/us-nhri/.

Power, Shannon. 2018. "One of Japan's Biggest Cities Will Officially Recognize Same-Sex Couples." *GSN*, February 10, 2018. https://www.gaystarnews.com/article/one-japans-biggest-cities-will-officially-recognize-sex-couples/#gs.jx5ph8.

UNGA (United Nations General Assembly). 2013. *Report of the Special Rapporteur on the Situation of Human Rights Defenders.* A/HRC/22/47. New York: United Nations General Assembly. https://undocs.org/A/HRC/22/47.

UNGA (United Nations General Assembly). 2019. *Report of the Independent Expert on Protection against Violence and Discrimination Based on Sexual Orientation and Gender Identity.* A/74/181. New York: United Nations General Assembly. https://undocs.org/A/74/181.

US Library of Congress. 2019. "Japan, Law Requiring Surgery for Legal Change of Gender Ruled Constitutional." *Global Legal Monitor*, April 12, 2019. https://www.loc.gov/item/global-legal-monitor/2019-04-12/japan-law-requiring-surgery-for-legal-change-of-gender-ruled-constitutional/.

Zappulla, Antonio. 2018. "Forgotten Twice: The Untold Story of LGBT Refugees." *World Economic Forum*, January 19, 2018. https://www.weforum.org/agenda/2018/01/forgotten-twice-lgbt-refugees.

6
Protection from Hate Crimes

KEY FINDINGS

Canada and Uruguay are the countries that protect sexual and gender minorities the most from hate crimes, followed by Mexico.

One-quarter of the sample countries criminalize hate crimes based on sexual orientation and gender identity (SOGI) and consider crimes based on a person's SOGI to be aggravating circumstances under the law.

Only Costa Rica and Mexico have laws or regulations that require government agencies to collect data on hate crimes against sexual and gender minorities or those perceived as such.

Mechanisms to report and monitor hate-motivated acts against sexual and gender minorities exist in seven of the countries studied.

Only four countries offer training to professionals in law enforcement on how to recognize hate crimes and provide programs and assistance to victims of hate crimes.

It is advised that countries enact or amend laws to specifically prohibit hate crimes against sexual and gender minorities.

Importance of the Protection against Hate Crimes Indicator Set

Hate crimes are criminal acts motivated by bias or prejudice toward particular groups of people. To be considered a hate crime, the offense must meet two criteria. First, the act must constitute an offense under criminal law, and second, the act must have been motivated by bias. *Bias motivations* can be broadly defined as preconceived, negative opinions, stereotypical assumptions, intolerance, or hatred directed to a particular group that shares a common characteristic, such as race, ethnicity, language, religion, nationality, sexual orientation, gender, or any other similar common factor (OSCE 2009). Hate crimes leave lasting scars not only victims but also on whole communities. They weaken the sense that all people share common values and a common future (Boram 2016). At the 59th Session of the UN General Assembly, the Secretary-General noted that "while freedom from want and fear is essential, they are not enough. All human beings have the right to be treated with dignity and respect" (UNGA 2005, 34). Furthermore, "... such dignity and respect [must be] afforded to people [...] and must be protected through the rule of law" (UNGA 2005).[1]

> "LGBTI people experience discrimination and poor treatment because of their SOGI in many areas of public life, and often change their behavior because they fear that they will experience discrimination."
>
> —*Bachmann and Gooch (2017, 20)*

Insufficient legal protection against hate crimes leaves vulnerable groups susceptible to violence, discrimination, harassment, exclusion, and stigmatization. Moreover, the victims' integrity and dignity, and the dignity of others who share the victims' characteristics, are undermined. Victims of hate crimes often lose their sense of self-worth and belonging to a community and feel excluded.[2] This exclusion leads to marginalized citizenry and poverty, particularly because the exclusion of a group from the development agenda diminishes the group's potential within the society. Societies and countries thus pay a considerable price for exclusion. Recent World Bank reports advance the notion that social inclusion matters because the cost of exclusion is very high (Badgett 2014; World Bank 2013).

Actively criminalizing hate crimes, either as aggravating circumstances or as separate crimes, sends a strong message that society as a whole is willing to protect its most vulnerable members. It also sends the message that sexual and gender minorities deserve recognition, respect, and equality.[3] Together, such measures ensure "community cohesion" and "social stability" (OSCE 2009). Conversely, a lack of hate crime legislation signals to the victims that hatred and bias based on their identity are condoned (Alongi 2017). The resulting fear and insecurity preclude this group from capitalizing on opportunities that would lead to a better life (World Bank 2013). When sexual and gender minorities are denied full participation in society, microlevel economic harm ensues. Similarly, such violations are likely to affect the country's level of economic development (Badgett and others 2014).

Discrimination in the form of personal attacks affects the individual foremost. But such discrimination is also expressed in the broader macroeconomic environment, translating into overall poor health and poverty and leading to a smaller labor force and higher health care costs. McFee and Galbraith (2016) establish that when sexual and gender minorities are targets of violence, their contribution to the whole country is diminished. The study concludes that individual-level connections between rights and economic development amount to negative impacts on a country's overall economic development. In addition, exclusionary practices—such as bullying, harassment, violence, and discrimination—translate into underinvestment in human capital; without human capital, countries cannot harness sustainable economic growth (Badgett and others 2014).

Hate crimes also have unique psychological consequences. Perpetrators of hate crimes want their victims to believe that they are social outcasts. Victims suffer psychological harm because they cannot change the characteristics that make them a target of the crimes (Badgett 2014). But victims of hate crimes do not suffer alone; the repercussions of the crimes are felt within the community as a whole because the community carries the burden of potential security and public order problems (OSCE 2009). The disruption that hate crimes create leads to social tensions, putting pressure on law enforcement resources and the government. Hate crimes also tend to exacerbate underlying tensions among groups that experience constant discrimination (OSCE 2009). If a targeted group begins to feel that crimes against it are socially acceptable, integration becomes more difficult. Perpetrators will also be emboldened to commit more hate crimes because vulnerable communities lack adequate legal protection.

Despite the known legal, societal, economic, and psychological consequences, sexual and gender minorities continue to suffer from discrimination, abuse, violence, and hatred.[4] It is well-documented that victims of hate crimes can suffer deep and long-lasting mental health issues. A study conducted by the Latvian Centre for Human Rights found that victims of hate crimes suffer multiple psychological traumas, ranging from reduced self-confidence to constant anxiety (Latvian Centre for Human Rights 2008). As Transgender Europe reports, there were 331 cases of reported killings of transgender and gender-diverse people between October 1, 2018, and September 30, 2019. The majority of the murders occurred in Brazil (130), Mexico (63), and the United States (30), adding up to a total of 3,314 reported cases in 74 countries worldwide between January 1, 2008, and September 30, 2019 (TGEU 2019).

The indicator set on protection against hate crimes is critical to determine the existence and effectiveness of laws and mechanisms that criminalize hate crimes and provide protection for sexual and gender minorities. The indicator set evaluates whether crimes based on a person's SOGI are considered aggravating circumstances under the law. It also assesses whether laws or regulations require government agencies to monitor and collect data or whether mechanisms for monitoring and reporting hate-motivated acts of violence against sexual and gender minorities (or those perceived to be sexual or gender minorities) exist. This is crucial during the COVID-19 pandemic, when sexual and gender minorities face restrictions that may confine them to hostile environments; tracking the laws that protect them is especially important at such times (box 6.1). Moreover, the indicator set examines whether existing regulations mandate the provision of legal assistance, shelter or housing, forensic or medical examinations, and medical certificates. Finally, it analyzes whether laws or regulations require the training of professionals, such as law enforcement officers and health care providers, to identify hate crimes.

A 2017 survey conducted by the World Bank revealed that one in three LGBTI persons across the five Western Balkan countries and two European Union member states had been a victim of physical and/or sexual violence or was threatened with violence within the past five years.

—*World Bank (2018)*

BOX 6.1 Links between Data on Protection from Hate Crimes and COVID-19

During the COVID-19 pandemic, sexual and gender minorities have been subjected to attacks, and civil society organizations (CSOs) advocating for the rights of sexual and gender minorities have been targeted in some countries (Ghoshal 2020). Recent reports suggest an increase in homophobic and transphobic rhetoric.

Some countries have put in place movement restrictions based on sex, with women and men allowed to leave their homes on alternate days. Such policies put nonbinary and transgender people at risk of heightened discrimination, as they may be subjected to harassment (Ott 2020). Furthermore, because of stay-at-home restrictions, many sexual and gender minorities are confined in hostile environments, often with unsupportive family members or cohabitants, causing excessive mental and physical strain and preventing them from reporting hate crimes and hate speech.

Tracking laws that protect sexual and gender minorities from hate crimes and hate speech is important, as are mechanisms for monitoring and reporting hate-motivated acts of violence against sexual and gender minorities. Only 7 of the 16 countries measured by the *Equality of Opportunity for Sexual and Gender Minorities* (EQOSOGI) report have mechanisms for monitoring and reporting hate-motivated acts of violence against sexual and gender minorities; 12 of the countries have laws or regulations criminalizing hate crimes based on sexual orientation and gender identity (SOGI). Accurate data ensure effective monitoring and reporting of hate-motivated acts of violence and allow the study of patterns of change in hate crime incidents. Insufficient legal protection against hate crimes leaves sexual and gender minorities susceptible to violence, discrimination, harassment, exclusion, and stigmatization.

At all times, but even more urgently during the pandemic, countries should ensure that perpetrators of hate crimes are held legally accountable. They should provide adequate mechanisms to facilitate effective investigations and find ways to protect victims from hate crimes and hate speech during times of isolation.

Hate Crime Legislation

> To be considered a hate crime, an offense must meet two criteria: the act must constitute an offense under criminal law, and the act must have been motivated by bias (OSCE 2014).[5] Countries should ensure that perpetrators of hate crimes are held legally accountable (EU FRA 2018).[6]

Hate crime laws are usually in the form of new substantive offenses or aggravating circumstances clauses for existing crimes (OSCE 2009). Aggravating circumstances clauses increase the penalty for a base offense when the base offense is committed with a bias motive (Alongi 2017). Countries that have enacted hate crime legislation realized the need to raise awareness, which translates into more effective implementation and better police–community relations (OSCE 2009). Of the 16 countries analyzed, only Canada, Kosovo, South Africa, and Uruguay (representing 25 percent) have laws or regulations that criminalize hate crimes based on SOGI. The remaining 75 percent (Bangladesh, Costa Rica, India, Indonesia, Jamaica, Japan, Lebanon, Mexico, Mozambique, Nigeria, Tunisia, and Ukraine) lack specific laws, constitutional provisions, or regulations criminalizing hate crimes based on sexual orientation, gender identity, gender expression, or sex characteristics. Additionally, only Canada, Kosovo, Mexico, and Uruguay consider crimes based on a person's SOGI as aggravating circumstances under the law (figure 6.1).

FIGURE 6.1

Number of Analyzed Countries with Laws or Regulations Criminalizing SOGI-Based Hate Crimes, 2021

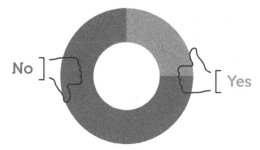

12 countries 4 countries

No   Yes

Source: World Bank Group, Equality of Opportunity database.

Note: SOGI = sexual orientation and gender identity.

Uruguay's Criminal Code provides enhanced penalties for crimes motivated by "sexual orientation" or "sexual identity." It criminalizes the incitement to hatred or any form of violence against a person or a group based on their sexual orientation or "sexual identity."[7] Furthermore, the law regulating audiovisual communication services prohibits the dissemination of content that promotes violence based on sexual orientation (among other grounds).[8] Kosovo's Criminal Code criminalizes hate crimes and hate speech against sexual and gender minorities and considers crimes committed on the basis of a person's gender identity and sexual orientation to be aggravating circumstances.[9] The South African Constitution prohibits discrimination based on sexual orientation.[10] Moreover, the Promotion of Equality and the Prevention of Unfair Discrimination Act (PEPUDA) prohibits hate speech on sexual orientation grounds.[11] However, crimes based on SOGI are not considered aggravating circumstances under the hate crime laws of South Africa.[12] Some contributors argue that although SOGI is not mentioned in PEPUDA, the legislation should be interpreted in tandem with the constitution, meaning that crimes committed against someone based on the person's SOGI will be considered to be aggravating circumstances under the law. In Canada, the Penal Code prohibits the promotion of genocide, defining it as killings or violence against a specific group. The term "group" is defined in the law as inclusive of sexual orientation, gender identity, or expression.[13] The Penal Code also provides that a sentence may be increased if a crime was motivated by hatred based on sex, sexual orientation, gender identity, or gender expression.[14] Finally, even though Mexico lacks national hate crime laws, in Mexico City and in the country's other 12 provinces, crimes committed based on a person's SOGI are considered to be aggravating circumstances.[15]

In early 2020, the government of Ukraine introduced three bills in the Ukrainian Parliament proposing amendments to the Criminal Code on the criminalization of hate crimes, including those based on SOGI.[16]

It is advised that countries adopt the following good practice policy actions:

■ Enact or amend laws to specifically prohibit hate crimes against sexual and gender minorities.

■ Recognize crimes committed against someone based on their SOGI as aggravating circumstances under the law.

■ Provide training to police and judges on hate crimes against sexual and gender minorities and amend sentencing guidelines to include aggravating circumstances for SOGI-motivated hate crimes (OSCE 2009).

Collecting Data, Monitoring, and Reporting Hate Crimes against Sexual and Gender Minorities

Accurate data ensure effective monitoring and reporting of hate-motivated acts of violence and allow the study of patterns or changes in hate crime incidents.[17] Maintaining reliable data is essential for effective policy formation and appropriate resource allocation in countering hate-motivated incidents (OSCE 2009). By providing a comprehensive picture of the problem and revealing the effectiveness of existing laws, data can help ensure the effective prosecution of hate-motivated acts of violence and egregious crimes committed against sexual and gender minorities. Collecting reliable data can also help authorities understand hate crimes and monitor the usefulness of programs designed to combat them. Finally, the existence of data assures victims that safe, reliable, accessible, and transparent reporting mechanisms have been put in place (OSCE 2014).[18]

Despite the importance of obtaining and analyzing relevant hate crimes data, only 2 of the 16 study countries (Costa Rica and Mexico) require government agencies to collect data on hate crimes against sexual and gender minorities or those perceived as such (figure 6.2). In Costa Rica, the Commissioner Office for LGBTI Affairs can collect data on gender identity and sexual orientation to adopt specific public policies that address the needs of sexual and gender minorities.[19] Similarly, Mexico's National Commission of Human Rights (Comisión Nacional de los Derechos Humanos) collects statistical data on the human rights situation in the country to improve relevant monitoring and reporting mechanisms.[20]

FIGURE 6.2

Number of Analyzed Countries That Require Agencies to Collect Data on Hate Crimes against Sexual and Gender Minorities, 2021

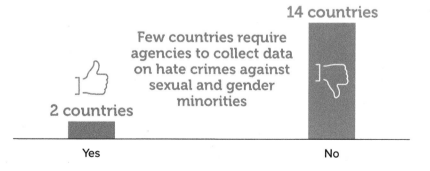

Source: World Bank Group, Equality of Opportunity database.

Seven countries (Canada, Costa Rica, India, Kosovo, Mexico, South Africa, and Uruguay) have mechanisms in place to report and monitor hate-motivated acts against sexual and gender minorities (figure 6.3). The Human Rights Commission in Ontario, Canada, for example, has a mandate to monitor the application of local laws and report human rights violations.[21] Relatedly, Costa Rica's Commissioner Office for LGBTI Affairs monitors discrimination and human rights violations faced by sexual and gender minorities in the country.[22] India's Human Rights Commission monitors ongoing threats against human rights.[23] Kosovo's Ombudsperson is explicitly authorized to monitor, defend, and protect individuals' rights and freedoms.[24] In Mexico, both the National Commission of Human Rights and the National Council to Prevent Discrimination (Consejo Nacional para Prevenir la Discriminación) are charged with monitoring and reporting all acts of violence against sexual and gender minorities.[25,26] Similarly, the South African Human Rights Commission monitors and assesses the observance of human rights in the country.[27] The commission is empowered by the South African Constitution to investigate and report the observance of human rights, take steps to secure appropriate redress when human rights have been violated, and carry out research and education.[28] Additionally, South Africa has established Equality Courts designated to hear matters relating to discrimination, hate speech, and harassment.[29] In Uruguay, the Honorary Commission against Racism, Xenophobia and Discrimination and All Other Forms of Discrimination (Comisión Honoraria contra el Racismo, la Xenofobia y toda otra forma de Discriminación) is responsible for recording acts that violate human rights and using these records to formulate judicial complaints if necessary.[30]

FIGURE 6.3

Analyzed Countries with Mechanisms for Monitoring Acts of Violence against Sexual and Gender Minorities, 2021

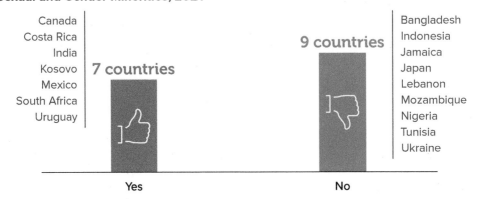

Source: World Bank Group, Equality of Opportunity dataset.

It is advised that countries adopt the following good practice policy actions:

- Adopt laws that authorize government agencies to collect data on hate crimes to counter hate-motivated crimes.

- Ensure effective monitoring and reporting of hate-motivated acts, such as harassment, bullying, and other forms of violence, to facilitate effective investigations and swift prosecutions.

- Monitor incidents of violence against people of diverse SOGI in places of detention and introduce policies to respect the self-identified gender identity and expression of transgender people.

Training Professionals in Law Enforcement and Victim Assistance to Recognize and Identify Hate Crimes and Provide Support Services to Hate Crime Victims

Training is an important step in hate crime prevention. Professionals in law enforcement and victim assistance agencies should be adequately trained to assist hate crime victims (McLaughlin and others 2000). Equipping professionals with the tools, strategies, and necessary information allows them to identify hate crimes and take appropriate actions to investigate, prosecute, and protect victims.[31] As first responders at a crime scene, police officers and health care professionals can properly assist the victim while reassuring the public of the government's genuine commitment to address and investigate hate crimes (OSCE 2009). Adequately trained professionals show empathy toward victims and initiate an immediate and thorough investigation, which sends a message to the community about the significance of the problem.

Similarly, legal professionals need sufficient training to recognize, investigate, and prosecute hate crimes. Most prosecutors must prove the bias element, which adds complexity to hate crime offenses compared with other criminal offenses. This complexity often leaves prosecutors unwilling or reluctant to charge perpetrators with hate crimes (Lopez 2017), violating the victim's right to equal justice. Assistance in legal matters, housing, medical examinations, and other forms of support are equally important for victims of hate crimes, especially for socially marginalized minorities.

Only Canada, Mexico, South Africa, and Uruguay legally mandate the training of professionals on hate crimes and other abuses (figure 6.4). Authorities in Ontario, Canada, designed a brochure for all police officers to supplement hate crimes training and have introduced hate crimes training for victim service workers.[32] Community legal services, such as Legal Aid Ontario, have also introduced guidelines for local police officers addressing SOGI issues, including a good practices manual on how to serve sexual and gender minorities (Ontario Association of Chiefs of Police 2013). In Mexico, both the National Commission of Human Rights (Ley de la Comisión Nacional de los Derechos Humanos) and the National Council to Prevent Discrimination (Ley Federal para Prevenir y Eliminar la Discriminación) provide education and training to prosecutors on abuses, including the rights of sexual and gender minorities.[33,34] In South Africa, the state is legally obliged to promote equality through assistance and training and to address complaints of discrimination, hate speech, or harassment against sexual and gender minorities.[35] Uruguay's national human rights institutions are mandated to offer training on identifying hate crimes to competent authorities, relevant ministries, and the courts.[36]

Canada, Mexico, South Africa, and Uruguay also provide support services—shelter and housing, legal assistance, medical or forensic examinations, and medical certificates—to victims of hate crimes. In Canada, access to legal aid in Ontario is regulated by the Legal Aid Services Act,[37] which offers legal aid to low-income individuals and disadvantaged communities in Ontario. Community legal clinics such as Legal Aid Ontario provide services to address the needs of low-income people and disadvantaged communities, including sexual and gender minorities who meet the criteria. In Uruguay, the law offers free legal assistance and shelter to female victims of crimes related to their sexual orientation and gender identity.[38] Similarly, the Honorary Commission against Racism, Xenophobia and Discrimination and All Other Forms

Analyzed Countries with Legally Mandated Training on Hate Crimes and Support Services to Victims, 2021

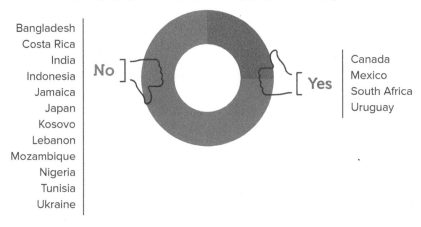

Source: World Bank Group, Equality of Opportunity dataset.

of Discrimination offers legal assistance and support to sexual and gender minority victims of abuses.[39] In South Africa, the state covers the cost of legal aid and advice, depending on the victim's personal circumstances, the nature and gravity of the charge, and whether other legal representation is available.[40] Similarly, Mexican law mandates the provision of services, such as legal assistance and housing, to any victim of a hate crime, including sexual and gender minorities.[41]

It is advised that countries adopt the following good practice policy actions:

- Enact laws and regulations that mandate training for professionals on recognizing hate crimes.

- Ensure that law enforcement professionals are equipped to effectively investigate hate crimes, identify bias or prejudice, show empathy, and protect victims when required. Provide community outreach programs and assistance to victims of hate crimes, such as free legal aid, shelter, forensics, medical examinations, and medical certificates.

Notes

1. See https://www.un.org/ruleoflaw/rule-of-law-and-human-rights.
2. See the Principles on the Application of International Human Rights Law in Relation to Sexual Orientation and Gender Identity (Yogyakarta Principles), 2006, available at http://yogyakartaprinciples .org/principles-en/about-the-yogyakarta-principles.
3. See the United Nations' Fact Sheet: International Human Rights Law and Sexual Orientation and Gender Identity at https://www.unfe.org/wp-content/uploads/2017/05/International-Human-Rights-Law.pdf.
4. See Human Rights Watch "LGBT Rights" available at https://www.hrw.org/topic/lgbt-rights.
5. The questions addressing hate crime legislation in the indicator set on protection from hate crimes include: Are there any laws, constitutional provisions, and/or regulations that criminalize hate crimes based on sexual orientation, gender identity, gender expression, and sex characteristics? Are crimes committed against someone based on that person's SOGI considered as aggravating circumstances by the law?
6. The EU 2018 report on hate crime says "[t]he proper identification and recording of hate crime is a vital step in ensuring that offenses are investigated and, where necessary, prosecuted and sanctioned, and that victims and their families are appropriately supported" (EU FRA 2018, 19).
7. Uruguay, Penal Code (as amended by Law 17.677). 2003. Article 149bis: "El que públicamente o mediante cualquier medio apto para su difusión pública incitare al odio, al desprecio, o a cualquier forma de violencia moral o física contra una o más personas en razón del color de su piel, su raza, religión, origen nacional o étnico, orientación sexual o identidad sexual, será castigado con tres a dieciocho meses de prisión." Article 149ter: "El que cometiere actos de violencia moral o física de odio o de desprecio contra una o más personas en razón del color de su piel, su raza, religión, origen nacional o étnico, orientación sexual o identidad sexual, será castigado con seis a veinticuatro meses de prisión."

8. Uruguay, Law No. 19.307. 2014. Article 28: "Los servicios de comunicación audiovisual no podrán difundir contenidos que inciten o hagan apología de la discriminación y el odio nacional, racial o religioso, que constituyan incitaciones a la violencia o cualquier otra acción ilegal similar contra cualquier persona o grupo de personas, sea motivada por su raza, etnia, sexo, género, orientación sexual, identidad de género, edad, discapacidad, identidad cultural, lugar de nacimiento, credo o condición socioeconómica."

9. Kosovo, Criminal Code, Law No. 06/L-074. 2019. Article 70, para. 2: "When determining the punishment the court shall consider, but not be limited by, the following aggravating circumstances . . . (12) if the criminal offense is a hate act, which is any crime committed against a person, group of persons, or property, motivated upon the race, color, gender, gender identity, language, religion, national or social origin, relation to any community, property, economic condition, sexual orientation, birth, disability or other personal status, or because of their affinity with persons who have the aforementioned characteristics, except if one of the enumerated characteristics constitutes an element of a criminal offense." Article 141: "Whoever publicly incites or publicly spreads hatred, discord and intolerance between national, racial, religious, ethnic and other groups or based on sexual orientation, gender identity and other personal characteristics, in a manner which is likely to disturb the public order shall be punished by a fine or imprisonment of up to five (5) years."

10. Constitution of South Africa. 1996. Article 9(3): "The state may not unfairly discriminate directly or indirectly against anyone on one or more grounds, including race, gender, sex, pregnancy, marital status, ethnic or social origin, colour, sexual orientation, age, disability, religion, conscience, belief, culture, language and birth."

11. South Africa, Promotion of Equality and the Prevention of Unfair Discrimination Act 4. 2000. Article 10(1): "(1) Subject to the provision in section 12, no person may publish, propagate, advocate or communicate words based on one or more of the prohibited grounds, against any person, that could reasonably be construed to demonstrate a clear intention to (a) be hurtful; (b) be harmful or to incite harm; (c) promote or propagate hatred. According to article 1, prohibited grounds are: race, gender, sex, pregnancy, marital status, ethnic or social origin, colour, sexual orientation, age, disability, religion, conscience, belief, culture, language and birth."

12. South Africa, Promotion of Equality and the Prevention of Unfair Discrimination Act 4. 2000. Article 28(1): "(1) If it is proved in the prosecution of any offence that unfair discrimination on the grounds of race, gender or disability played a part in the commission of the offence, this must be regarded as an aggravating circumstance for purposes of sentence."

13. Canada, Criminal Code. 1985. Article 318(1): "Everyone who advocates or promotes genocide is guilty of an indictable offence and liable to imprisonment for a term not exceeding five years." Article 318(2): "In this section, genocide means any of the following acts committed with intent to destroy in whole or in part any identifiable group, namely, (a) killing members of the group; or (b) deliberately inflicting on the group conditions of life calculated to bring about its physical destruction." Finally, Article 318(4): "In this section, identifiable group means any section of the public distinguished by colour, race, religion, national or ethnic origin, age, sex, sexual orientation, gender identity or expression, or mental or physical disability."

14. Canada, Criminal Code. 1985. Article 718.2: "A court that imposes a sentence shall also take into consideration the following principles: (a) a sentence should be increased or reduced to account for any relevant aggravating or mitigating circumstances relating to the offense or the offender, and, without limiting the generality of the foregoing, (i) evidence that the offense was motivated by bias, prejudice or hate based on race, national or ethnic origin, language, color, religion, sex, age, mental or physical disability, sexual orientation, or gender identity or expression, or any other similar factor."

15. Mexico, Código Penal para el Distrito Federal. 2002 (amended in 2016). Article 138: "El homicidio y las lesiones son calificadas cuando se cometan con: ventaja, traición, alevosía, retribución, por el medio empleado, saña, en estado de alteración voluntaria u odio...VIII. Existe odio cuando el agente lo comete

por la condición social o económica; vinculación, pertenencia o relación con un grupo social definido; origen étnico o social; la nacionalidad o lugar de origen; el color o cualquier otra característica genética; sexo; lengua; género; religión; edad; opiniones; discapacidad; condiciones de salud; apariencia física; orientación sexual; identidad de género; estado civil; ocupación o actividad de la víctima."

16. Ukraine, Bills 3316, 3316-2, and 3316-3. See http://w1.c1.rada.gov.ua/pls/zweb2/webproc4_1?pf3511=68552.

17. Questions addressing collecting data, monitoring, and reporting hate crimes against sexual and gender minorities in this indicator set are: Are there any laws and/or regulations that require government agencies to collect data on hate crimes committed against sexual and gender minorities or those perceived to be sexual or gender minorities? Are there mechanisms in your country for monitoring and reporting hate-motivated acts of violence against sexual and gender minorities?

18. See also IACP (2016).

19. Costa Rica, Decreto Ejecutivo 41158-MP. 2018. Article 2: "Las principales funciones del Comisionado serán: i) Coordinar con distintas instancias públicas, tales como el Sistema Nacional de Información y Registro Único de Beneficiarios del Estado (SINIRUBE) y el Instituto Nacional de Estadística y Censo (INEC), a fin de recolectar datos sobre identidad de género y orientación sexual para poder alimentar políticas públicas específicas de acuerdo con las distintas necesidades particulares."

20. Mexico, Ley de la Comisión Nacional de los Derechos Humanos. 1992 (amended 2018). Article 6: "La Comisión Nacional tendrá las siguientes atribuciones: XII. Supervisar el respeto a los derechos humanos en el sistema de reinserción social del país mediante la elaboración de un diagnóstico anual sobre la situación que éstos guarden. En dicho diagnóstico deberán incluirse, además de las evaluaciones que la Comisión pondere, datos estadísticos sobre el número, las causas y efectos de los homicidios, así como de las riñas, motines, desórdenes, abusos y quejas documentadas que sucedan en las prisiones, centros de detención y retención federales y locales. El diagnóstico se hará del conocimiento de las dependencias federales y locales competentes en la materia para que éstas elaboren, considerando las opiniones de la Comisión, las políticas públicas tendientes a garantizar el respeto de los derechos humanos de los internos."

21. Ontario's Human Rights Code. 1962. Article 1: "Every person has a right to equal treatment with respect to services, goods and facilities, without discrimination because of race, ancestry, place of origin, color, ethnic origin, citizenship, creed, sex, sexual orientation, gender identity, gender expression, age, marital status, family status or disability." Article 29: "The functions of the Commission are to promote and advance respect for human rights in Ontario, to protect human rights in Ontario and, recognizing that it is in the public interest to do so and that it is the Commission's duty to protect the public interest, to identify and promote the elimination of discriminatory practices and, more specifically, (a) to forward the policy that the dignity and worth of every person be recognized and that equal rights and opportunities be provided without discrimination that is contrary to law; (b) to develop and conduct programs of public information and education to, (i) promote awareness and understanding of, respect for and compliance with this Act, and (ii) prevent and eliminate discriminatory practices that infringe rights under Part I; (c) to undertake, direct and encourage research into discriminatory practices and to make recommendations designed to prevent and eliminate such discriminatory practices; …(e) to initiate reviews and inquiries into incidents of tension or conflict, or conditions that lead or may lead to incidents of tension or conflict, in a community, institution, industry or sector of the economy, and to make recommendations, and encourage and co-ordinate plans, programs and activities, to reduce or prevent such incidents or sources of tension or conflict; …(j) to report to the people of Ontario on the state of human rights in Ontario and on its affairs."

22. Costa Rica, Decreto Ejecutivo 41158-MP. 2018. Article 2: "Las principales funciones del Comisionado serán: a) Dar seguimiento y evaluar los planes contra todo tipo de discriminación por orientación sexual e identidad y expresión de género en las instituciones públicas. f) Dar seguimiento a las políticas contra discriminación hacia la población LGBTI establecidas en los Decretos Ejecutivos N° 38999 del 12 de mayo de 2015 y N° 40422 del 25 de mayo de 2017. g) Coordinar con los diferentes Ministerios e

instituciones de gobierno, y otros organismos nacionales e internacionales, todas las actividades relacionadas con garantizar la igualdad plena a las personas LGBTI en el país y el disfrute de sus derechos."

23. India, Protection of Human Rights Act. 1993. Article 12: "The Commission shall perform all or any of the following functions, namely: …(d) review the safeguards provided by or under the Constitution or any law for the time being in force for the protection of human rights and recommend measures for their effective implementation; (e) review the factors, including acts of terrorism, that inhibit the enjoyment of human rights and recommend appropriate remedial measures; …(g) undertake and promote research in the field of human rights."

24. Constitution of Kosovo. 2008. Article 132: "Role and Competencies of the Ombudsperson (1) The Ombudsperson monitors, defends and protects the rights and freedoms of individuals from unlawful or improper acts or failures to act of public authorities."

25. Mexico, Ley de la Comisión Nacional de los Derechos Humanos. 1992 (amended 2018). Article 6: "La Comisión Nacional tendrá las siguientes atribuciones: I.- Recibir quejas de presuntas violaciones a derechos humanos; II.- Conocer e investigar a petición de parte, o de oficio, presuntas violaciones de derechos humanos en los siguientes casos: a) Por actos u omisiones de autoridades administrativas de carácter federal; b) Cuando los particulares o algún otro agente social cometan ilícitos con la tolerancia o anuencia de algún servidor público o autoridad, o bien cuando estos últimos se nieguen infundadamente a ejercer las atribuciones que legalmente les correspondan en relación con dichos ilícitos, particularmente en tratándose de conductas que afecten la integridad física de las personas; XII. Supervisar el respeto a los derechos humanos en el sistema de reinserción social del país mediante la elaboración de un diagnóstico anual sobre la situación que éstos guarden. En dicho diagnóstico deberán incluirse, además de las evaluaciones que la Comisión pondere, datos estadísticos sobre el número, las causas y efectos de los homicidios, así como de las riñas, motines, desórdenes, abusos y quejas documentadas que sucedan en las prisiones, centros de detención y retención federales y locales. El diagnóstico se hará del conocimiento de las dependencias federales y locales competentes en la materia para que éstas elaboren, considerando las opiniones de la Comisión, las políticas públicas tendientes a garantizar el respeto de los derechos humanos de los internos; XV. Investigar hechos que constituyan violaciones graves de derechos humanos, cuando así lo juzgue conveniente o lo pidiere el Ejecutivo Federal, alguna de las Cámaras del Congreso de la Unión, el Gobernador de un Estado, el Jefe de Gobierno del Distrito Federal o las legislaturas de las entidades federativas."

26. Mexico, Ley Federal para Prevenir y Eliminar la Discriminación. 2003. Article 20: "Son atribuciones del Consejo: XXX. Promover una cultura de denuncia de prácticas discriminatorias."

27. South Africa, Human Rights Commission Act No. 40. 2013. Article 2: "The objects of the Commission are …(c) to monitor and assess the observance of human rights in the Republic."

28. South African Human Rights Commission. Programmes. https://www.sahrc.org.za/index.php/what-we-do/programmes.

29. For more details, see South Africa, Department of Justice and Constitutional Development, Equality Courts. https://www.justice.gov.za/eqcact/eqc_main.html.

30. Uruguay, Law 17.817 Lucha contra el racismo, la xenofobia y toda otra forma de discriminación. 2004. Article 5: "A esos efectos, será asimismo competencia de la Comisión Honoraria: G) Recibir y centralizar información sobre conductas racistas, xenofóbicas y discriminatorias; llevar un registro de las mismas y formular la correspondiente denuncia judicial si eventualmente correspondiere."

31. The questions addressing training professionals in law enforcement in this indicator set include: Are there any laws and/or regulations that mandate training of the following professionals on recognizing and identifying hate crimes (for example, police officers, prosecutors, judges, social workers, and paramedics/doctors)? Are there any laws and/or regulations that mandate the provision of any of the following services to victims of hate crimes (for example, legal assistance [including asylum applications and completing court forms] shelter/housing, forensic or medical examinations, and medical certificates)?

32. For more information about this brochure, see Ontario Human Rights Commission, the Hate Crimes Community Working Group Report and Initiatives in Schools, available at http://www.ohrc.on .ca/en/fishing-without-fear-report-inquiry-assaults-asian-canadian-anglers/appendix.

33. Mexico, Ley de la Comisión Nacional de los Derechos Humanos. 1992 (amended 2018). Article 6: "La Comisión Nacional tendrá las siguientes atribuciones: IX.- Promover el estudio, la enseñanza y divulgación de los derechos humanos en el ámbito nacional e internacional; XI.- Elaborar y ejecutar programas preventivos en materia de derechos humanos."

34. Mexico, Ley Federal para Prevenir y Eliminar la Discriminación. 2003. Article 20: "Son atribuciones del Consejo: XXXIX. Proporcionar orientación, formación y capacitación bajo diversas modalidades; XL. Sensibilizar, capacitar y formar a personas servidoras públicas en materia de no discriminación; XLI. Instrumentar la profesionalización y formación permanente del personal del Consejo."

35. South Africa, Promotion of Equality and Prevention of Unfair Discrimination Act 4. 2000. Article 25: "(1) The State must, where necessary with the assistance of the relevant constitutional institutions: (a) develop awareness of fundamental rights in order to promote a climate of understanding, mutual respect and equality; (b) take measures to develop and implement programs in order to promote equality; and (c) where necessary or appropriate (i) develop action plans to address any unfair discrimination, hate speech or harassment; (ii) enact further legislation that seeks to promote equality and to establish a legislative framework in line with the objectives of this Act; (iii) develop codes of practice as contemplated in this Act in order to promote equality, and develop guidelines, including codes in respect of reasonable accommodation; (iv) provide assistance, advice and training on issues of equality; (v) develop appropriate internal mechanisms to deal with complaints of unfair discrimination, hate speech or harassment; (vi) conduct information campaigns to popularize this Act. Contributors argued that section 25 of PEPUDA extends to all professionals tasked with the mandate of preventing hate crime."

36. Uruguay, Ley 17.817 Lucha contra el racismo, la xenofobia y toda otra forma de discriminación. 2004. Article 5: "A esos efectos, será asimismo competencia de la Comisión Honoraria: (J) Proporcionar al Ministerio Público y a los Tribunales Judiciales el asesoramiento técnico especializado que fuere requerido por estos en los asuntos referidos a la temática de su competencia;" Uruguay Ley 18.446. 2008. Institución Nacional de Derechos Humanos." Article 4: "La INDDHH será competente para N) Colaborar con las autoridades competentes en la educación en derechos humanos en todos los niveles de enseñanza y, especialmente, colaborar con la Dirección de Derechos Humanos del Ministerio de Educación y Cultura en los programas generales y especiales de formación y capacitación en derechos humanos destinados a los funcionarios públicos, particularmente en los previstos en el artículo 30 de la Ley No 18.026, de 25 de setiembre de 2006."

37. Ontario Legal Aid Services Act. 1998. Article 1: "The purpose of this Act is to promote access to justice throughout Ontario for low-income individuals by means of, (a) providing consistently high quality legal aid services in a cost-effective and efficient manner to low-income individuals throughout Ontario; (b) encouraging and facilitating flexibility and innovation in the provision of legal aid services, while recognizing the private bar as the foundation for the provision of legal aid services in the areas of criminal law and family law and clinics as the foundation for the provision of legal aid services in the area of clinic law; (c) identifying, assessing and recognizing the diverse legal needs of low-income individuals and of disadvantaged communities in Ontario; and (d) providing legal aid services to low-income individuals through a corporation that will operate independently from the Government of Ontario but within a framework of accountability to the Government of Ontario for the expenditure of public funds."

38. Uruguay, Law No. 19.580 Violence Against Women. 2017. Article 1: "Esta ley tiene como objeto garantizar el efectivo goce del derecho de las mujeres a una vida libre de violencia basada en género. Comprende a mujeres de todas las edades, mujeres trans, de las diversas orientaciones sexuales, condición socioeconómica, pertenencia territorial, creencia, origen cultural y étnico-racial o situación de discapacidad,

sin distinción ni discriminación alguna. Se establecen mecanismos, medidas y políticas integrales de prevención, atención, protección, sanción y reparación." Article 7: "Además de los derechos reconocidos a todas las personas en la legislación vigente, nacional e internacional aplicable, toda mujer víctima de alguna de las formas de violencia basada en género, tiene derecho: (G) A recibir orientación, asesoramiento y patrocinio jurídico gratuito, dependiendo de la posición socioeconómica de la mujer. Dicha asistencia deberá ser inmediata, especializada e integral, debiendo comprender las diversas materias y procesos que requiera su situación."

39. Uruguay, Law 17.817 Lucha contra el racismo, la xenofobia y toda otra forma de discriminación. 2004. Article 5: "A esos efectos, será asimismo competencia de la Comisión Honoraria: (I) Brindar un servicio de asesoramiento integral y gratuito para personas o grupos que se consideren discriminados o víctimas de actitudes racistas, xenofóbicas y discriminatorias."

40. Legal Aid South Africa Act. 2014. Article 22: "(1) A court in criminal proceedings may only direct that a person be provided with legal representation at state expense, if the court has (a) taken into account (i) the personal circumstances of the person concerned; (ii) the nature and gravity of the charge on which the person is to be tried or of which he or she has been convicted, as the case may be; (iii) whether any other legal representation at state expense is available or has been provided; and (iv) any other factor which in the opinion of the court should be taken into account."

41. Mexico, Ley General de Víctimas. 2013. Article 12: "Las víctimas gozarán de los siguientes derechos : (iv) A ser asesoradas y representadas dentro de la investigación y el proceso por un Asesor Jurídico. En los casos en que no quieran o no puedan contratar un abogado, les será proporcionado por el Estado a solicitud de la víctima de acuerdo al procedimiento que determine esta Ley y su Reglamento; esto incluirá su derecho a elegir libremente a su representante legal; La Comisión Ejecutiva, así como las Comisiones de víctimas de las entidades federativas, podrán cubrir los gastos que se originen con motivo de la contratación de expertos independientes o peritos a que se refiere el párrafo anterior, con cargo al Fondo o al Fondo Estatal, según corresponda." Article 117: "En materia de acceso a la justicia, corresponde al Gobierno Federal y a las entidades federativas, en el ámbito de sus respectivas competencias: (i) Promover la formación y especialización de agentes de la Policía Federal Investigadora, agentes del Ministerio Público, Peritos y de todo el personal encargado de la procuración de justicia en materia de derechos humanos; (ii) Proporcionar a las víctimas orientación y asesoría para su eficaz atención y protección, de conformidad con la Ley Orgánica de la Procuraduría General de la República, su Reglamento y demás ordenamientos aplicables; (iii) Dictar las medidas necesarias para que la Víctima reciba atención médica de emergencia; (iv) Proporcionar a las instancias encargadas de realizar estadísticas las referencias necesarias sobre el número de víctimas atendidas; (v) Brindar a las víctimas la información integral sobre las instituciones públicas o privadas encargadas de su atención; (vi) Proporcionar a las víctimas información objetiva que les permita reconocer su situación; (vii) Promover la cultura de respeto a los derechos humanos de las víctimas y garantizar la seguridad de quienes denuncian; (viii) Celebrar convenios de cooperación, coordinación y concertación en la materia, y (ix) Las demás previstas para el cumplimiento de la presente Ley, y las normas reglamentarias aplicables."

References

Alongi, Briana. 2017. "The Negative Ramification of Hate Crime Legislation." *Pace Law Review* 37 (1).

Bachmann, Chaka L., and Becca Gooch. 2017. *LGBTI in Britain: Hate Crime and Discrimination*. London: Stonewall. https://www.stonewall.org.uk/system/files/lgbt_in_britain_hate_crime.pdf.

Badgett, M.V. Lee. 2014. "The Economic Cost of Stigma and the Exclusion of LGBT People: A Case Study of India (English)." World Bank, Washington, DC.

Badgett, M.V. Lee, Sheila Nezhad, Kees Waaldijk, and Yana van der Meulen Rodgers. 2014. "The Relationship between LGBT Inclusion and Economic Development: An Analysis of Emerging Economies." The Williams Institute, UCLA School of Law, Los Angeles. https://williamsinstitute.law.ucla.edu/wp-content/uploads/lgbt-inclusion-and-development-november-2014.pdf.

Boram, Meredith. 2016. "The Matthew Shepard and Hames Byrd, Jr., Hate Crimes Prevention Act: A Criminal Perspective." *University of Baltimore Law Review* 45 (2): 343.

EU FRA (European Union Agency for Fundamental Rights). 2018. *Hate Crime Recording and Data Collection Practice across the EU.* Luxembourg: Publications Office of the European Union. https://fra.europa.eu/sites/default/files/fra_uploads/fra-2018-hate-crime-recording_en.pdf.

Ghoshal, Neela. 2020. "Uganda LGBT Shelter Residents Arrested on COVID-19 Pretext." Human Rights Watch Dispatches, April 3, 2020. https://www.hrw.org/news/2020/04/03/uganda-lgbt-shelter-residents-arrested-covid-19-pretext.

IACP (International Association of Chiefs of Police). 2016. "Investigation of Hate Crimes Model Policy Concepts & Issues Paper." Law Enforcement Policy Center, IACP, Alexandria, Virginia. https://www.theiacp.org/sites/default/files/2018-08/HateCrimesBinder2016v2.pdf.

Latvian Centre for Human Rights. 2008. *Psychological Effects of Hate Crime.* Latvian Centre for Human Rights. http://cilvektiesibas.org.lv/site/attachments/30/01/2012/Naida_noziegums_ENG_cietusajiem_Internetam.pdf.

Lopez, German. 2017. "Why It's So Hard to Prosecute a Hate Crime." *Vox*, May 23. https://www.vox.com/identities/2017/4/10/15183902/hate-crime-trump-law.

McFee, Rochelle, and Elroy Galbraith. 2016. "The Developmental Cost of Homophobia: The Case of Jamaica." *Washington Blade,* January, 2016. http://www.washingtonblade.com/content/files/2016/01/he-Developmental-Cost-of-Homophobia-The-Case-of-Jamaica_2016-1.pdf.

McLaughlin, K. A., S. M. Malloy, K. J. Brilliant, and C. Lang 2000. *Responding to Hate Crime: A Multidisciplinary Curriculum for Law Enforcement and Victim Assistance Professionals.* Newton, MA: National Center for Hate Crime Prevention, Education Development Center. https://www.ncjrs.gov/ovc_archives/reports/responding/files/ncj182290.pdf.

Ontario Association of Chiefs of Police. 2013. "Best Practices in Policing and LGBTQ Communities in Ontario."

OSCE (Organization for Security and Co-operation in Europe). 2009. *Hate Crime Laws, A Practical Guide.* Warsaw: OSCE. https://www.osce.org/odihr/36426?download=true.

OSCE (Organization for Security and Co-operation in Europe). 2014. *Prosecuting Hate Crimes: A Practical Guide.* Warsaw: OSCE. https://www.osce.org/odihr/prosecutorsguide?download=true.

Ott, Haley. 2020. "Trans Woman Fined for Violating Panama's Gender-Based Coronavirus Lockdown, Rights Group Says." *CBS News*, April 10, 2020. https://www.cbsnews.com/news/trans-woman-fined-for-violating-panamas-gender-based-coronavirus-lockdown-rights-group-says-2020-04-10/.

TGEU (Transgender Europe). 2019. "TMM Update Trans Day of Remembrance 2019." Transrespect versus Transphobia Worldwide (TvT), November 11, 2019. https://transrespect.org/en/tmm-update-trans-day-of-remembrance-2019.

UNGA (United Nations General Assembly). 2005. *Report in Larger Freedom: Towards Development, Security and Human Rights for All, Report of the Secretary-General.* New York: United Nations General Assembly. https://undocs.org/A/59/2005.

World Bank. 2013. *Inclusion Matters: The Foundation for Shared Prosperity.* Washington, DC: World Bank. https://openknowledge.worldbank.org/handle/10986/16195.

World Bank. 2018. *Life on the Margins: Survey Results of the Experiences of LGBTI People in Southeastern Europe (English).* Washington, DC: World Bank. http://documents.worldbank.org/curated/en/123651538514203449/Life-on-the-Margins-Survey-Results-of-the-Experiences-of-LGBTI-People-in-Southeastern-Europe.

Glossary

The glossary of terms and definitions provides a common basis of understanding and terminology related to sexual orientation, gender identity, gender expression, and sex characteristics (SOGIESC).

The terms are presented here in categories for clarity of comparison. These are common terms and definitions captured in the English language. It is important to note that sexual orientation and gender identity terms of identification vary across cultures and languages. Therefore, the list is by no means complete or exhaustive. The terms and definitions included below are in standard English.

Term/acronym	Definition
Acronyms	
EQOSOGI	Equality of Opportunity for Sexual and Gender Minorities
SOGI	Sexual orientation and gender identity
SOGIESC	Sexual orientation, gender identity, gender expression, and sex characteristics
LGBTI	Lesbian, gay, bisexual, transgender, and intersex people
LGBTI+	Lesbian, gay, bisexual, transgender, and intersex people, with "+" denoting everything on the gender and sexuality spectrum
LGB	Lesbian, gay, bisexual
LBT women	Lesbian, bisexual, and transgender women
Sex Classifications	
Sex	*Sex* refers to the classification of a person as female, male, or intersex. Infants are usually assigned a sex at birth based on the appearance of their external anatomy. A person's sex is a combination of bodily characteristics, including the person's chromosomes (typically XY chromosomes = male, XX chromosomes = female), reproductive organs, and secondary sex characteristics.
Sex assigned at birth	This phrase refers to the sex classification of people at birth, which is usually assigned by a medical practitioner after a brief review of a newborn's genitalia.
Sex characteristics	This phrase refers to each person's physical features relating to sex, including genitalia and other sexual and reproductive anatomy, chromosomes, hormones, and secondary physical features emerging from puberty.
Intersex	*Intersex* is an umbrella term that refers to people possessing one or more of a range of variations of physical sex characteristics that fall outside traditional conceptions of male or female bodies. Some intersex characteristics are identified at birth, while others may be discovered later in life. Note that *intersex* is not synonymous with *transgender*.

Gender Identity

Gender	*Gender* refers to social, behavioral, and cultural attributes, as well as expectations and norms associated with being male or female.
	The historical and contemporary record in many places indicates that various societies have understood gender beyond the binary concept of men and women.
Gender identity	This term refers to each person's profound internal and individual experience of gender (for example, of being a man, a woman, in-between, neither, or something else), which may or may not correspond with the sex they were assigned at birth or the gender attributed to them by society. It includes the personal sense of the body (which may involve, if freely chosen, modification of appearance or function by medical, surgical, or other means) and expressions of gender, including dress, speech, and mannerisms.
	Note that sense of self is separate from the sex assigned at birth and is unrelated to sexual orientation. In other words, gender identity is internal and is not necessarily visible to others.
Gender expression	*Gender expression* is the means through which individuals show their gender to the world, including through clothing, hairstyles, and mannerisms, among others.
Gender neutral	This term refers to the state of not identifying or being associated with being a man, a woman, or another gender.
	The term can apply to people, objects, language, policies, and institutions. For example, a gender-neutral bathroom can be accessed by people of any gender identity and expression.
Gender nonconforming	This term refers to people who do not follow other people's ideas or stereotypes about how they should look or act based on the female or male sex they were assigned at birth.
Gender binary	This term is the classification of gender into two distinct, opposite forms of masculine and feminine. As understanding of gender evolves, it has become increasingly clear that gender is a spectrum, and the binary approach fails to capture the nuances of lived gender experiences.
Gender diverse	This term refers to people whose gender identity and/or sex characteristics fall outside the traditional range of masculinity and femininity.
Masculinity/femininity	These terms refer to the possession of the socially, historically, and politically constructed qualities associated with men and women, or maleness and femaleness. The definitions change over time and from place to place.
Cis, cisgender	*Cis* or *cisgender* are used for people whose gender identity is in alignment with the sex assigned to them at birth, *cis* meaning "in alignment with" or "on the same side."
Transgender	*Transgender* refers to a person whose sex assigned at birth does not match their gender identity. The term *trans* is often used as shorthand.
Trans man	This is a person whose sex assigned at birth was female, but who identifies as male.
Trans woman	This is a person whose sex assigned at birth was male, but who identifies as female.
Transphobia	*Transphobia* is the irrational fear of those who are gender variant, or the inability to deal with gender ambiguity. It also describes discriminatory treatment of individuals who do not conform in presentation or identity to conventional conceptions of gender and/or those who do not identify with or express their assigned sex.

Cross-dresser, crossdresser	This term refers to an individual who generally identifies with his/her assigned sex but at times identifies with or personifies a different sex in gender presentation and dress. Cross-dressing is not necessarily indicative of sexual orientation or gender identity. Rather, cross-dressing is a form of gender expression.

Sexual Orientation

Sexual orientation	This term refers to each person's enduring capacity for profound romantic, emotional, and/or physical feelings for, or attraction to, person(s) of a particular sex or gender. It encompasses hetero-, homo-, and bisexuality and a wide range of other expressions of sexual orientation.
Queer	*Queer* is an umbrella term that includes lesbian, gay, bisexual, transgender, and intersex people, among others. For decades, *queer* was used solely as a pejorative for gays and lesbians but was reclaimed by activists as a term of self-identification.
Sexual and gender minorities	This term refers to persons whose sex, gender, sexual orientation, gender identity, and/or gender expression differ from those of the majority of the surrounding society.
Lesbian	*Lesbian* describes a woman who predominantly has the capacity for romantic, emotional, and/or physical attraction to other women.
Gay	*Gay* describes a man who predominantly has the capacity for romantic, emotional, and/or physical attraction to other men. The term is also sometimes used to describe women who are attracted to other women.
Heterosexual	*Heterosexual* describes people who are attracted to individuals of a different sex and/or gender identity from their own (also referred to as *straight*).
Bisexual	*Bisexual* describes people who have the capacity for romantic, emotional, or physical attraction to person(s) of the same sex or gender, as well as to person(s) of a different sex or gender.
Homophobia	*Homophobia* is the fear, hatred, or intolerance of homosexual people as a social group or as individuals. It also describes discrimination on the basis of sexual orientation.
Biphobia	*Biphobia* is the fear, hatred, or intolerance of bisexuality and bisexual people as a social group or as individuals.
Interphobia	*Interphobia* refers to negative attitudes and feelings toward people who are believed to possess biological sex traits that are not typically male or female, known as *intersex traits*.

Common Terms and Definitions

Child benefits	*Child benefits* may include but are not limited to maternity allowances, weekly or monthly child benefit allowances, and parental benefits to take care of children.
Hate crimes	*Hate crimes* are crimes that manifest prejudice against sexual or gender minorities and usually are typified in two ways: (1) in the form of a substantive hate crime law, such as in a separate provision within the law that includes the bias motive as an integral element of the offense. For example, if the offense of "assault" exists, but is different from a specific offense of "assault motivated by sexual orientation"; and (2) in the form of penalty enhancement laws, such as an "aggravating circumstance" such as increasing the penalty for a basic crime when it is committed with a bias motive.

Social housing	*Social housing* may include but is not limited to direct government-funded subsidies, rent supplements paid to private landlords, government-owned public housing, and caps or limits to rent increases.
Social pensions	*Social pensions* may include but are not limited to conditional or unconditional cash transfers for older individuals, different retirement ages, or the ability to combine part-time pension benefits with part-time jobs.
Subsidized health insurance	*Subsidized health insurance* may include but is not limited to government financial assistance for health insurance, insurance programs for individuals over a certain age, and health care coverage for pregnant women.
Unemployment insurance	*Unemployment insurance* may include but is not limited to a determined number of weeks of paid benefits, direct cash transfers, and petrol allowances.
Victim by association	A *victim by association* is an individual who may or may not belong to the protected category but is related to someone whom the perpetrator has a bias against. Because of that, the individual becomes a target of a hate crime. An example is a human rights defender or activist who is attacked for advocating the interests of certain groups or a particular issue.
Conversion therapy	Sometimes referred to as "reparative therapy," *conversion therapy* is any of several dangerous and discredited practices aimed at changing an individual's sexual orientation or gender identity.
Gender reassignment surgery	This phrase is the act or process of changing from living as a person of one sex to living as a person of the opposite sex by undergoing surgery, hormone treatment, and so on, to obtain the physical appearance of the opposite sex. Also known as *gender affirming surgery*.
Same-sex civil union	A *same-sex civil union* is a legally recognized arrangement similar to marriage, created primarily as a means to provide recognition in law for same-sex couples.
Same-sex partners	A *same-sex partner* is a domestic partner of the same genotypic sex.
Gender marker	A *gender marker* is an individual's efforts to convey gender identity.

Appendix A. Acknowledgments

This study was made possible by the generous contributions of lawyers, judges, academics, and civil society representatives from 16 countries. The names of local partners wishing to be acknowledged individually are listed below.

BANGLADESH

Dr. Monirul Azam
Stockholm University,
Department of Law

Bandhu Social Welfare
Society

Bangladesh Legal Aid and
Services Trust (BLAST)

Dr. Meghna Guhathakurta

Mohsina Hossain
Bangladesh Judicial Service

Dr. Shahnaz Huda
University of Dhaka,
Department of Law

Mr. Mustakimur Rahman
Notre Dame University
Bangladesh

Dr. Dinah Siddiqi
New York University

Ms. Sadiya Sultana Silvee
Bangladesh Institute of Law
and International Affairs
(BILIA)

CANADA

Mr. Lee Akazaki
Gilbertson Davis LLP

Mr. Michael Battista
Battista Smith Migration
Law Group

Ms. Andrea Luey
Justice for Children and
Youth

Ms. O'Neall Massamba
Eurovia Canada Inc. (VINCI
GROUP)

Mr. Marcus McCann
Symes Street & Millard LLP

N. Nicole Nussbaum
N. Nicole Nussbaum Barrister
& Solicitor

Ryan Peck
HALCO

Ms. Joanna Radbord
Martha McCarthy &
Company LLP

Mr. Shakir Rahim

Ms. Sabrina Rewald

Ms. Caroline Rivard

Amy Wah
HALCO

COSTA RICA

Mrs. Irene Aguilar
BLP Legal

Ms. Gabriela Arguedas
Ramírez
Universidad de Costa Rica

Mr. Manrique Blen
BLP Legal

Mr. Pedro Castro
BLP Legal

Mr. Herman Duarte
HDuarte Legal / Fundación Igualitos

Mr. Gabriel Duran
BLP Legal

Ms. Aleshka Isabella González Soto

Ms. Natasha Jiménez Mata
Mulabi/Latin American Space for Sexualities and Rights

Mr. José Mario Muñoz Araya

Ms. Alexa Narvaez
Lexincorp

Ms. Larissa Arroyo Navarrete
Asociación Ciudadana ACCEDER

Ms. Edna Julia Rodriguez Alvarado

Mr. Luis Salazar

Mr. Alonso Vargas
Lexincorp

Ms. Ana Luis Villegas
BLP Legal

INDIA

Mr. Nikhil Anand
Juris Chamber

Mr. Harsh Bajpai
The Dialogue

Shubha Chacko
Solidarity Foundation

Ms. Manpreet Chadha
Dhir & Dhir Associates

Ms. Katyayani Chandola

Mx. Avinaba Dutta
Sappho for Equality

Human Rights Law Network

KPS Kohli
Dhir & Dhir Associates

Ms. Anusha Madhusudhan

Mx. Gopi Shankar Madurai
Srishti Madurai LGBTQIA+ Student Volunteer Movement, Tamil Nadu, India

Dr. Sutapa Majumdar
Centre for Advocacy and Research

Ms. Rutuja Pol

Minakshi Sanyal
Sappho for Equality

Ms. Akhila Sivadas
Centre for Advocacy and Research

Prashant Singh
Advocate, Supreme Court of India

Ms. Rhea Suri
Enhesa SA

Mr. Siddharth Tewari
Tax N Legal Partner LLP

Gyan Tripathi
Symbiosis International University

Mr. Eklavya Vasudev

Mr. Ajay Verma
Juris Chamber

Mr. V. Daniel Vinod Kumar
Centre for Advocacy and Research

INDONESIA

Rangga Adityawarman
Suhardi Somomoeljono & Associates

Mr. Diovio Alfath
Sandya Institute for Peace and Human Rights

Bas Dejong
PNB Law Firm

Mr. Philo Dellano
PNB Law Firm

Ms. Jihan Fairuz
Youth Interfaith Forum on Sexuality (YIFoS)

Mr. Ricky Gunawan
LBH Masyarakat (LBHM)

Jurisdito Hutomo Hardy
Suhardi Somomoeljono & Associates

Moch Fahmi Try Hindami

Suhardi Somomoeljono & Associates

Indonesia Legal Aid Foundation-Pekanbaru Legal Aid Institution

Perkumpulan Keluarga Berencana Indonesia (PKBI)

Mr. Dianyndra Kusuma Hardy
Suhardi Somomoeljono & Associates

Gede Widya Mintaraga
Suhardi Somomoeljono & Associates

Faris Muhammad Rabbani
Suhardi Somomoeljono & Associates

Mr. Fernando Sihotang

JAMAICA

Ms. Katrian Clarke
Stand Up for Jamaica

Mr. Alexander Corrie
Livingston, Alexander & Levy

Mr. Ivan Cruickshank
Caribbean Vulnerable Communities Coalition (CVC)

Ms. Maria Carla Gullotta
Stand Up for Jamaica

Mr. Neish McLean
OutRight Action International

Mr. Glenroy Murray
J-FLAG

Ms. Jodi-Ann Quarrie

Ms. Kathryn Williams
Livingston, Alexander & Levy

JAPAN

Dr. Ronni Alexander
Kobe University

Ms. Yukari Ando
Osaka University

Ai Mori
Aso Himawari Foundation Legal Office

Youmi Moriya
Japan Alliance for Legislation to Remove Social Barriers based on Sexual Orientation and Gender Identity (J-ALL)

Akira Nishiyama
Japan Alliance for Legislation to Remove Social Barriers based on Sexual Orientation and Gender Identity (J-ALL)

Ms. Shizuka Onoyama
Junpo Law Office

Mr. Fumino Sugiyama
NPO Tokyo Rainbow Pride

Dr. Hiroyuki Taniguchi
Kanazawa University

Mika Yakushi
Certified NPO ReBit

Shinya Yamagata
NPO Tokyo Rainbow Pride

Ms. Azusa Yamashita
Hirosaki University

KOSOVO

Genc Boga
Boga and Associates

Sokol Elmazaj
Boga and Associates

Mr. Habit Hajredini
Office for Good Governance, Human Rights, Equal Opportunities and Gender Issues, Office of the Prime Minister of Kosovo

Ms. Rina Kika
Kika & Associates Sh.p.k.

Mr. Besim Morina

Ms. Ariana Qosaj Mustafa
Kosovar Institute for
Policy Research and
Development-KIPRED

Delvina Nallbani
Boga and Associates

Mr. Kushtrim Palushi
Ramaj & Palushi LLC

Ms. Vjosa Pllana
Raiffeisen Bank

Mr. Nezir Sinani
BIC Europe

Mr. Liridon Veliu
Center for Social Group
Development (CSGD)

Blendi Zhitija
Boga and Associates

LEBANON

Mario Abboud
MOSAIC

Mr. Georges Azzi
Arab Foundation for
Freedoms and Equality

Mrs. Brigitte Chelebian
Justice Without Frontiers

Pia Maria el Dabbak
MOSAIC

Mr. Fadel Fakih
Lebanese Center for Human
Rights

Mr. George Ghali
ALEF act for human rights

Mr. Nabil Halabi
Lebanese Institute for
Democracy and Human
Rights (LIFE)

Mrs. Djurdja Lazic
Moarbes LLP

Dr. Charbel Maydaa
MOSAIC

Mr. Charbel Moarbes
Moarbes LLP

Mr. Karim Nammour

Layal Sakr
SEEDS for Legal Initiatives

Ms. Myriam Sfeir
Arab Institute for Women
at the Lebanese American
University

Mr. Tarek Zeidan
Helem

MEXICO

Dr. Laura Alicia Camarillo
Govea
Universidad Autónoma de
Baja California

Comisión de Derechos
Humanos de la Ciudad de
México

Consejo para Prevenir y
Eliminar la Discriminación
de la Ciudad de México
(COPRED)

Mr. Marco Antonio Corral

Mr. Juan Pablo Delgado
AMICUS DH, A.C.

Ms. Rebeca Lorea
AMICUS DH, A.C.

Mr. Javier Meléndez
AMICUS DH, A.C.

Dr. Juan Carlos Mendoza
Pérez
Universidad Nacional
Autónoma de México

Mr. Roberto Perez Baeza
Fundación Arcoíris por el
Respeto AC

Mr. Enrique Torre Molina
Colmena 41

Ms. Estefania Vela Barba
Intersecta

MOZAMBIQUE

Mr. Frank Bernardo Amade Lileza
LAMBDA

Joyce Cossa
SAL & Caldeira Advogados, Lda

Ms. Maria Fernanda Lopez
FL & A Advogados

Ms. Zaida Lumbela
FL & A Advogados

Ms. Gimina Mahumana Langa
SAL & Caldeira Advogados, Lda

Ms. Deisy Massango
Foundation for Community Development

Diana Ramalho
SAL & Caldeira Advogados, Lda

Dionisio Varela
Foundation for Community Development

Gercia Xavier
Foundation for Community Development

NIGERIA

Temidayo Adewoye
Perchstone & Graeys LP

Adeola Ajayi
Udo Udoma & Belo-Osagie

Mr. Manuel Akinshola
Jacobs & Bigaels

Michael Amalumilo
Access to Good Health Initiative (AGHI)

Mr. Olusola Jegede
Resolution Law Firm

Mr. Folabi Kuti
Perchstone & Graeys LP

Kike Lamidi
HURILAWS

Ozofu Ogiemudia
Udo Udoma & Belo-Osagie

Mr. Collins Okeke
HURILAWS

Mr. Tochukwu Okereke
Centre for the Right to Health

Ogechi Onyeonoro
Machidoles Health Organization

Damilola Oyelade
Perchstone & Graeys LP

Ms. Chinenye Monde-Anumihe

Morenike Saula
George Washington University Law School

SOUTH AFRICA

Dr. Oyeniyi Abe
Centre for Human Rights, University of Pretoria

Jacquie Cassette
Cliffe Dekker Hofmeyr

Mr. Jose Jorge
Cliffe Dekker Hofmeyr

Busi Kamolane
Centre for Applied Legal Studies (CALS) WITS University

Mr. Neil Kirby
Werksmans Attorneys

Ms. Charlene May
Women's Legal Centre

Virginia Magwaza

Vuyo Mntonintshi
Centre for Applied Legal Studies (CALS) WITS University

Ms. Zamathiyane Mthiyane
Werksmans Attorneys

Thabisani Ncube
AIDS Foundation

Lebina Phukuille

Alana Porter

Ms. Sheena Swemmer
Centre for Applied Legal Studies (CALS) WITS University

Siyabonga Tembe
Cliffe Dekker Hofmeyr

Anastasia Vatalidis
Werksmans Attorneys

Mr. Anthony Waldhausen
Gay and Lesbian Network

Daniella Van Wyk
Werksmans Attorneys

TUNISIA

Badr Baabou
Damj, pour la justice et
l'égalité

Ms. Yosr El Benna

Chaima Bouhlel

Eric Goldstein

UKRAINE

Mr. Oleh Andreikiv
Kinstellar Ukraine

Ms. Olena Bondarenko
Social Action Centre NGO

Anna Kirey
Amnesty International -
Regional Office for Eastern
Europe and Central Asia

Ms. Olena Mykhalchenko

Oksana Pokalchuk
Amnesty International
–Ukraine

Volodymyr Selivanenko
Amnesty International
–Ukraine

Ms. Olena Shevchenko
Insight

Aminat Suleymanova
Avellum

Anna Synytsya
Syntyk & Partners LLC

Mr. Denys Sytnyk
Syntyk & Partners LLC

URUGUAY

Ms. Lilián Abracinskas
Mujer y Salud en Uruguay

Mr. Mauricio Coitiño

Colectivo Ovejas Negras

Ms. Ana Gabriela Fernández
Facultad Latinoamericana de
Ciencias Sociales (FLACSO)

Lic. Enf. Florencia Forrisi
Ministerio de Salud

Mr. Heber Tito Gálvez

Mr. Federico José Graña
Viñoly
Ministerio de Desarrollo
Social

Sr. Sergio Miranda
Cámara de Comercio y
Negocios LGBT de Uruguay

Mr. Santiago Puyol
Mujer y Salud en Uruguay

Dr. Martin Risso Ferrand
Catholic University of
Uruguay (U.C.U.)

Mr. Diego Sempol
Universidad de la República

Ms. Dahyana Suárez
Mujer y Salud en Uruguay

Appendix B. Country Score Tables and Indicator Sets

The first group of tables in this appendix summarize the Equality of Opportunity for Sexual and Gender Minorities (EQOSOGI) scores for each of the countries analyzed.

TABLE B.1

Bangladesh EQOSOGI Scores

Indicator set	EQOSOGI score
Criminalization and SOGI	2.5
Access to Inclusive Education	0
Access to the Labor Market	0.75
Access to Public Service and Social Protection	1.25
Civil and Political Inclusion	4
Protection from Hate Crimes	0

TABLE B.2

Canada EQOSOGI Scores

Indicator set	EQOSOGI score
Criminalization and SOGI	10
Access to Inclusive Education	8.8
Access to the Labor Market	8.25
Access to Public Service and Social Protection	10
Civil and Political Inclusion	7.5
Protection from Hate Crimes	6.8

TABLE B.3

Costa Rica EQOSOGI Scores

Indicator set	EQOSOGI score
Criminalization and SOGI	10
Access to Inclusive Education	8.8
Access to the Labor Market	7.75
Access to Public Service and Social Protection	8.75
Civil and Political Inclusion	8
Protection from Hate Crimes	3.2

TABLE B.4

India EQOSOGI Scores

Indicator set	EQOSOGI score
Criminalization and SOGI	7.5
Access to Inclusive Education	7.6
Access to the Labor Market	6.75
Access to Public Service and Social Protection	5
Civil and Political Inclusion	5.5
Protection from Hate Crimes	1.6

TABLE B.5

Indonesia EQOSOGI Scores

Indicator set	EQOSOGI score
Criminalization and SOGI	7.5
Access to Inclusive Education	0
Access to the Labor Market	0.75
Access to Public Service and Social Protection	1.25
Civil and Political Inclusion	3.5
Protection from Hate Crimes	0

TABLE B.6

Jamaica EQOSOGI Scores

Indicator set	EQOSOGI score
Criminalization and SOGI	2.5
Access to Inclusive Education	0
Access to the Labor Market	4.5
Access to Public Service and Social Protection	1.25
Civil and Political Inclusion	3
Protection from Hate Crimes	0

TABLE B.7

Japan EQOSOGI Scores

Indicator set	EQOSOGI score
Criminalization and SOGI	10
Access to Inclusive Education	1.2
Access to the Labor Market	0.75
Access to Public Service and Social Protection	1.25
Civil and Political Inclusion	4
Protection from Hate Crimes	0

TABLE B.8

Kosovo EQOSOGI Scores

Indicator set	EQOSOGI score
Criminalization and SOGI	10
Access to Inclusive Education	5.2
Access to the Labor Market	7.75
Access to Public Service and Social Protection	8.75
Civil and Political Inclusion	4
Protection from Hate Crimes	5.2

TABLE B.9

Lebanon EQOSOGI Scores

Indicator set	EQOSOGI score
Criminalization and SOGI	2.5
Access to Inclusive Education	0
Access to the Labor Market	0.75
Access to Public Service and Social Protection	1.25
Civil and Political Inclusion	2
Protection from Hate Crimes	0

TABLE B.10

Mexico EQOSOGI Scores

Indicator set	EQOSOGI score
Criminalization and SOGI	10
Access to Inclusive Education	4.4
Access to the Labor Market	7.5
Access to Public Service and Social Protection	10
Civil and Political Inclusion	7.5
Protection from Hate Crimes	6.4

TABLE B.11

Mozambique EQOSOGI Scores

Indicator set	EQOSOGI score
Criminalization and SOGI	10
Access to Inclusive Education	0
Access to the Labor Market	3
Access to Public Service and Social Protection	1.25
Civil and Political Inclusion	2
Protection from Hate Crimes	0

TABLE B.12

Nigeria EQOSOGI Scores

Indicator set	EQOSOGI score
Criminalization and SOGI	2.5
Access to Inclusive Education	0
Access to the Labor Market	0.75
Access to Public Service and Social Protection	0
Civil and Political Inclusion	1
Protection from Hate Crimes	0

TABLE B.13

South Africa EQOSOGI Scores

Indicator set	EQOSOGI score
Criminalization and SOGI	10
Access to Inclusive Education	7.6
Access to the Labor Market	8.5
Access to Public Service and Social Protection	10
Civil and Political Inclusion	7
Protection from Hate Crimes	5.2

TABLE B.14

Tunisia EQOSOGI Scores

Indicator set	EQOSOGI score
Criminalization and SOGI	2.5
Access to Inclusive Education	0
Access to the Labor Market	0.75
Access to Public Service and Social Protection	1.25
Civil and Political Inclusion	2
Protection from Hate Crimes	0

TABLE B.15

Ukraine EQOSOGI Scores

Indicator set	EQOSOGI score
Criminalization and SOGI	10
Access to Inclusive Education	0
Access to the Labor Market	6
Access to Public Service and Social Protection	1.25
Civil and Political Inclusion	3
Protection from Hate Crimes	0

TABLE B.16

Uruguay EQOSOGI Scores

Indicator set	EQOSOGI score
Criminalization and SOGI	10
Access to Inclusive Education	7.6
Access to the Labor Market	6.75
Access to Public Service and Social Protection	10
Civil and Political Inclusion	7
Protection from Hate Crimes	8.4

The following group of tables present the six indicator sets along with each of the analyzed countries' response to the questions.

TABLE B.17

Data Points for the Criminalization and SOGI Indicator Set

Country	1. Criminalization and SOGI questions			
	1.1 Are there any laws, constitutional provision, and/or regulations that criminalize people on the basis of sexual orientation, gender identity, gender expression, and sex characteristics?	1.2 Does your country criminalize same-sex relations between consenting adults?	1.3 Is the legal age for consensual sex the same for heterosexuals as for sexual and gender minorities?	1.4 Are sexual and gender minorities targeted with other laws such as vagrancy, public nuisance, or public morals?
Bangladesh	Yes	Yes	Yes	Yes
Canada	No	No	Yes	No
Costa Rica	No	No	Yes	No
India	No	No	Yes	Yes
Indonesia	No	No	Yes	Yes
Jamaica	Yes	Yes	Yes	Yes
Japan	No	No	Yes	No
Kosovo	No	No	Yes	No
Lebanon	Yes	Yes	Yes	Yes
Mexico	No	No	Yes	No
Mozambique	No	No	Yes	No
Nigeria	Yes	Yes	Yes	Yes
South Africa	No	No	Yes	No
Tunisia	Yes	Yes	Yes	Yes
Ukraine	No	No	Yes	No
Uruguay	No	No	Yes	No

TABLE B.18

Data Points for the Access to Inclusive Education Indicator Set

Country	2. Access to inclusive education questions						
	2.1 Are there any laws, constitutional provisions, and/or regulations that prohibit discrimination against students and/or teachers in educational settings on the basis of sexual orientation, gender identity, gender expression, and sex characteristics?	2.2 Are there any laws and/or regulations that prohibit discrimination in school admission on the basis of SOGI?	2.3 Are there any laws and/or or regulations preventing and addressing bullying and harassment against students and/or teachers in the educational system that include students based on actual or perceived SOGI?	2.4 Are there any laws and/or regulations that mandate the revision of national textbooks/national curriculum in primary and secondary education to eliminate discriminatory language (homophobic or transphobic language, for example)?	2.5 Are there any laws and/or regulations that mandate training of schoolteachers and other school staff in primary and secondary education on antidiscrimination of students who are sexual and gender minorities, or those perceived as such?	2.6 Are there any laws and/or or regulations that mandate the creation of courses on sex education in a SOGI-inclusive manner in secondary and tertiary education?	2.7 Are there any concrete mechanisms (national or local) for reporting cases of SOGI-related discrimination, violence, and bullying toward students, including incidents perpetrated by representatives of the education sector such as teachers and other school staff?
Bangladesh	No	No	No	No	No	No	No
Canada	Yes	Yes	Yes	Yes	Yes	No	Yes
Costa Rica	Yes	Yes	Yes	No	Yes	Yes	Yes
India	Yes	Yes	Yes	No	Yes	No	Yes
Indonesia	No	No	No	No	No	No	No
Jamaica	No	No	No	No	No	No	No
Japan	No	No	No	Yes	No	No	No
Kosovo	Yes	Yes	Yes	No	No	No	No
Lebanon	No	No	No	No	No	No	No
Mexico	Yes	Yes	No	No	No	No	Yes
Mozambique	No	No	No	No	No	No	No
Nigeria	No	No	No	No	No	No	No
South Africa	Yes	Yes	Yes	No	Yes	No	Yes
Tunisia	No	No	No	No	No	No	No
Ukraine	No	No	No	No	No	No	No
Uruguay	Yes	Yes	Yes	Yes	Yes	Yes	No

TABLE B.19

Data Points for the Access to the Labor Market Indicator Set

Country	3. Access to the labor market											
	3.1 Are there any laws, constitutional provisions, and/ or regulations prohibiting discrimination on the basis of sexual orientation, gender identity, gender expression, and sex characteristics in public and private sector workplaces at the national level?	3.2 Are there any laws and/ or regulations prohibiting discrimination in recruitment in the public sector on the basis of SOGI?	3.3 Are there any laws and/ or regulations prohibiting discrimination in recruitment in the private sector on the basis of SOGI?	3.4 Are there any laws and/or regulations prohibiting sexual and gender minorities from obtaining employment in specific industries?	3.5 Are there any laws and/or regulations prohibiting an employer from asking an individual's SOGI and/ or marital status during the recruitment process?	3.6 Are there any laws, constitutional provisions, and/or regulations prescribing equal remuneration for work of equal value for sexual and gender minorities?	3.7 Are there any laws and/or regulations prohibiting the dismissal of employees on basis of their perceived or actual SOGI?	3.8 Are there any laws and/or regulations that allow an employee to bring a claim for employment discrimination on SOGI grounds in the public sector?	3.9 Are there any laws and/or regulations that allow an employee to bring a claim for employment discrimination on SOGI grounds in the private sector?	3.10 Do victims of employment discrimination based on SOGI grounds have a right to free or reduced legal assistance (if proven they do not have the necessary means to cover the cost of the claim)?	3.11 Is there a national equality body or national human rights institution responsible for handling charges of employment discrimination related to SOGI?	3.12 Does the pension system for civil servants provide the same benefits to same-sex partners provided to different- sex spouses?
Bangladesh	No	No	No	No	No	No	No	No	No	No	No	No
Canada	Yes	Yes	Yes	No	Yes	No	No	Yes	Yes	Yes	Yes	Yes
Costa Rica	Yes	Yes	Yes	No	No	Yes	Yes	Yes	Yes	No	No	Yes
India	Yes	Yes	Yes	No	No	No	No	Yes	Yes	No	Yes	No
Indonesia	No	No	No	No	No	No	No	No	No	No	No	No
Jamaica	Yes	Yes	No	No	No	No	No	Yes	No	No	Yes	No
Japan	No	No	No	No	No	No	No	No	No	No	No	No
Kosovo	Yes	Yes	Yes	No	No	Yes	Yes	Yes	Yes	No	Yes	No
Lebanon	No	No	No	No	No	No	No	No	No	No	No	No
Mexico	Yes	Yes	Yes	No	No	Yes	No	Yes	Yes	No	Yes	Yes
Mozambique	No	No	No	No	Yes	No	No	No	No	No	No	No
Nigeria	No	No	No	No	No	No	No	No	No	No	No	No
South Africa	Yes	Yes	Yes	No	No	Yes	Yes	Yes	Yes	No	Yes	Yes
Tunisia	No	No	No	No	No	No	No	No	No	No	No	No
Ukraine	Yes	Yes	Yes	No	No	Yes	No	Yes	Yes	No	No	No
Uruguay	Yes	Yes	Yes	No	No	No	No	Yes	Yes	Yes	Yes	Yes

TABLE B.20

Data Points for the Access to the Public Services and Social Protection Indicator Set

Country	4.1 Are there any laws, constitutional provisions, and/or regulations that prohibit discrimination based on sexual orientation, gender identity, gender expression, and sex characteristics in accessing health care, social housing, public transportation, electricity, water supply, waste disposal services, microcredits, subsidized health insurance, social pensions, unemployment insurance, child benefits, other social services, and so on?	4. Access to public services and social protection questions											
		4.1.1 In health care?	4.1.2 In social housing?	4.1.3 In public transportation?	4.1.4 In electricity?	4.1.5 In water supply?	4.1.6 In waste disposal services?	4.1.7 In microcredits?	4.1.8 In subsidized health insurance?	4.1.9 In social pensions?	4.1.10 In unemployment insurance?	4.1.11 In child benefits?	4.1.12 In other services?
Bangladesh	No	No	No	No	No	No	No	No	No	No	No	No	No
Canada	Yes	Yes	Yes	Yes	Yes	Yes	Yes	No	Yes	Yes	Yes	Yes	Yes
Costa Rica	Yes	Yes	Yes	No	No	No	No	Yes	Yes	Yes	No	No	No
India	Yes	Yes	Yes	No	No	No	No	No	No	No	No	No	No
Indonesia	No	No	No	No	No	No	No	No	No	No	No	No	No
Jamaica	No	No	No	No	No	No	No	No	No	No	No	No	No
Japan	No	No	No	No	No	No	No	No	No	No	No	No	No
Kosovo	Yes	Yes	Yes	Yes	Yes	Yes	No	No	No	No	No	No	Yes
Lebanon	No	No	No	No	No	No	No	No	No	No	No	No	No
Mexico	Yes	Yes	Yes	Yes	Yes	Yes	Yes	Yes	Yes	Yes	Yes	Yes	N/A
Mozambique	No	No	No	No	No	No	No	No	No	No	No	No	No
Nigeria	No	No	No	No	No	No	No	No	No	No	No	No	No
South Africa	Yes	Yes	Yes	Yes	Yes	Yes	Yes	Yes	Yes	Yes	Yes	Yes	Yes
Tunisia	No	No	No	No	No	No	No	No	No	No	No	No	No
Ukraine	No	No	No	No	No	No	No	No	No	No	No	No	No
Uruguay	Yes	Yes	Yes	Yes	Yes	Yes	Yes	Yes	Yes	Yes	Yes	Yes	Yes

TABLE B.20

Data Points for the Access to the Public Services and Social Protection Indicator Set (continued)

Country	4.2 Are there any laws and/or regulations that allow civil society organizations to provide social services specifically to sexual and gender minorities? (for example, vaccinations, sanitation, transportation, family planning, health services—psychological, physiological, and sexual and reproductive; HIV preventive services [for example, condoms, lubricants, pre-exposure prophylaxis and so on]; and information on vulnerable sexual practices, antiretrovirals, medication for gender-reassignment surgery, support for transgender people during/after gender reassignment surgery)	4. Access to public services and social protection questions												4.3 Are there any laws and/or regulations imposing funding limitations on civil society organizations on the provision of such services?	4.4 Is there a national equality body or national human rights institution responsible for handling charges of SOGI-based discrimination in public services?
		4.2.1 Vaccinations?	4.2.2 Sanitation?	4.2.3 Transportation?	4.2.4 Family planning?	4.2.5 Health services (psychological)?	4.2.6 Health services (physiological)?	4.2.7 Health services (sexual and reproductive)?	4.2.8 HIV prevention services & information on vulnerable sexual practices?	4.2.9 Antiretrovirals?	4.2.10 Medication for gender-reassignment surgery?	4.2.11 Support for transgender individuals during/after gender reassignment surgery?	4.2.12 Other?		
Bangladesh	No	No	No	No	No	No	No	No	No	No	No	No	No	No	No
Canada	No	No	No	No	No	No	No	No	No	No	No	No	No	No	Yes
Costa Rica	No	No	No	No	No	No	No	No	No	No	No	No	No	No	No
India	Yes	No	No	No	No	No	No	No	Yes	No	No	No	No	No	Yes
Indonesia	No	No	No	No	No	No	No	No	No	No	No	No	No	No	No
Jamaica	No	No	No	No	No	No	No	No	No	No	No	No	No	No	No
Japan	No	No	No	No	No	No	No	No	No	No	No	No	No	No	No
Kosovo	No	No	No	No	No	No	No	No	No	No	No	No	No	No	No
Lebanon	No	No	No	No	No	No	No	No	No	No	No	No	No	No	No
Mexico	No	No	No	No	No	No	No	No	No	No	No	No	No	No	Yes
Mozambique	No	No	No	No	No	No	No	No	No	No	No	No	No	No	No
Nigeria	No	No	No	No	No	No	No	No	No	No	No	No	No	Yes	No
South Africa	No	No	No	No	No	No	No	No	No	No	No	No	No	No	Yes
Tunisia	No	No	No	No	No	No	No	No	No	No	No	No	No	No	No
Ukraine	No	No	No	No	No	No	No	No	No	No	No	No	No	No	No
Uruguay	No	No	No	No	No	No	No	No	No	No	No	No	No	No	Yes

TABLE B.21

Data Points for the Civil and Political Inclusion Indicator Set

Country	5.1 Are there laws and/or regulations that establish national human rights institutions that include sexual orientation, gender identity, gender expression, and sex characteristics within their mandate and/or specific institutions with expertise on and a mandate to deal with sexual and gender minority rights and inclusion?	5. Civil and political inclusion questions										
		5.2 Are organizations (NGOs and so on) related to (i) sexual minority rights, (ii) transgender rights, and (iii) intersex rights permitted under the law?	5.2.1 Sexual minority rights	5.2.2 Transgender rights	5.2.3 Intersex rights	5.2.4 If yes, are the NGOs subject to limitation by the state on the basis of national security, public order, morality, or other grounds?	5.3 How many members of parliament or other national, elected representative body openly self-identify as a sexual or gender minority?	5.4 Does the law mandate quotas for sexual and gender minorities in parliament?	5.5 Are there national action plans on SOGI?	5.6 Are there any laws and/or regulations that restrict expression, civic participation, or association related to SOGI?	5.7 Are there any centralized protocols for updating sex/gender in official certifications without pathologizing requirements?	5.8 Can same-sex couples enter into a registered partnership or civil union?
Bangladesh	No	Yes	Yes	Yes	Yes	Yes	None	No	Yes	Yes	Yes	No
Canada	Yes	Yes	Yes	Yes	Yes	No	~5	No	No	No	No	Yes
Costa Rica	Yes	Yes	Yes	Yes	Yes	No	1	No	Yes	No	Yes	Yes
India	Yes	Yes	Yes	Yes	Yes	Yes	None	No	Yes	No	Yes	No
Indonesia	No	Yes	Yes	Yes	Yes	Yes	None	No	No	No	No	No
Jamaica	No	Yes	Yes	Yes	Yes	No	None	No	No	No	No	No
Japan	No	Yes	Yes	Yes	Yes	No	1 or 2	No	No	No	No	No
Kosovo	Yes	Yes	Yes	Yes	Yes	No	None	No	No	No	No	No
Lebanon	No	Yes	Yes	Yes	Yes	Yes	None	No	No	Yes	No	No
Mexico	Yes	No	No	No	No	No	~10	No	No	No	No	Yes
Mozambique	No	No	No	No	No	No	None	No	No	No	No	No
Nigeria	No	No	No	No	No	Yes	None	No	No	Yes	No	No
South Africa	Yes	Yes	Yes	Yes	Yes	Yes	1	No	No	No	No	Yes
Tunisia	No	Yes	Yes	Yes	Yes	Yes	None	No	No	Yes	No	No
Ukraine	No	Yes	Yes	Yes	Yes	No	None	No	No	No	No	No
Uruguay	Yes	Yes	Yes	Yes	Yes	No	2	No	Yes	No	Yes	Yes

Note: NGOs = nongovernmental organizations.

TABLE B.21

Data Points for the Civil and Political Inclusion Indicator Set (continued)

Country	5.9 Can same-sex couples get legally married?	5.10 Is second-parent and/ or joint adoption by same-sex partner(s) legally possible?	5.11 Do laws and/or regulations relating to any of these categories differ between sexual and gender minorities and the rest of the population?	5.11.1 Obtaining citizenship?	5.11.2 Obtaining a passport?	5.11.3 Obtaining an ID card?	5.12 When applying for a passport or ID cards, are there only two options for "male or female"?	5.12.1 Passports	5.12.2 ID cards	5.13 Are there any laws and/ or regulations that require the assigned gender on the passport and/ or ID card to match the expression of one's gender?	5.14 Are there any laws and/or regulations that require gender-reassignment surgery for intersex children in order to receive a birth certificate?	5.15 Are there any laws and/ or regulations prohibiting/ banning/ protecting against sexual orientation and gender identity "conversion therapy"?	5.16 Are there any laws and/ or regulations that allow an individual to obtain a new ID card or passport after gender reassignment?	5.17 Does your country recognize persecution based on SOGI as one of the grounds for asylum?
Bangladesh	No	No	No	No	No	No	No	No	No	No	No	No	No	No
Canada	Yes	Yes	No	No	No	No	No	No	No	No	No	Yes	Yes	Yes
Costa Rica	Yes	Yes	No	No	No	No	Yes	Yes	No	No	No	No	Yes	Yes
India	No	No	No	No	No	No	No	No	No	No	No	No	No	No
Indonesia	No	No	No	No	No	No	Yes	Yes	Yes	No	No	No	Yes	No
Jamaica	No	No	No	No	No	No	Yes	Yes	Yes	No	No	No	No	No
Japan	No	No	No	No	No	No	Yes	Yes	Yes	Yes	No	No	Yes	No
Kosovo	No	No	No	No	No	No	Yes	Yes	Yes	No	No	No	No	Yes
Lebanon	No	No	No	No	No	No	Yes	Yes	Yes	No	No	No	No	No
Mexico	Yes	Yes	No	No	No	No	Yes	Yes	Yes	Yes	No	Yes	Yes	Yes
Mozambique	No	No	No	No	No	No	Yes	Yes	Yes	No	No	No	No	No
Nigeria	No	No	No	No	No	No	Yes	Yes	Yes	Yes	No	No	No	No
South Africa	Yes	Yes	No	No	No	No	Yes	Yes	Yes	No	No	No	Yes	Yes
Tunisia	No	No	No	No	No	No	Yes	Yes	Yes	No	No	No	No	No
Ukraine	No	No	No	No	No	No	Yes	Yes	Yes	No	No	No	No	No
Uruguay	Yes	Yes	No	No	No	No	Yes	Yes	Yes	No	No	No	Yes	Yes

5. Civil and political inclusion questions

TABLE B.22

Data Points for the Protection against Hate Crimes Indicator Set

Country	6. Protection against hate crimes questions						
	6.1 Are there any laws, constitutional provisions, and/or regulations that criminalize hate crimes on the basis of sexual orientation, gender identity, gender expression, and sex characteristics?	6.2 Are there any laws and/or regulations that require government agencies to collect data on hate crimes committed against sexual and gender minorities or those perceived to be sexual or gender minorities?	6.3 Are there mechanisms in your country for monitoring and reporting hate-motivated acts of violence against sexual and gender minorities?	6.4 Are crimes committed against someone based on that person's SOGI considered as aggravating circumstances by the law?	6.5 Are there any laws and/or regulations that mandate training of the following professionals on recognizing and identifying hate crimes? (for example, police officers, prosecutors, judges, social workers, and paramedics/doctors)	6.5.1 Police officers?	6.5.2 Prosecutors?
Bangladesh	No	No	No	No	No	No	No
Canada	Yes	No	Yes	Yes	Yes	Yes	No
Costa Rica	No	Yes	Yes	No	No	No	No
India	No	No	Yes	No	No	No	No
Indonesia	No	No	No	No	No	No	No
Jamaica	No	No	No	No	No	No	No
Japan	No	No	No	No	No	No	No
Kosovo	Yes	No	Yes	Yes	No	No	No
Lebanon	No	No	No	No	No	No	No
Mexico	No	Yes	Yes	Yes	Yes	No	No
Mozambique	No	No	No	No	No	No	No
Nigeria	No	No	No	No	No	No	No
South Africa	Yes	No	Yes	No	Yes	Yes	Yes
Tunisia	No	No	No	No	No	No	No
Ukraine	No	No	No	No	No	No	No
Uruguay	Yes	No	Yes	Yes	Yes	Yes	Yes

TABLE B.22

Data Points for the Protection against Hate Crimes Indicator Set (*continued*)

Country	6.5.3 Judges?	6.5.4 Social workers?	6.5.5 Paramedics/ doctors?	6.5.6 Other?	6.6 Are there any laws and/or regulations that mandate the provision of any of the following services to victims of hate crimes? (for example, legal assistance [including asylum applications and completing court forms], shelter/housing, forensic or medical examinations, and medical certificates)	6.6.1 Legal assistance (including asylum applications and completing court forms)?	6.6.2 Shelter/ housing?	6.6.3 Forensic or medical examinations?	6.6.4 Medical certificates?	6.6.5 Other?
Bangladesh	No	No	No	No	No	No	No	No	No	No
Canada	No	No	No	No	Yes	Yes	No	No	No	No
Costa Rica	No	No	No	No	No	No	No	No	No	No
India	No	No	No	No	No	No	No	No	No	No
Indonesia	No	No	No	No	No	N\o	No	No	No	No
Jamaica	No	No	No	No	No	No	No	No	No	No
Japan	No	No	No	No	No	No	No	No	No	No
Kosovo	No	No	No	No	No	No	No	No	No	No
Lebanon	No	No	No	No	No	No	No	No	No	No
Mexico	No	No	No	Yes	Yes	Yes	No	No	No	No
Mozambique	No	No	No	No	No	No	No	No	No	No
Nigeria	No	No	No	No	No	No	No	No	No	No
South Africa	Yes	Yes	Yes	Yes	No	No	No	No	No	No
Tunisia	No	No	No	No	No	No	No	No	No	No
Ukraine	No	No	No	No	No	No	No	No	No	No
Uruguay	Yes	No	No	Yes	Yes	Yes	Yes	No	No	No

Appendix C. Additional Readings

Burleson, Elizabeth. 2009. "International Human Rights Law: Co-parent Adoption, and the Recognition of Gay and Lesbian Families." *Loyola Law Review* 55: 792.

Eisenberg, Avlana. 2014. "Expressive Enforcement." *UCLA Law* Review 61: 858–60.

Florida, Richard. 2002a. *The Rise of the Creative Class: And How It's Transforming Work, Leisure, Community and Everyday Life*. New York: Basic Books.

Florida, Richard. 2002b. "Bohemia and Economic Geography." *Journal of Economic Geography* 2 (1): 55–71.

Florida, Richard. 2003. "Cities and the Creative Class." *City & Community* 2 (1): 319.

Florida, Richard. 2004. "Revenge of the Squelchers." *The Next American City* 5. http://creativeclass.com/rfcgdb/articles/Revenge_of_the_Squelchers_long%20report.pdf.

Florida, Richard, and Gary Gates. 2001. "Technology and Tolerance: The Importance of Diversity to High-Technology Growth." The Brookings Institution, Washington, DC.

Florida, Richard, and Charlotta Mellander. 2010. "There Goes the Metro: How and Why Bohemians, Artists and Gays Affect Regional Housing Values." *Journal of Economic Geography* 10 (2): 167–88.

Gross, Aeyal. 2017. "Gay Governance: A Queer Critique." In *Governance Feminism: An Introduction*. Minnesota University Press (forthcoming). https://ssrn.com/abstract=3065422.

Human Rights Watch. 2019. "Don't Punish Me for Who I Am: Systemic Discrimination Against Transgender Women in Lebanon." September 3. https://www.hrw.org/report/2019/09/03/dont-punish-me-who-i-am/systemic-discrimination-against-transgender-women-lebanon.

Inglehart, Ronald, Miguel E. Basáñez, Jaime Diez-Medrano, Loek Halman, and Ruud Luijkx. 2004. *Human Beliefs and Values: A Cross-Cultural Sourcebook Based on the 1999–2002 Values Surveys*. Mexico: Siglo XXI Editores.

Lind, Amy, ed. 2010. *Development, Sexual Rights and Global Governance*. Taylor and Francis.

O'Malley, Jeffrey, and Andreas Holzinger. 2018. "Sexual and Gender Minorities and the Sustainable Development Goals." United Nations Development Programme, New York.

United Nations. 1948. Universal Declaration of Human Rights. General Assembly Resolution 217A. New York: United Nations General Assembly. https://www.ohchr.org/EN/UDHR/Documents/UDHR_Translations/eng.pdf.

United Nations. 2016. *Living Free & Equal: What States Are Doing to Tackle Violence and Discrimination against Lesbian, Gay, Bisexual, Transgender and Intersex People*. New York and Geneva: United Nations. https://www.ohchr.org/Documents/Publications/LivingFreeAndEqual.pdf.

United Nations. 2017. *Fact Sheet: International Human Rights Law and Sexual Orientation & Gender Identity*. https://www.unfe.org/wp-content/uploads/2017/05/International-Human-Rights-Law.pdf.

United Nations. 2018. *Quality Education: Why it Matters.* https://www.un.org/sustainabledevelopment/wp-content/uploads/2018/09/Goal-4.pdf.